Visual Language Guide
Italian

Barron's

Grammar Overview 6

Quick Overview 9

General Information 15

Conversation 25

On the Move 47

Overnight Accommodations 85

Eating and Drinking 105

Shopping 137

Beach, Sports, and Nature 179

Culture and Entertainment 195

Offices and Institutions 201

Health 207

Business Travel 217

Glossary 221

ℹ️

Italian is a very melodious language. It is for good reason that Italy is the country of famous opera composers such as Rossini, Verdi, and Puccini.

Sentence Structure

Sentence structure follows (more or less) what applies to all Romance languages:

Article	Subject	Adjective	Verb	Adverb	Object
The	policeman	tall	spoke	slowly	with my husband.
Il	poliziotto	alto	parlava	lentamente	con mio marito.

Articles

The definite article changes according to number and gender:

  the window – la finestra / the windows – le finestre
  the dog – il cane / the dogs – i cani
  the uncle – lo zio / the uncles – gli zii
  the snack – lo spuntino / the snacks – gli spuntini

The definite article **lo** is used before all masculine nouns that start with **z** or **s** followed by a consonant. The feminine article **la** and the masculine article **il** are shortened to **l'** before words that begin with a vowel. Similarly, there are three basic forms for the indefinite article: **un, una,** and **uno,** which function like the definite articles. As with the definite articles, **una** is shortened to **un'** before words that start with a vowel.

Nouns

Singular and plural are formed in accordance with the grammatical gender of the words:

  ragazzo – ragazzi (boys)
  ragazza – ragazze (girls)

... but not necessarily:

  cane – cani (dogs)

There are a number of exceptions to these basic rules. **Bambino**, for example, has two forms: **bambino** for a boy and **bambina** for a girl.

Often there is a difference in spelling between singular and plural for both nouns and adjectives:

  bottega – botteghe
  bacio – baci
  fungo – funghi

This generally occurs to preserve similar pronunciation in both forms.

Adverbs

Adverbs generally (but not always) are formed by adding the ending **–mente** to the feminine form of an adjective, or simply by adding it to the end of an adjective:

  candido – candidamente
  utile – utilmente
  piacevole – piacevolmente

Possessives and Indirect Objects

These are constructed using the prepositions **di** and **a** in combination with the nouns in the proper gender and number:

La casa del Sig. Rossi – Mr. Rossi's house
una bottiglia di vino – a bottle of wine
la bottega degli scampoli – the remnants store

Pronouns

There are quite a number of pronouns; the following chart is a simplified summary:

Subject		Object (stressed)		Possessive 1 (unstressed)	Possessive 2
I	io	a me / di me	mi	mio / miei mia / mie	mio / miei mia / mie
you (fam./formal)	tu /lei	a te / di te a lei / di lei	ti	tuo / tuoi tua / tue	tuo / tuoi tua / tue
he	lui	a lui / di lui	gli	suo / suoi sua / sue	suo / suoi sua / sue
she	lei	a lei / di lei	le	sua / sue	sua / sue
we	noi	a noi / di noi	ci	il nostro i nostri la nostra le nostre	nostro nostri nostra nostre
you (pl.)	voi / loro	a voi di voi / di loro a loro / di loro	vi	il vostro / i vostri la vostra / le vostre il loro / la loro i loro / le loro	vostro
they	loro	a loro / di loro	loro	loro	loro

Possessive 1 is used as an adjective before nouns (*mia macchina*); Possessive 2 is used alone as a possessive pronoun (*è mia*). Usually the appropriate form of the article is placed before the possessive pronoun.

Adjectives

Adjectives (which generally follow the nouns they modify) change according to gender and number:

un cane grande – a large dog
cani grandi – large dogs

The comparative is generally formed using **più**:

grande – più grande

i

Helping Verbs and Modal Verbs

essere	avere	fare
to be	to have	to make, to do
sono	ho	faccio
sei	hai	fai
è	ha	fa
siamo	abbiamo	facciamo
siete	avete	fate
sono	hanno	fanno

Verbs

There are three regular verb conjugations; those ending in **–ire** are conjugated differently. In addition, there are a great number of irregular verbs.

	comprare	vendere	finire	mentire
io	compro	vendo	finisco	mento
tu	compri	vendi	finisci	menti
lui / lei	compra	vende	finisce	mente
noi	compriamo	vendiamo	finiamo	mentiamo
voi	comprate	vendete	finite	mentite
loro / essi	comprano	vendono	finiscono	mentono

Negation

Sentences are made negative using **non,** e.g., **Non fumo.**

Pronunciation

We have consciously avoided phonetic spelling. Experience shows that tiresome stammering with phonetic spelling produces poor results. Moreover, you can just point to most things in this book. Here, however, are the most important pronunciation rules:

	Rule	Example	Pronunciation
c	before e and i, like **ch** in **chew**	bacio	bahchio
	otherwise like **k**	cane	kahneh
ch	like **k**	chiesa	kiehsah
ci	before a, o, and u, like **ch**	ciao	chahoh
g	before e or i, like **j** in **jungle**	gelato	jelahtoh
	otherwise like **g** in **gift**	gala	gahlah
gh	like **g** in **gala**	ghia	geeah
gl	like **ll** in **million**	figlio	feelleeoh
qu	like **k**	cinque	cheenkweh
r	rolled	Roma	Rrohmah
s	between two vowels, like the **s** in **rose**	casa	kahsah
	otherwise like a sibilant **s**	smussare	smoossahreh
		sete	sehteh
sc	before a, o, u, like **sk**	scusi	skoosee
	before e or i, like **sh**	pesce	pehsheh
sch	like **sk**	Ischia	eeskeeah
z	like the **s** in **rose**	zucchero	sookehroh
	a bit stronger when doubled	pazzo	pahtzoh

The 11 Most Important Words

yes **sì**

no **no**

please **per favore**

Thank you! / Thanks! **grazie**

I'm sorry! / Sorry! **Scusi! / Scusa!**

Don't mention it! **Di niente**

Good-bye! **Arrivederci!**

How are you? **Come sta? / Come stai?**

Fine, thanks. **Bene, grazie.**

Help! **Aiuto!**

Hello!
Buon giorno!

The 22 Most Important Expressions

My name is ...
Mi chiamo ...

I'm from the United States / Canada.
Vengo degli Stati Uniti / del Canadà.

Can you please help me?
Può aiutarmi per favore?

Pardon?
Come, prego?

What is that?
Cos'è (questo)?

How much does that cost?
Quanto costa (questo)?

Do you speak English?
(Lei) parla inglese?

I don't understand you.
Non La comprendo.

I only speak a little bit of Italian.
Io conosco solo un po' di italiano.

Please speak slowly.
Per favore, parli lentamente.

Can you please repeat that?
Può ripetere per favore?

Can you write that down?
Può scrivermelo?

How do you say that in Italian?
Come si dice (questo) in italiano?

Please show me that in this book.
Per favore me lo mostri in questo libro.

Just a minute.
Un momento.

I'm hungry.
Ho fame.

I'm thirsty.
Ho sete.

Leave me alone!
Mi lasci in pace!

Go away!
Levati dai piedi!

What would you recommend?
Cosa mi consiglia?

Where are the toilets?
Dov'è la toilette?

I got lost.
Mi sono perso(a).

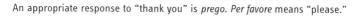

An appropriate response to "thank you" is *prego*. *Per favore* means "please."

What You Often Hear

Can I help you?
Posso aiutarLa?

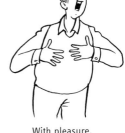

With pleasure.
Con piacere.

Don't mention it.
Di niente.

I'm sorry.
Mi dispiace.

We are completely full.
Siamo al completo. É tutto esaurito.

Doesn't matter. / That's all right.
Non fa niente. / Non si preoccupi.

Where are you from?
Da dove viene?

Too bad!
Peccato!

Italians usually are less concerned with terrorism than Americans. Expect greater airport security measures in the U.S. than in Italy.

The 33 Most Important Verbs

work **lavorare**

get **ricevere**

think **pensare**

recommend **consigliare**

tell **raccontare**

eat **mangiare**

find **trovare**

ask **chiedere**

feel **sentire**

give **dare**

go **andare**

believe **credere**

have **avere**

hear **sentire**

buy **comprare**

come **enire**

can **potere**

let **lasciare**

read **leggere**

like **piacere**

must / have to... **dovere**

take **prendere**

smell **sentire**

say **dire**

taste **assaggiare**

write **scrivere**

see **vedere**

speak **parlare**

look for ... **cercare**

do **fare**

sell **vendere**

know **sapere**

listen **ascoltare**

Constructing Sentences

Even if you don't know much about languages you can easily construct the easiest sentences. These formulas will help you. Plug in the words you need to replace the underlined words. It's courteous to begin questions and requests by saying, "Pardon me..."

Excuse me, do you have ...
Scusi, ha ...

I'm hungry.
Ho fame.

I would like to have a pair of sunglasses.
Vorrei degli occhiali da sole.

I would like a double room.
Vorrei una camera doppia.

Do you have track shoes / running shoes?
Ha delle scarpe da ginnastica?

Are there any oranges?
Ha delle arance?

I would rather have bananas.
Preferirei delle banane.

Can I have some mineral water?
Mi può portare dell'acqua minerale?

I need a band-aid.
Avrei bisogno di un cerotto.

I'm looking for a hotel.
Cerco un albergo.

Can you tell me what time it is?
Mi può dire l'ora, per cortesia?

Do you please bring me a fork?
Mi porta una forchetta per favore?

hear **sentire**

Casual clothing is the norm in Italy, but when you visit their wonderful churches and basilicas, remember that they are houses of worship.

Everyday Conversation

Achoo!
Ecci!
Bless you!
Salute!

Have a nice day!
Buona giornata!
Same to you!
Altrettanto.

I'll have the special of the day.
Io prendo il piatto del giorno.
So will I.
Anch'io.

I don't feel well today.
Non mi sento bene oggi.
Get well soon!
Auguri!

Have fun!
Buon divertimento!
You, too!
Anche a lei!

The sign *Toilette* does not appear everyplace there is a toilet. You will often see *Donne* (Ladies) and *Uomini* (Men).

Comparatives

old, older, oldest
vecchio, più vecchio, il più vecchio

good, better, best
buono, migliore, il migliore

hot, hotter, hottest
caldo, più caldo, il più caldo

high, higher, highest
alto, più alto, il più alto

young, younger, youngest
giovane, più giovane, il più giovane

cold, colder, coldest
freddo, più freddo, il più freddo

short, shorter, shortest
corto, più corto, il più corto

long, longer, longest
lungo, più lungo, il più lungo

slow, slower, slowest
lento, più lento, il più lento

bad, worse, worst
cattivo, più cattivo, il più cattivo

fast, faster, fastest
veloce, più veloce, il più veloce

beautiful, more beautiful, most beautiful
bello, più bello, il più bello

deep, deeper, deepest
profondo, più profondo, il più profondo

far, farther, farthest
distante, più distante, il più distante

Opposites

all – nothing
tutto – niente

old – young
vecchio – giovane

old – new
vecchio – nuovo

outside – inside
fuori – dentro

early – late
presto – tardi

big – small
grande – piccolo

good – bad
buono – cattivo

right – wrong
giusto – sbagliato

fast – slow
veloce – lento

beautiful – ugly
bello – brutto

strong – weak
forte – debole

expensive – cheap
caro – conveniente

much – little
molto – poco

full – empty
pieno – vuoto

warm – cold
caldo – freddo

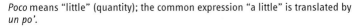

Poco means "little" (quantity); the common expression "a little" is translated by *un po'*.

Important Vocabulary

all **tutt-i / -e**

as **come**

other **altr-i / -e**

on **su**

out (of) **fuori**

at **con**

then **poi**

that **quell-o / -a**

therefore **quindi**

these **quest-i / -e**

through **mediante; attraverso**

a, an **un / uno / una**

some / a few **alcun-i / -e**

for **per**

same **stess-o / -a**

their **suo / sua / suoi / sue**

in **in**

each **ognun-o / -a**

now **ora, adesso**

with **con**

still **ancora**

only **solo, soltanto, solamente**

although **anche se**

or **o, oppure**

without **senza**

very **molto**

such **tali**

and **e**

of / from **di; da**

before **prima di; davanti a**

because **perché**

little **poco**

if **se**

like **come**

again **di nuovo**

Questions About Questions

when? **Quando?**

what? **Cosa?**

why? **Perché?**

who? **Chi?**

where? **Dove?**

how? **Come?**

how much? **Quanto?**

how many? **Quanti?**

how far? **Quanto dista?**

how long? **Quanto tempo?**

there **là**

This and That

this one **questo**

that one **quello**

here **qui**

"How long?" (*Quanto tempo?*) in this instance refers to time rather than to such things as the length of a skirt.

General Information

Cardinal Numbers

zero **zero**

one **uno**

two **due**

three **tre**

four **quattro**

five **cinque**

six **sei**

seven **sette**

eight **otto**

nine **nove**

ten **dieci**

twenty **venti**

thirty **trenta**

forty **quaranta**

fifty **cinquanta**

sixty **sessanta**

seventy **settanta**

eighty **ottanta**

ninety **novanta**

one hundred **cento**

one thousand **mille**

ten thousand **diecimila**

one hundred thousand **centomila**

one million **un milione**

one billion **un miliardo**

Ordinal Numbers

first (1st) **primo**

second (2nd) **secondo**

third (3rd) **terzo**

fourth (4th) **quarto**

fifth (5th) **quinto**

sixth (6th) **sesto**

seventh (7th) **settimo**

eighth (8th) **ottavo**

ninth (9th) **nono**

tenth (10th) **decimo**

twentieth (20th) **ventesimo**

thirtieth (30th) **trentesimo**

Fractions and Quantities

one eighth **un ottavo**

one quarter **un quarto**

one half **mezzo**

three quarters **tre quarti**

once **una volta**

twice **due volte**

three times **tre volte**

half **mezzo**

half **metà**

double **il doppio**

a little **un po' di**

a pair **un paio**

a dozen **una dozzina**

enough **abbastanza**

too much **troppo**

more **molt-i / -e**

many **molt-i / -e**

The page numbers in this book are written out. That will help you find the number you want.

Weights

gram **grammo**
pound **mezzo chilo**
kilo **chilo**
ton **tonnellata**
ounce **oncia**

Fluids

liter **litro**
one half liter **mezzo litro**
one quarter liter **un quarto di litro**

Length

millimeter **millimetro**
centimeter **centimetro**
meter **metro**
kilometer **chilometro**
inch **pollice**
foot **piede**
yard **iarda**
mile **miglio**

Area

square meter **metro quadrato**
square kilometer **chilometro quadrato**

Conversions

1 ounce (oz)		= 28,35 g
1 pound (lb)	= 16 ounces	= 453,59 g
1 ton	= 2000 pounds	= 907 kg
¼ pound		= 113 g
½ pound		= 227 g
100 g	= 3.527 oz	
1 kg	= 2.205 lb	
1 inch (in)		= 2,54 cm
1 foot (ft)	= 12 inches	= 0,35 m
1 yard (yd)	= 3 feet	= 0,9 m
1 mile (mi)	= 1760 yards	= 1,6 km
1 cm	= 0.39 in	
1 km	= 0.62 mi	
1 square foot (ft^2)		= 930 cm^2
1 acre (A)		= 4047 m^2
1 m^2	= 0.386 mi^2	
1 ha	= 2.471 acres	
1 pint (pt)		= 0,47 l
1 quart (qt)	= 2 pints	= 0,95 l
1 gallone (gal)	= 4 quarts	= 3,79 l
¼ l	= 0.26 qt	
½ l	= 0.53 qt	
1 l	= 1.057 qt	
	= 0.264 gal	

In specifying dates, only the first of a month is given using an ordinal number; after that the cardinal numbers are used, such as *due* and so forth.

Date and Time

When will you arrive?
Quando arrivate?

We will arrive on the 15th of July.
Arriviamo il 15 luglio.

That is, in 14 days.
Cioè tra 15 giorni.

What is the date today?
Quanti ne abbiamo oggi?

Today is the 1st of July.
Oggi è il 1° luglio.

At about what time must we be there?
A che ora dobbiamo essere lì?

At 3 o'clock (in the afternoon).
Alle tre.

How long will you stay?
Quanto tempo rimanete?

We will stay until the 12th of August.
Rimaniamo fino al 12 agosto.

For the Italians, 14 days are always considered to be 15 days; that's their designation for a period of two weeks.

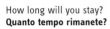

Days of the Week

Monday **lunedì**
Tuesday **martedì**
Wednesday **mercoledì**
Thursday **giovedì**
Friday **venerdì**
Saturday **sabato**
Sunday **domenica**

Months

January **gennaio**
February **febbraio**
March **marzo**
April **aprile**
May **maggio**
June **giugno**
July **luglio**
August **agosto**
September **settembre**
October **ottobre**
November **novembre**
December **dicembre**

Holidays

New Year's Day **Anno nuovo / capodanno**
Good Friday **Venerdì santo**
Easter **Pasqua**
Whitsun, Pentecost **Pentecoste**
Christmas **Natale**
Happy Easter! **Buona Pasqua!**
New Year's eve **San Silvestro / la Vigilia di capodanno**
Merry Christmas! **Buon Natale!**
Happy New Year! **Buon anno!**

Times

in the evening **di sera**
That is too early. **È troppo presto.**
That is too late. **È troppo tardi.**
earlier **prima**
yesterday **ieri**
today **oggi**
in fourteen days **tra quindici giorni**
year **anno**
now **ora, adesso**
at noon **a mezzogiorno**
midnight **mezzanotte**
month **mese**
tomorrow **domani**
afterward **dopo**
in the afternoon **di pomeriggio**
at night **di notte**
sunrise **alba**
sunset **tramonto**
later **più tardi**
hourly **ogni ora**
day **giorno**
daily **quotidiano; quotidianamente**
during the day **durante la giornata / di giorno**
the day after tomorrow **dopodomani**
the day before yesterday **l'altro ieri**
previously **prima**
in the morning **di mattina**
weekend **fine settimana**

Seasons

spring **primavera**
summer **estate**
autumn / fall **autunno**
winter **inverno**
in season / high season **alta stagione**
off season / low season **bassa stagione**

Easter is *Pasqua*; Easter Monday is *Pasquetta*, or "Little Easter."

Telling Time

Can you tell me what time it is?
Mi può dire l'ora, per cortesia?

Ten minutes past three.
Sono le tre e dieci.

Is your watch working?
Funziona il Suo orologio?

Of course.
Certamente.

My watch is slow.
Il mio orologio è indietro.

I am sorry, I'm late.
Mi dispiace, sono in ritardo.

For questions such as "Can you tell me what time it is?" it is always good to end them with "please"—that is, *per cortesia* or *per favore.*

two o'clock
le due

five past two
le due e cinque

ten past two / two ten
le due e dieci

quarter past two
le due e un quarto

two thirty
le due e mezza

two thirty-five
**le due e trentacinque / tre meno
venticinque**

In telling time in the afternoon and evening, Italians commonly use the same numbers as in the morning, in other words, *alle tre*.

twenty to four
le tre e quaranta / le quattro meno venti

quarter to four
le tre e quarantacinque / le quattro meno un quarto

five to three
le due e cinquantacinque / le tre meno cinque

12 noon
mezzogiorno

Can you please tell me the time?
Può dirmi l'ora, per cortesia?

hour
ora

minute
minuto

second
secondo

in ten minutes
in / tra dieci minuti

in an hour
in / tra un'ora

in half an hour
in / tra (una) mezz'ora

Since 12:00 noon for Italians is *mezzogiorno*, it follows that midnight is *mezzanotte*.

The Weather

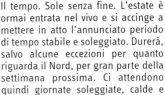

The weather: Endless sunshine. Summer has now reached its peak and we'll continue having sunshine and stable weather, which will last during most of next week save for some areas in the north of the country. We are therefore waiting for sunny, hot and humid days. Today: Sunshine all over the Italian peninsula, except for some cloudy weather that will develop in the Alpine areas and also around the Apennines. Widespread fog. The daily temperatures will slightly rise in the north and the Tyrrhenian Sea. Weak winds and a breezy sea with moderate waves.

Il tempo. Sole senza fine. L'estate è ormai entrata nel vivo e si accinge a mettere in atto l'annunciato periodo di tempo stabile e soleggiato. Durerà, salvo alcune eccezioni per quanto riguarda il Nord, per gran parte della settimana prossima. Ci attendono quindi giornate soleggiate, calde e afose. Oggi. Tempo soleggiato su tutta la penisola, salvo della nuvolosità ad evoluzione diurna sulle zone alpine e quelle appenniniche. Foschie diffuse. Temperature diurne in lieve aumento al Nord. E sulle regioni tirreniche. Venti deboli di brezza e mari poco mossi.

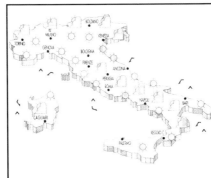

How will the weather be today? **Oggi come sarà il tempo?**	It is 15 degrees Celsius. **(Ci sono) 15 gradi.**
It will stay nice. **Rimarrà bello / Rimarrà bel tempo.**	Is it always so hot? **Fa sempre così caldo?**
It will become nice. **Farà bello / Farà bel tempo.**	It is freezing at night. **Di notte si gela.**
It's supposed to rain. **Dicono che pioverà.**	The streets are … **Le strade sono …**
How long has it been raining? **Da quanto tempo è che piove?**	wet. **bagnate.**
How much longer will it rain? **Per quanto tempo pioverà ancora?**	slippery. **ghiacciate.**
What is the temperature today? **Quanti gradi ci sono oggi?**	snow-covered. **coperte di neve.** dry. **asciutte.**

The weather report is often shortened to *previsioni*, forecast.

clearing **la schiarita**
lightning **il lampo**
thunder **il tuono**
ice **il ghiaccio**
frost **il gelo**
regional **regionale**
thunderstorm **il temporale**
sheet ice **le strade ghiacciate**
sleet **il nevischio**
hail **la grandine**
heat **il calore**
high **l'alta pressione**
maximum (values) **i valori massimi**
high tide **l'acqua alta**
air **l'aria**
humidity **l'umidità**
moderately warm **temperato**
fog **la nebbia**
drizzle **la pioviggine**
ozone **l'ozono**
puddle **la pozzanghera**
powder (snow) **la neve farinosa**
rain **la pioggia**
showers **lo scroscio di pioggia**
snow **la neve**
snow chains **le catene da neve**
sun **il sole**
storm **la tempesta**
typhoon **il tifone**
thaw **il disgelo**
low **la bassa pressione**
minimum (values) **i valori minimi**
flood **l'inondazione**
fairly stable **abbastanza stabile**
wind **il vento**
tornado **il tornado**
clouds **le nubi, nuvole**

Fahrenheit and Celsius

Temperatures in the United States are measured in degrees Fahrenheit, but in Italy they measure in degrees Celsius. To convert degrees Fahrenheit to degrees Celsius, deduct 32 and multiply by $5/9$. To convert degrees Celsius to degrees Fahrenheit, multiply by $9/5$ and add 32.

°F	°C	°F	°C
0	−17.8	78	25.6
10	−12.2	79	26.1
15	−9.4	80	26.7
20	−6.7	81	27.2
25	−3.9	82	27.8
30	−1.1	83	28.3
32	0.0	84	28.9
35	1.7	85	29.4
40	4.4	86	30.0
45	7.2	87	30.6
50	10.0	88	31.1
60	15.6	89	31.7
61	16.1	90	32.2
62	16.7	91	32.8
63	17.2	92	33.3
64	17.8	93	33.9
65	18.3	94	34.4
66	18.9	95	35.0
67	19.4	96	35.6
68	20.0	97	36.1
69	20.6	98	36.7
70	21.1	99	37.2
71	21.7	100	37.8
72	22.2	101	38.3
73	22.8	102	38.9
74	23.3	103	39.4
75	23.9	104	40.0
76	24.4	105	40.6
77	25.0	106	41.1

"What's the temperature...?" Here the Italians start with *Ci sono...*, which literally means "there are..."

Don't Forget!

rubber boots
gli stivali di gomma

umbrella
l'ombrello

It is ... **È ...**
  cloudy. **È nuvoloso.**
  hazy. **C'è foschia.**
  hot. **Fa molto caldo.**
  cold. **Fa freddo.**
  foggy. **C'è nebbia.**
  muggy. **È afoso.**
  sunny. **C'è il sole.**
  stormy. **C'è aria di tempesta.**
  dry. **È asciutto.**
  warm. **Fa caldo.**
  variable / changeable. **È instabile.**
  windy / breezy. **C'è il vento.**

It is raining. **Piove.**
It is snowing. **Nevica.**

sun glasses
gli occhiali da sole

parasol / sun umbrella
l'ombrellone

Pronunciation

apple **Ancona**	jam **Jersey**	snow **Savona**
ball **Bologna**	kitten **kilo**	toy **Torino**
cat **Como**	lamb **Livorno**	ooze **Udine**
dog **Domodossola**	money **Milano**	victory **Venezia**
elephant **Empoli**	nut **Napoli**	wing **Washington**
fox **Firenze**	orange **Otranto**	xylophone **Xeres**
golf **Genova**	paper **Padova**	yellow **York**
house **Hotel**	queen **Quarto**	zebra **Zara**
ice **Imola**	rabbit **Roma**	

In speaking of the weather—e.g., The weather is nice/it's hot, Italians use the verb *fare* (to make); thus, *Fa caldo*, etc.

Conversation

First Contact

By nature, Italians are curious and receptive, helpful, and friendly. But the "man on the street" doesn't always know much about foreign languages.

Formerly, French was the primary foreign language in Italy, but recently English has taken its place, and you can use English successfully with most young people. That is especially true in tourist areas.

In Italy greetings depend on the degree of familiarity between people. The usual greeting during the day is *buon giorno*; in the evening, it is *buona sera*.

If the people know each other a little better, they may use the greeting *salve* (which was used by the ancient Romans).

With close acquaintances and friends it is common to use the simple and international *ciao*.

In saying good-bye, people commonly say *arrivederci*.

After the initial greeting, you can hardly go wrong by saying something like *Come va?* or *Come sta?*, which correspond to the English "How's it going?" For people with whom you are on familiar terms, you can say *Come stai?*

And what do you talk about when you want to make small talk with a native? One subject that will always hit home with your acquaintance is soccer.

Hello!
Ciao!

Good morning.
Buon giorno.

Good day.
Buon giorno.

Good evening.
Buona sera.

Good night.
Buona notte.

How are you?
Come sta?

Fine, thank you.
Bene, grazie.

What is your name?
Come si chiama Lei?

Good-bye.
Arrivederci.

Pardon me?
Come (prego)?

Do you speak English?
(Lei) parla inglese?

I did not understand.
Non ho capito.

I speak only a little Italian.
Parlo solo un po' d'italiano.

Can you please repeat that?
Può ripetere per favore?

Can you please write that down?
Può scrivermelo per favore?

For "Pardon me?" you can also say *Che cosa?* or *Cosa?* by itself. That means, "What?" but of course it is not as polite.

Hello!
Ciao!

Good day!
Buon giorno!

How are you?
Come sta?

Fine, thanks.
Bene, grazie.

Nice meeting you.
Mi fa piacere incontrarLa.

Same here!
Anche a me.

Good-bye!
Arrivederci!

It was nice to meet you.
È stato un piacere incontrarLa.

If you meet a close acquaintance you can also say something like *Ciao bello* or *Ciao bella*. Italian has an abundance of salutations.

What You Hear

Da dove viene?
Where are you from?

Da quanto tempo è qui?
How long have you been here?

Le piace?
Do you like it?

È la prima volta che viene qui?
Is it your first time here?

Quanto tempo rimane?
How long are you staying?

Posso presentarmi?
May I introduce myself?

Familiar Greetings

How is it going?
Come va?

What's happening? / What's going on?
Cosa c'è?

Hi, there!
Ciao a tutt-i / -e!

Hi folks!
Ciao a tutt-i / -e!

Hi pal!
Ciao!

Good to see you!
Sono contento di vederti!

What's new?
Come va?

Great!
Sto benissimo!

Okay.
Così così.

Have a nice day.
Buona giornata!

See you later!
A presto!

Take care!
Stammi bene!

Bye!
Ciao!

Set Phrases

Oh, really?
Oh, davvero?

That is right.
È giusto.

That is interesting.
È interessante.

That is new to me.
Mi giunge nuovo.

I agree.
Sono d'accordo.

I don't agree.
Non sono d'accordo.

I like that.
Mi piace.

That would be nice.
Sì, grazie molto cortese.

Great!
Benissimo!

Could be.
Potrebbe essere.

Maybe.
Forse.

Probably.
È probabile.

I don't know.
Non so.

Just a minute, please.
Un momento per favore.

May I? / Excuse me!
Permette?

Good luck!
Buona fortuna!

Have fun!
Buon divertimento!

All the best!
Auguri!

A hearty welcome!
Benvenut-o / -a / -i / -e!

Unfortunately, I have no time.
Mi spiace, non ho tempo.

I must step away for a minute.
Scusi un attimo, dovrei andare in bagno.

An expression such as "That's news to me" can be expressed more economically using *Non sapevo* (I didn't know that).

Excuse Me!

Excuse me, how much do
these shoes cost?
**Scusi, quanto costano queste
scarpe?**

I'm sorry, I don't work here.
**Mi spiace, non faccio parte del
personale.**

Excuse me please!
Oh, mi scusi!

No problem!
Di niente!

To say "Pardon me!" in such places as a streetcar you can simply say *Permesso*.

Introductions

My name is ...
Mi chiamo ...

What is your name?
Come si chiama?

How old are you?
Quanti anni ha?

I am 25 years old.
Ho 25 anni.

Are you married?
È sposato?

I am single.
Sono celibe / nubile.

Do you have any children?
Ha figli?

What do you do for a living?
Che professione fa?

Where are you travelling to?
Dove è diret-o / -a?

How long will you stay?
Quanto tempo rimane?

I am on ...
Sono qui per ...
  a business trip.
  un viaggio d'affari.
  vacation.
  una vacanza.
  I am travelling on to ...
  Proseguo per ...

I would like to visit the following cities.
Vorrei visitare le seguenti città.

I am spending the night ...
Alloggio ...
  in a hotel.
  in albergo.
  with friends.
  da amici.

It was very nice to meet you.
È stato un piacere conoscerLa!

May I introduce?
Posso presentarmi / presentare?

Forms of Address

	Singular	Abbreviation	Plural	Abbreviation
Mr.	signor	sig.	signori	sigg.
Mrs.	signora	sig.ra	signore	sig.re
Miss	signorina	sig.na	signorine	sig.ne
Ladies and Gentlemen	Egregi signori,			

In speaking of someone's age the helping verb *avere* is always used—not the verb "to be" as in English.

Where Are You From?

Where are you from?
Da dove viene?

I'm from the United States.
Vengo dagli Stati Uniti.

I'm from Canada.
Vengo dal Canadà.

I'm from Italy.
Vengo dall'Italia.

In Italy the national ID is called *la carta di identità.*

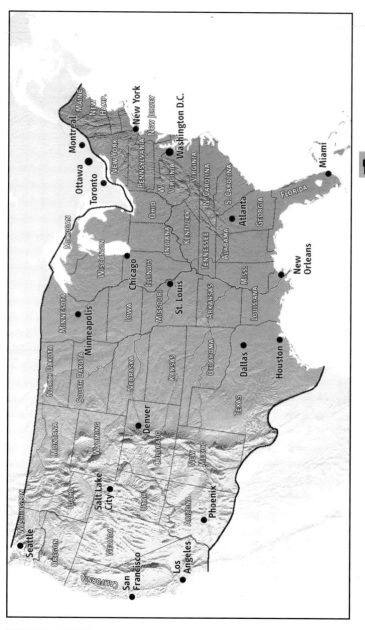

If you ever need to show personal identification, of course your passport will suffice.

Relatives

husband **marito**
wife **moglie**
friend **amico**
friend / acquaintance **conoscente**
fiancée **fidanzata**
fiancé **fidanzato**
daughter **figlia**
son **figlio**
brother **fratello**
sister **sorella**
father **padre**
mother **madre**
grandfather **nonno**
grandmother **nonna**
son-in-law **genero**
daughter-in-law **nuora**
father-in-law **suocero**
mother-in-law **suocera**
uncle **zio**

aunt **zia**
grandson **nipote**
cousin **cugina**
cousin **cugino**
nephew **nipote**
niece **nipote**

Occupations

What do you do for a living?
Che professione fa?

I work in a factory.
Lavoro in fabbrica.

I work for the XYZ company.
Lavoro presso la ditta XYZ.

I work in retail sales.
Lavoro nel commercio al minuto.
Sono commerciante.

I'm still at school.
Vado ancora a scuola.

What are you studying?
Cosa studia?

I'm studying architecture.
Studio architettura.

I am an official / a civil servant.
Sono impiegato pubblico.

The word *nipote* has the double meaning of "nephew/niece" and "grandson/granddaughter."

Professions

doctor
**il dottore /
medico**

construction worker
il lavoratore edile

cook
il cuoco

painter
l'imbianchino

mason
il muratore

chimney sweep
lo spazzacamino

department head **il capo (di) reparto**

geriatric nurse **l'assistente geriatrico**

employee **l'impiegato**

lawyer **l'avvocato**

worker **il lavoratore**

unemployed **il disoccupato**

architect **l'architetto**

architecture **l'architettura**

army **l'esercito**

doctor's assistant **l'assistente del medico**

trainee **l'apprendista**

car mechanic **il meccanico per automobili**

author **l'autore**

baker **il panettiere**

official / civil servant **l'impiegato pubblico**

management expert **il commercialista**

biologist **il biologo**

bookkeeper **il contabile**

bookseller **il libraio**

chemistry **la chimica**

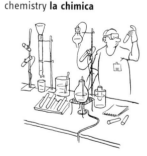

chemist **il chimico**

roofer **il muratore / copritetto**

decorator **il decoratore**

druggist **il droghiere**

computer expert **l'esperto EDP**

In Italian there is a distinction between workers: *lavoratore* is someone who works hard, and *operaio* is a factory worker.

Professions

retail **il commercio al minuto**

electrician **l'elettricista**

teacher **l'istitutore / istitutrice / maestra d'asilo**

skilled worker / specialist **il lavoratore specializzato**

photographer **il fotografo**

freelancer **il libero professionista**

hairdresser **il parrucchiere**

management level **il livello direttivo**

gardener **il giardiniere**

hotelier **l'albergatore**

German language & literature specialist **il germanista**

glazier **il vetraio**

craftsperson **l'artigiano**

housewife **la casalinga**

homemaker **il casalingo**

lawyer **il dottore in legge**

jeweler **il gioielliere**

businessman / merchant **il commerciante**

waiter **il cameriere**

motor vehicle mechanic **il meccanico per automobili**

nurse **l'infermiera**

artist **l'artista**

farmer **l'agricoltore**

midwife **l'ostetrica**

healer ("alternative medicine") **il guaritore**

college **l'università**

industry **l'industria**

engineer **l'ingegnere**

plumber **l'idraulico**

journalist **il giornalista**

law **la giurisprudenza**

teacher **l'insegnante**

broker / agent **il sensale**

manager **il manager**

mechanic **il meccanico**

medicine **la medicina**

master **il capo**

butcher **il macellaio**

musician **il musicista**

notary **il notaio**

government service / public service **il servizio pubblico**

optician **l'ottico**

priest **il prete**

In Italy a farmer is *un agricoltore*; however, you will still encounter the term *contadino*.

Professions

pharmacy **la farmacia**
philosophy **la filosofia**
physics **la fisica**
police officer **il poliziotto**
president **il presidente**
production **la produzione**
professor **il professore**
programmer **il programmatore**
psychologist **lo psicologo**

tailor **il sarto**
carpenter **il falegname**
author **lo scrittore**
shoemaker **il calzolaio**
student **lo scolaro**
tax advisor **il consulente fiscale**
student **lo studente**
taxi driver / cab driver **il tassista**
veterinarian **il veterinario**
watchmaker **l'orologiaio / orefice**
retraining **la riqualificazione**
entrepreneur / businessman **l'imprenditore**
salesperson **il commesso**
administration **l'amministrazione**
scientist **lo scienziato**
dentist **il dentista**
dental technician **l'odontotecnico**
carpenter **il carpentiere**

psychology **la psicologia**
lawyer **l'avvocato**
retired person **il pensionato**
judge **il giudice**
actor **l'attore**
locksmith **il fabbro**

Italians make a distinction between a painter who's an artist (*un pittore*) and a house painter (*un imbianchino*).

CONVERSATION

...ou?

...e you?
...e va?

So-so.
Così così.

tired.
stanco.
sick.
ammalato.
angry.
arrabbiato.
annoyed.
annoiato.

I am cold.
Ho freddo.

I am warm.
Ho caldo.

I am worried.
Sono preoccupato.

Super!
Benissimo.

I feel terrific!
Sono in piena forma.

On top of the world!
Mi sento euforico.

I am in love.
Sono innamorato.

I'm not feeling very well.
Non mi sento molto bene.

I am ...
Sono ...
depressed.
depresso.
frustrated.
frustrato.

Terms of Endearment

sweetheart
tesoro

darling
amore

The Italian for "I have" is *Ho*.

Congratulations

All the best!
Auguri!

Lots of success!
Tanto successo!

Good luck!
Buona fortuna!

Get well soon!
Auguri di pronta guarigione!

Congratulations
Congratulazioni / Auguri
  on your birthday.
  di buon compleanno.
  on your promotion.
  per la promozione.
  on the birth of your son / daughter.
  per la nascita del figlio / della figlia.
  on your engagement.
  per il fidanzamento.
  on your wedding.
  di felice matrimonio.
  on your silver wedding anniversary.
  per le nozze d'argento.
  on your golden wedding anniversary.
  per le nozze d'oro.

Opinion

What is your opinion?
Cosa ne pensa?

I totally agree with you.
La penso come Lei.

I have a different opinion.
Non sono d'accordo con Lei.

In my opinion ...
Secondo me ...
  we should go back.
  dovremmo tornare indietro.
  we should turn back.
  dovremmo tornare indietro.
  we should drive home.
  dovremmo tornare a casa.
  that is wrong.
  è sbagliato.
  that is right.
  è giusto.

That is outrageous!
Che sfacciato!

Enthusiasm

amazing
sorprendente

fantastic
fantastico

gorgeous
magnifico

great
eccellente, ottimo

super
bellissimo

terrific
formidabile

Indignation

Nonsense!
Sciocchezze!

Stop that!
Lasci perdere!

Leave me alone!
Mi lasci in pace!

Don't you dare!
Guai a Lei!

What nerve!
Che impertinente!

What a mess!
Che porcheria!

In Italy people congratulate each other on their saints' days, the *onomastico*.

Problems

Can you please help me!
Per favore mi aiuti!

I don't see well.
Non vedo (più) bene.

I don't hear well.
Non sento (più) bene.

I feel sick.
Mi sento male.

I am dizzy.
Ho le vertigini / Mi gira la testa.

Please call a doctor.
Per favore chiami un dottore.

Insults

Fool!
Imbecille!

Shit!
Merda!

Idiot!
Idiota!

Imbecile!
Cretino!

Nonsense!
Deficiente!

Dumb bitch!
Brutta strega!

First Approach

May I join you?
Posso sedermi vicino a lei?

Are you travelling alone?
Viaggia da sola?

Are you married?
È sposata?

Do you have a boyfriend?
È fidanzata?

I think you're very nice.
La trovo molto simpatica.

You are really sweet.
(Tu) sei davvero carina / carino.

Do you have anything planned for this evening?
Ha già programmi per questa sera?

Shall we do something together?
Le va di fare qualcosa insieme?

Shall we go out together this evening?
Le andrebbe di uscire con me questa sera?

May I invite you lunch / dinner?
Posso invitarLa a pranzo / cena?

When should we meet?
A che ora ci vediamo?

At eight o'clock in front of the movie theatre.
Alle otto davanti al cinema.

I can pick you up.
Passo a prenderLa io.

I am looking forward to it.
Ne sono lieta.

Thank you for a wonderful evening.
Grazie per la bella serata.

I would be very happy if we could see each other again.
Mi farebbe molto piacere rivederLa.

Can I bring you home?
Posso accompagnarLa a casa?

Italians can expand their supply of curses by combining the word *porco(a)* (pig) with some other word.

Agreement

May I join you?
Posso sedermi qui?

Sure, why not?
Certo! / Perchè no?

Would you like something to drink?
Vuole bere qualcosa?

Yes, that's a good idea.
Sì, volentieri.

I think you're very nice.
La trovo veramente molto simpatica.

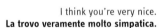

Do you have anything planned for this evening?
Ha già programmi per questa sera?

I am meeting my husband.
Sì, ho un appuntamento con mio marito.

In Italian the distinction between acquaintances and friends is not very important; the word for "friend" is usually used.

Polite but Firm

I am waiting for ...
Sto aspettando ...
my husband.
mio marito.
my wife.
mia moglie.
my (boy)friend.
il mio amico.
my (girl)friend.
la mia amica.

It was nice meeting you, but unfortunately I have to go now.
Mi ha fatto piacere incontrarLa, ma adesso devo proprio andare.

Unfortunately, I have no time.
Mi spiace, non ho tempo.

I already have something else planned.
Mi spiace, ho già altri programmi.

Leave me alone please!
La prego, mi lasci in pace!

Please go now.
Se ne vada adesso per favore.

You are being pushy.
Sei uno scocciatore.

Impolite and Very Firm

Stop that!
Mi lasci in pace!

Stop that immediately!
Smettila!

Go away!
Vattene!

Get out!
Levati dai piedi!

Take your hands off me!
Tenga a posto le mani!

I'll call the police!
Chiamo la polizia!

This person is becoming offensive.
Aiuto! Questa persona mi sta molestando!

This person is threatening me.
Aiuto! Mi ha minacciato!

Things Are Getting Serious!

I have fallen in love with you.
Mi sono innamorato di te.

I would like to go to bed with you.
Ho voglia di fare l'amore con te.

Your place or mine?
Andiamo da te o da me?

But only with a condom!
Ma solo se usi il preservativo!

There is a major jump in the quality of the relationship between *amico* and *amica* to *fidanzato* and *fidanzata*, which correspond roughly to boy/girlfriend.

On the Phone

Good day. This is Barron's Publishing House. May I help you?
Buon giorno. Qui è la casa editrice Barron's. In cosa posso esserLe utile?

I would like to speak to Mr. Pavone.
Vorrei parlare con il sig. Pavone.

Who is calling?
Chi lo desidera?

My name is Giovanni Bianchi.
Mi chiamo Giovanni Bianchi.

Just a minute, I'll connect you.
Un momento, glielo passo.

Unfortunately, the line is busy. Would you like to hold?
Purtroppo è occupato. Può attendere?

I'll call again later.
Richiamo io più tardi.

Direct dialing to extensions is indicated by *interno* or *numero interno*.

Using the Telephone

Is Paul there?
C'è Paolo?

Paul speaking.
Sono io.

To whom am I speaking?
Con chi parlo?

Could you connect me with Mr. Smith?
Può passarmi il sig. Smith?

Please stay on the line / Please hold.
Certo, rimanga in linea.

There is no reply.
Non risponde nessuno.

He is on another line.
É al telefono.

Can I leave a message?
Posso lasciare un messaggio?

Can you please repeat the phone number slowly?
Può ripetermi lentamente il numero di telefono per favore?

I'm sorry, I have dialled the wrong number.
Scusi, ho sbagliato numero.

Excuse me, I didn't get your name.
Scusi, non ho capito il Suo nome.

Can I call you back?
Posso richiamarLa?

Thanks for your phone call.
Grazie per aver chiamato.

There is no such number.
Il numero da lei selezionato è inesistente.

cell phone, cellular
il cellulare

receiver
la cornetta

dial tone **il signale libero**

phone call **la chiamata telefonica**

answering machine **la segreteria telefonica**

information **le informazioni**

busy signal **il tono (di) occupato**

classified directory / yellow pages **le pagine gialle**

direct dialling **l'interno**

unit **lo scatto**

long-distance call **la (comunicazione) interurbana**

charge **la tariffa di addebito**

card telephone **il telefono a scheda**

telephone connection / telephone line **la linea**

pay phone / coin-operated telephone **il telefono a gettoni**

emergency **la chiamata di emergenza**

local call **la (comunicazione) urbana**

collect call **la chiamata a carico del destinatario**

telephone book **l'elenco telefonico**

phone card **la scheda telefonica**

telephone booth **la cabina telefonica**

switchboard **il centralino**

area code **il prefisso**

The telephone receiver is not to be confused with other receivers (such as a radio); in those cases the word is *ascoltatore*.

A Personal Letter

Bianchi Giovanni
Via Dante 15
10100 Torino
Italia

June 6, 2001

Dear Giovanni,

Thanks for your letter and your kind invitation.
As we discussed, we will arrive at your place next Thursday at about 6:00 p.m. We're really looking forward to it!

Yours truly,
Maria

Bianchi Giovanni
Via Dante 15
10100 Torino
Italia

6 giugno 2001

Caro Giovanni,

vorrei ringraziarti per la tua lettera e per il tuo cortese invito.
Come stabilito, ci troveremo da voi giovedì prossimo verso le 18.00.
Non vediamo l'ora di vedervi!

Salutoni,
Maria

In speaking of close relatives such as parents and children, the article is omitted: my cousin, *mia cugina;* my brother, *mio fratello.*

A Business Letter

June 6, 2001
Re: your letter of June 4, 2001

Dear Mr. Bianchi,

Thank you for your letter.
We confirm our appointment for this Thursday at about 6 p.m. Please find attached a few documents that will be useful in preparing for our discussions.
If you have any further questions, please feel free to call on me at any time.

Sincerely,
Maria Ross
Manager

6 giugno 2001
Rif.: Vs. lettera del 4 luglio 2001

Egregio Signor Bianchi,

desidero ringraziarLa per la Sua lettera.
Confermo il nostro incontro per giovedì prossimo verso le 18.00. In allegato troverà alcuni documenti per la preparazione del nostro colloquio.
In caso di ulteriori domande, mi può contattare telefonicamente in qualsiasi momento.

Distinti saluti
Amministratrice
Maria Ross

Intestazione is the Italian for "letterhead."

Salutations

Dear Ms. Bianchi ...
(Egregia) Gentile Sig.ra Bianchi ...

Dear Mr. Bianchi ...
Egregio Sig. Bianchi ...

Dear Ms. Bianchi ...
Cara Sig.ra Bianchi ...

Dear Sirs / To whom it may concern
Egregi signori,

Greetings

Very formal:
Illustrissimo Sig. / Illustrissima Sig.ra

Less formal:
Egregio Sig. / Egregia Sig.ra

Personal:
Caro ... / Cara ...

Casual:
Carissimo ... / Carissima ...

Important Vocabulary

sender
il mittente

address
l'indirizzo

enclosure
l'allegato

salutation
titolo

address
l'indirizzo

reference
il riferimento

letterhead
l'intestazione

envelope
la busta

date
la data

registered mail
la raccomandata

recipient
il destinatario

greeting
la formula di saluto

post office box (P.O. Box)
la casella postale

zip code
il codice postale

stamp
il francobollo

The representative in Parliament is addressed as *Onorevole* (Honorable Sir).

Subjects

ballet **il balletto**

television **la televisione**

film **il film**

jazz **jazz**

cinema **il cinema**

concert **il concerto**

culture **la cultura**

literature **la letteratura**

music **la musica**

news **le notizie**

opera **l'opera**

politics **la politica**

press **la stampa**

radio **la radio**

religion **la religione**

sports **lo sport**

theater **il teatro**

economy / finance **l'economia**

magazine **la rivista**

newspaper **il giornale**

Politics

Italy is a parliamentary democracy. The country is divided into twenty regions, some of which have special status as so-called autonomous regions because of their ethnic characteristics.

Two interesting anomalies are the Vatican, a sovereign state located in Rome and headed by the Pope (who holds legislative and executive powers), and the tiny principality of San Marino, also independent, and located east of Florence. The latter is known to most people because of its colorful postage stamps.

Italy has a president, who is chosen by elected delegates and who has more constitutional powers than some of his European counterparts. Parliament consists of two chambers (a senate and a house of representatives). At the head of the government is the prime minister (*il presidente del consigilio dei ministri* – the head of the ministers' council).

Federal President **il Presidente federale**

Chancellor **il Cancelliere**

House of Representatives **la Camera dei deputati**

Federal Council **il Consiglio federale**

representative / congressman **il deputato**

vote **la votazione**

political refugee **il richiedente di asilo politico**

citizens' action / citizens' initiative **il comitato civico**

democracy **la democrazia**

immigration **l'immigrazione**

coalition **la coalizione**

monarchy **la monarchia**

parliament **il parlamento**

government **il governo**

taxes **le tasse**

constitution **la costituzione**

elections **le elezioni**

In the Italian governmental system, the senate, *il senato*, corresponds to the same branch of our government.

At the Border

Your passport, please!
Il (Suo) passaporto, prego!

Your passport has expired
Il Suo passaporto è scaduto.

How long are you staying?
Quanto tempo rimane?

How much money do you have with you?
Quanto denaro porta con sè?

Do you have anything to declare?
Ha qualcosa da dichiarare?

Please open your suitcase.
Apra la valigia per favore.

Can you show me a receipt?
Ha una fattura da presentare?

You have to declare that.
Questo deve essere dichiarato.

There are no more border checks within the European Union. However, spots checks may occur.

Therefore, always keep your personal identification papers or passport and your auto insurance papers with you.

If you arrive by plane, you still have to go through customs and border control. You will see a special counter set aside for citizens of European Union countries.

You can go through.
Può passare.

Even Italian is interspersed with anglicisms; as a result, you will often see *meeting point* instead of *punto di incontro*.

Customs Regulations

Within the European Union, you may transport goods for personal use in practically unlimited quantities.

If you exceed the following quantities, in the case of a spot check you may have to prove convincingly that the items are really for your personal use, which may prove difficult considering how generous these limits are:

Alcoholic drinks

20 liters of liquor under 22% vol.
10 liters of liquor over 22% vol.
90 liters wine (including a maximum of 60 liters of sparkling wine)
110 liters of beer

Tobacco

800 cigarettes
400 cigarillos
200 cigars
1 kg tobacco

Coffee, tea, and perfume

No limit

Customs

I have nothing to declare.
Non ho niente da dichiarare.

These are gifts.
Questi sono regali.

These are personal belongings.
Questi sono oggetti personali.

I want to declare merchandise in the value of ...
Devo dichiarare merci di un valore di ...

departure
uscita

arrival
entrata

export
esportazione

import
importazione

declarable goods
merci da dichiarare

customs
dogana

customs declaration
dichiarazione doganale

customs regulations
regolamentazioni doganali

customs check
controllo doganale

duty-free
esente da dazio doganale

dutiable
soggetto a dazio doganale

You have had too much to drink? In more familiar terms you would say, *Lei è ubriaco* or *Lei è ciuco* (tipsy).

Booking a Flight

I would like to make a reservation to Milan.
Vorrei prenotare un volo per Milano.

For when?
Per quando?

Next Tuesday.
Per martedì prossimo.

One way?
Sola andata?

Round trip.
Andata e ritorno.

The flight leaves at 3:40 P.M.
C'è un aereo (verso le) 15.40.

Is there an earlier flight?
Prima non c'è niente?

I'm sorry, that flight is booked full.
Mi spiace, il volo precedente è già al completo.

If you want to rent an apartment, the word is *affittare*; but if you want to rent a car, you say *noleggiare*.

Booking a Flight

Where is the Alitalia counter?
Dove è lo sportello dell'Alitalia?

When is the next flight to Milan?
Quando parte il prossimo volo per Milano?

Are seats still available?
Ci sono ancora dei posti liberi?

What does the flight cost?
Quanto costa il biglietto?

I would like to confirm my flight to Milan.
Vorrei confermare il volo per Milano.

Is there a stopover?
È previsto uno scalo?

Is there a connecting flight?
Devo prendere un volo di coincidenza?

My flight number is ...
Il mio numero di volo è ...

How much baggage can I take?
Quanti bagagli posso portare?

Can I take this as hand baggage?
Questo posso portarlo come bagaglio a mano?

I would like to change my flight to Milan.
Vorrei cambiare la prenotazione del mio volo per Milano.

At what time must I be at the airport?
Quando devo trovarmi all'aeroporto?

How long is the flight?
Quanto tempo dura il volo?

Is there an extra charge for this?
Per questo è previsto un supplemento?

Are there any reduced rates?
Ci sono offerte più economiche?

Do children pay the full fare?
I bambini pagano il biglietto intero?

If the flight is overbooked, I would be prepared to take the next flight.
Se il volo è al completo, prenoto per quello successivo.

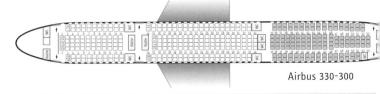

Airbus 330-300

There is no doubt that *weekend* has been adopted by the Italian language.

Security Check

Last call for flight LH465 to Milan.
Ultima chiamata per il volo LH465 per Milano.

Excuse me, my flight leaves in a few minutes. Would you please let me through?
Scusi, il mio volo parte tra pochi minuti. Mi potrebbe far passare?

I am in a hurry myself.
Anch'io ho fretta.

Put all objects into this receptacle.
Metta tutti gli oggetti in questo contenitore.

Open your bag.
Apra la Sua borsa.

Switch on your notebook.
Accenda il Suo notebook.

Passenger Bianchi, traveling to Milan, is requested to proceed immediately to gate 12.
Il passeggero Bianchi, prenotato per Milano, è richiesto urgentemente all'uscita 12.

If *un ingorgo* (tie-up) develops, there is often mention of *una coda* (a line).

On the Plane

Please extinguish all cigarettes.
Si prega di spegnere le sigarette.

Please fasten your seat-belts!
Allacciare le cinture di sicurezza!

Where can I put this?
Dove posso mettere questo?

Could I please have something to drink?
Mi potrebbe portare qualcosa da bere, per cortesia?

Could you please pour me another coffee?
Mi può versare un altro po' di caffè?

Could you please bring me a blanket?
Può portarmi una coperta, per cortesia?

Do you have any toys for my children?
Ha dei giocattoli per i miei figli?

Can you heat up the baby food?
Mi potrebbe scaldare il latte / l'omogeneizzato per il bambino?

Do you also have vegetarian meals?
Ci sono anche cibi vegetariani?

Can you give me something for my nausea?
Mi può dare una compressa per il mal d'aria?

What is our cruising altitude?
A quale quota stiamo volando?

Will we arrive on time?
Arriveremo puntuali?

When can I use my notebook?
A partire da quando potrò usare il mio notebook?

Arrival

When does my connecting flight leave?
Quando parte il mio volo di coincidenza?

I have missed my flight.
Ho perso l'aero.

I can't find my baggage.
Non riesco a trovare i miei bagagli.

My baggage has been lost.
Sono stati persi i miei bagagli.

My suitcase has been damaged.
La mia valigia è stata danneggiata.

Italians like superlatives, so instead of saying *bene, grazie*, you may also say *benissimo, grazie*.

Important Vocabulary

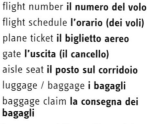

suitcase
la valigia

traveling bag
la borsa da viaggio

backpack / knapsack
lo zaino

flight number **il numero del volo**
flight schedule **l'orario (dei voli)**
plane ticket **il biglietto aereo**
gate **l'uscita (il cancello)**
aisle seat **il posto sul corridoio**
luggage / baggage **i bagagli**
baggage claim **la consegna dei bagagli**
baggage cart **il carrello portabagagli**
belt **la cintura**

takeoff **il decollo**
departure time **l'orario di decollo**
arrival time **l'orario di arrivo**
connecting flight **il volo di coincidenza**
crew **l'equipaggio**
boarding pass **la carta d'imbarco**
landing / disembarkation form **la carta di sbarco**

window seat **il posto accanto al finestrino**

hand baggage **il bagaglio a mano**
landing **l'atterraggio**
non-smoking section **non fumatori**
passenger **il passeggero**
smoking section **i fumatori**
return flight **il volo di ritorno**
counter **lo sportello**
life jacket **il giubbotto di salvataggio**
security check **il controllo di sicurezza**
meeting place **il punto di incontro**
excess baggage **il (pacco di consegna) sovraccarico**
delay **il ritardo**
stopover **lo scalo**

If you are in a situation where you have to spell a name for an Italian person, use the Italian terms whenever possible.

Taxi

Where is the nearest taxi stand?
Dove è la prossima fermata del taxi?

Taxi!
Taxi!

I would like to order a taxi for 10 o'clock.
Vorrei prenotare un taxi per le 10.00.

Can you please send a taxi immediately?
Può inviare immediatamente un taxi, per cortesia?

Please take me...
Mi porti ...

    to the hotel...
    all'albergo ...
    to this street...
    in questa via ...
    downtown.
    al centro.
    to the airport.
    all'aeroporto.
    to the railway station.
    alla stazione ferroviaria.

What will the fare cost, approximately?
Quanto costa il tragitto più o meno?

Take the shortest / fastest route.
Prenda la strada più corta / più rapida.

Straight ahead here, please.
Prosegua diritto.

Turn right / left here.
Svolti qui a destra / a sinistra.

Please stop here.
Si fermi qui.

Stop at the next crossroad.
Si fermi al prossimo incrocio.

Please wait for me here.
Mi aspetti qui.

How much do I owe to you?
Quanto Le devo?

We agreed on another amount.
Ma si era parlato di un'altra cifra!

That seems too much!
Mi sembra un po' troppo caro!

I would like a receipt.
Vorrei la ricevuta, per cortesia.

Keep the change!
Tenga il resto!

That is for you.
Questa è per Lei.

You can keep the change.
Può tenere il resto.

Could you please put our luggage into the trunk?
Le dispiacerebbe mettere le nostre valigie nel bagagliaio?

Could you please help me to get in?
Potrebbe aiutarmi a salire, per cortesia?

Do you know a reasonably priced hotel in the neighborhood?
Conosce un albergo economico nelle vicinanze?

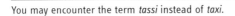

You may encounter the term *tassi* instead of *taxi*.

Renting a Car

I would like to rent a car for a week.
Vorrei noleggiare una macchina per una settimana.

Which price category would
you like?
**Quale categoria di prezzo
desidera?**

A medium-size car.
Quello di un'utilitaria.

Let's see what we have. That will
cost 200 euros per week.
**Vediamo un po' i prezzi. Sono 200
euro alla settimana.**

Can I see your driver's license?
Può mostrarmi la patente?
Please sign here.
Firmi qui per favore.

Una utilitaria is a small car; the designation for midsize cars is less common in
Italian than in English.

Renting a Car

Do you have weekend rates?
Sono previste delle tariffe per il fine settimana / Ha delle tariffe week-end?

Do you have any special offers?
Ci sono offerte speciali?

Do you have any better offers?
Ci sono anche offerte più convenienti?

Can I return the car elsewhere?
Posso restituire il veicolo anche presso un'altra sede?

At what time do I have to return the vehicle?
A che ora devo restituire il veicolo?

Is this with unlimited mileage?
Quanti chilometri posso percorrere al massimo?

Do I have to leave a deposit?
Devo lasciare una caparra?

Is the gas tank full?
Ha fatto il pieno?

Do I have to return the car with a full tank?
Devo restituire la macchina con il serbatoio pieno?

Could you explain to me what the different types of insurance are?
Può spiegarmi le varie assicurazioni esistenti?

I would like comprehensive insurance.
Vorrei un'assicurazione contro tutti i rischi.

How much is the deductible?
A quanto ammonta la franchigia?

Can my partner drive the car too?
Il mio partner è autorizzato a guidare la macchina?

Does the car have ...
Il veicolo è dotato di ...
  air conditioning?
  aria condizionata?
  power steering?
  servosterzo?
  ABS?
  ABS?

  anti-theft device?
  dispositivo antifurto?

Do you have a map?
Ha una cartina?

What's the fastest way through the city?
Dove devo passare per attraversare rapidamente la città?

Can I bypass the city center?
É possibile evitare il centro?

What's the best way to go downtown?
Come si arriva al centro?

The Italians use the expression *fare il pieno* for "to fill it up."

The Car

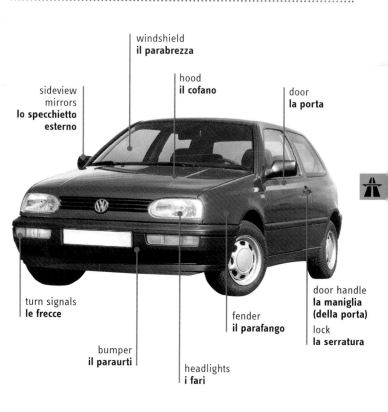

windshield
il parabrezza

hood
il cofano

sideview
mirrors
**lo specchietto
esterno**

door
la porta

turn signals
le frecce

door handle
**la maniglia
(della porta)**

lock
la serratura

fender
il parafango

bumper
il paraurti

headlights
i fari

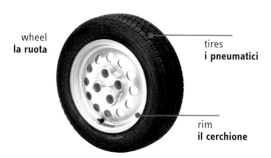

wheel
la ruota

tires
i pneumatici

rim
il cerchione

In using the directional lights for a right or left turn, the expression is *mettere la freccia a destra* or *a sinistra*; *freccia* is the word for *arrow*.

The Car

steering wheel
il volante

gearshift lever
la leva del cambio

exhaust
lo scarico

brake
il freno

tachometer
il contagiri

gas pedal
l'acceleratore

hand brake / emergency brake
il freno a mano

glove compartment
il vano posaoggetti

rear
la parte posteriore

rear windshield
il lunotto

trunk
il bagagliaio

clutch
la frizione

motor
il motore

rearview mirrors
lo specchietto retrovisore

windshield wiper
il tergicristallo

seat belt
la cintura di sicurezza

speedometer
il tachimetro

fuel gauge
la spia serbatoio

emergency flashers
l'impianto lampeggio emergenza

When you flash your headlights, you use the *lampiluce* function.

The Motorcycle

exhaust **lo scarico**
flasher / blinker **le frecce**
brake light **gli stop (luci freno)**
brake cable **la fune freno**
motor **il motore**
taillight **le luci retromarcia**
headlight **il faro**
tank **il serbatoio**
drum brake **il freno a tamburo**
carburetor **il carburatore**

Lead-free gasoline is also called *benzina verde* in Italy.

On the Move

Excuse me, how do I get to ...
Scusi, come si arriva a ...

Can you show me that on the map?
Può indicarmi il posto sulla cartina?

Can you show me where I am on the map?
Può indicarmi il punto in cui mi trovo sulla cartina?

Where is the nearest gas station?
Dove si trova il prossimo distributore (di benzina)?

Where is the nearest repair shop?
Dove si trova la prossima officina?

traffic light
semaforo

highway
autostrada

national highway
strada statale

crossroad
incrocio

country road
strada provinciale

Is that the street that goes to ...?
Vado bene per ...?

How far is it to ...?
Quanto dista ...?

Directions

You took the wrong road.
Ha sbagliato strada.

You must drive back.
Deve tornare indietro.

Straight ahead.
Prosegua sempre diritto.

Go to the first crossroad.
Vada fino al primo incrocio.

Turn right at the next corner.
Quindi svolti a destra all'angolo successivo.

Follow the signs.
Segua le indicazioni.

Turn left at the traffic lights.
Svolti a sinistra al semaforo.

"I'm out of gas" can be expressed more picturesquely as *Sono al secco* (I'm on empty.)

Notices and Traffic Signs

Caution! **Attenzione!**

Exit **Uscita**

Keep Driveway Clear **Tenere libero il passaggio**

Construction **Lavori in corso**

One-Way Street **Strada a senso unico**

Junction **Sbocco**

Form Lanes **Disporsi su un'unica corsia**

Single-Lane Traffic **Strada percorribile su una sola corsia**

End of No Parking Zone **Fine del divieto di parcheggio**

Road Narrows **Restringimento della carreggiata**

Pedestrian Footbridge **Passaggio pedonale**

Pedestrian Zone **Zona pedonale**

Danger **Pericolo**

Dangerous Curve **Curva pericolosa**

Hill **Discesa**

Speed Limit **Limite di velocità**

Hairpin Bend **Curva a 180 gradi**

No Stopping **Divieto di sosta**

No Entry **Divieto di accesso**

Rotary Traffic **Circolazione rotatoria**

Crossing **Incrocio**

Slow Lane **Corsia per veicoli lenti**

Slow Down **Decelerare**

Slow Ahead **Decelerare ulteriormente**

Trucks Only **Autocarro / camion**

No Parking **Divieto di parcheggio**

Parking Garage **Autosilo**

Parking Lot **Parcheggio**

Ticket Vending Machine **Distributore del ticket di parcheggio**

Radar Control **Controllo radar**

Keep Rght **Guidare a destra**

Right Lane Has Right of Way **Diritto di precedenza a destra**

No Right Turn **Divieto di svolta a destra**

Loose Gravel **Pietrisco**

Road Slippery When Wet **Strada sdrucciolevole**

Dead End **Strada senza uscita**

Turn on Headlights **Accendere i fari**

Danger of Skidding **Strada sdrucciolevole**

Expressway **Superstrada**

School-Bus Stop **Fermata scuolabus**

Traffic **traffico / coda**

Road Construction **Lavori in corso**

Underground Parking Garage **Garage sotterraneo**

No Passing **Divieto di sorpasso**

Bypass **Circonvallazione**

Detour **Deviazione**

Traffic Light **Semaforo**

Right of Way **Diritto di precedenza**

Yield **Dare precedenza**

Caution! **Attenzione!**

No U-Turn **Divieto di svolta**

Toll Booth **Pagamento pedaggio**

The sign announcing *velocità controllata elettronicamente* (speed checked electronically) is the equivalent of our signs for radar-controlled speed.

Parking

Can I park here?
Posso parcheggiare qui?

How long can I park here?
Per quanto tempo posso parcheggiare?

Where is there ...
Mi può indicare ...
  a parking lot?
  un parcheggio?
  an underground parking garage?
  un garage sotterraneo?
  a parking garage?
  un autosilo?

What are the parking charges ...
Quant'è la tariffa di parcheggio ...
  per hour?
  all'ora?

per day?
al giorno?

Is the parking lot attended?
Il parcheggio è custodito?

During what hours is the parking garage open?
Per quanto tempo rimane aperto l'autosilo?

Is the parking garage open the whole night?
L'autosilo rimane aperto anche di notte?

Where is the cashier?
Dove è la cassa?

Where is the automatic ticket vending machine?
Dove si trova il distributore automatico del ticket di parcheggio?

Can you give me change?
Può cambiarmi la moneta?

I have lost my parking ticket.
Ho perso il ticket.

parking meter
Parchimetro

At the Gas Station

gas pump
il distributore

gas can
la tanica di benzina

gas
la benzina

oil
l'olio

super
la benzina Super

regular
la benzina normale

unleaded
senza piombo

diesel
Diesel

brake fluid
il liquido dei freni

A parking lot that's guarded is *un parcheggio custodito.*

Filling Up

Where is the nearest gas station?
Dove si trova il prossimo distributore (di benzina)?

Please fill it up.
Mi fa il pieno per favore?

Give me 10 euros' worth please.
Mi mette la benzina / il gasolio per 10 euro?

I need one quart of oil.
Vorrei un litro di olio.

  Can you check ...
  Per favore mi può controllare ...
  the oil.
  il livello dell'olio?
  the tire pressure.
  la pressione dei pneumatici?
  the water.
  l'acqua di raffreddamento?

Please fill the windshield washer fluid.
Mi può rimboccare il serbatoio dell'impianto di lavaggio?

Can you do an oil change?
Mi può cambiare l'olio?

Would you please clean the windshield?
Mi può pulire il parabrezza?

Can I have the car washed?
Mi può lavare la macchina?

Octane Ratings

In the US, gasolines have the following octane ratings:

Regular: 89

Mid-grade: 91

Super: 94

Compare these ratings with those of Italy.

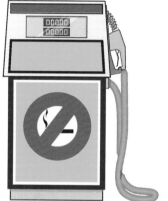

How much do I owe you?
Quanto Le devo?

Do you have a map?
Ha una cartina?

Where are the toilets?
Dov'è la toilette?

At a car wash you will generally be asked about exterior or interior cleaning:
all'esterno or *all'interno.*

Breakdowns

Can you help me? I've
had a breakdown.
**Può aiutarmi? Ho un
guasto.**

What is wrong?
Cos'è successo?

The motor won't start.
Il motore non si avvia.

Let me have a look.
Mi faccia vedere.

I think you have to take it
to the repair shop.
**Mi sa che dovrà andare in
officina.**

Can you tow my car?
Può rimorchiarmi?

The sign *Assistenza stradale* often refers to roadside assistance for breakdowns.

I've had a breakdown.
Ho un guasto.

I have a problem ...
Ho dei problemi ...
   with the battery.
   con la batteria.
   with the steering.
   con lo sterzo.
   when starting.
   con l'avvio.
   with the lights.
   con l'impianto luci.
   with the brakes.
   con i freni.
   with changing gears.
   col cambio.

I have a flat tire.
Ho una ruota bucata.

It won't start.
La macchina non si avvia.

The motor splutters / misses.
Il motore gira a strappi.

I'm out of gas.
Non c'è più benzina nel serbatoio.

Do you know of a repair shop nearby?
Sa se c'è un'officina (riparazioni) nelle vicinanze?

Can you take me to the nearest gas station?
Può portarmi al prossimo distributore (di benzina)?

Can you tow me?
Può rimorchiarmi?

Can you push me?
Può darmi una spinta?

Can you repair it?
Può ripararlo?

Can I drive any further with the car?
Posso proseguire in macchina?

When will it be ready?
Per quando sarà pronta?

Can I phone from here?
Posso fare una telefonata?

Please connect me with my car rental agency.
Può mettermi in contatto con la mia agenzia di autonoleggio?

gas can
la tanica di benzina

warning-triangle
il triangolo

tool
attrezzo

breakdown / towing service **il servizio rimorchio**

towing cable **la fune di rimorchio**

breakdown assistance **l'assistenza meccanica**

jumper cables **il cavo per avviamento con cavi ponte**

jack **il martinetto**

emergency flashers **l'impianto lampeggio emergenza**

For the expression "I have a flat," you can say either *Ho una ruota bucata* or *Ho una ruota a terra.*

In the Repair Shop

There's something wrong with the brakes.
I freni sono difettosi.

My car is losing oil.
La mia macchina perde olio.

The warning light is on.
La spia è accesa.

Change the spark plugs please.
Mi può cambiare le candele?

Can you recharge the battery?
Mi può caricare la batteria?

Can you fix the tire?
Mi può riparare la ruota bucata?

Can you take a look at it?
Può dare un'occhiata?

Can you repair it?
Può ripararlo?

Something is wrong with the motor.
Il motore non funziona bene.

How long will it take?
Quanto tempo ci impiegherà?

What will it cost?
Quanto costa la riparazione?

starter **il motorino di avviamento**	light bulb **la lampadina**
brake lining **la guarnizione del freno**	heater **il riscaldamento**
brakes **i freni**	rear axle **l'assale posteriore**
brake fluid **il liquido del freno**	horn **il clacson**
brake light **la luce freno**	cables **il cavo**
gasket **la guarnizione**	v-belt **la cinghia trapezoidale**
fuel injector pump **l'iniettore**	air conditioning **il climatizzatore**
spare tire **la ruota di scorta**	radiator **il radiatore**
spare parts **i ricambi (parti di ricambio)**	coolant / water **l'acqua di raffreddamento**
backfire **l'accensione difettosa**	short circuit **il cortocircuito**
gears / transmission **il cambio**	steering **lo sterzo**

Do you think Italians say "I need a liter of oil?" No, in such cases they say *chilo* (kilo).

battery
la batteria

distributor
il distributore

piston
il pistone

water pump
la pompa dell'acqua

shock absorber
il paraurti

spark plugs
le candele

headlight flasher
il lampeggiatore

locking system
il fusibile

dynamo
la dinamo

seat
il sedile

motor
il motore

valve
la valvola

oil filter
il filtro dell'olio

carburetor
il carburatore

taillight
la luce posteriore

front axle
l'assale anteriore

ignition
l'accensione

cylinder head
la testata cilindri

sunroof
il tettuccio scorrevole

If you want to get a ride as a hitchhiker, the best thing to say is, *Può darmi un passaggio, per cortesia?*

Traffic Regulations, Violations

Like so many things in the European Union, even the traffic regulations are "harmonized," as the official usage would term it. Just the same, Italy, like every other country, has maintained its own special characteristics. Here are some traffic regulations to which you need to pay particular attention: Headlights are required in poorly lighted tunnels and passageways. Using a telephone while driving is permitted only with a hands-free headset. Streetcars always have right of way. Parking is prohibited by black-and-green painted curbs, which are reserved for buses and taxis. You must signal to change lanes or pull over.

Legal alcohol limit
   0.8

Speed limit
   in town, 50 km/h
   outside town, 90 km/h
   divided highways, 130 km/h

Seat belt law in effect

In Italy drivers are required to pay promptly in case of traffic violations. The traffic police are likely to deal summarily with tourists.

Current fines
   DWI, up to 1225 euros
   20 km/h over the speed limit, 125 euros and higher
   red light infraction, 60 euros and higher
   passing violation, 60 euros and higher;
   parking violation, 30 euros and higher.

Police emergency: 112

Accident assistance: 118

You were driving too fast.
Guidava con eccesso di velocità.

You went through a red light.
É passato con il rosso.

You didn't yield the right of way.
Non ha rispettato la precedenza.

You cannot park here.
Ha parcheggiato in sosta vietata.

This is a no-passing area.
Qui è vietato sorpassare.

You have had too much to drink.
Guidava in stato di ubriachezza.

In Italy traffic lights are a kind of sacred cow, but more for foreign tourists than for the natives, who have a tendency to overlook red.

Accidents

There has been an accident.
C'è stato un incidente.

I've had an accident.
Ho avuto un incidente.

Some people have been injured.
Ci sono dei feriti.

Do you have any bandages?
Ha delle bende?

Please call ...
Per favore chiami ...
   the police.
   la polizia.
   an ambulance.
   un'ambulanza.
   breakdown assistance.
   il soccorso stradale.

My name is ...
Mi chiamo ...

I am a tourist.
Sono un turista.

What is your name and address?
Mi può dire il Suo nome e indirizzo?

Please give me your insurance number.
Mi dia il Suo numero di polizza(assicurativa).

I need witnesses.
Ho bisogno di testimoni.

I have witnesses.
Ho dei testimoni.

It was my fault.
È stata colpa mia.

It was your fault.
È stata colpa Sua.

I had the right of way.
Io avevo la precedenza.

You came too close.
Lei si è avvicinato troppo alla mia macchina.

You braked suddenly.
Lei ha frenato all'improvviso.

Please inform my family. The number is ...
Può informare la mia famiglia per favore?

A hairpin turn is known as a *tornante*.

The Bicycle

saddle
la sella

handlebars
il manubrio

saddlebags
la borse porta-attrezzi

chain
la catena

pedal
il pedale

tires
i pneumatici

gearshift
l'innesto marce

reflector
il riflettore

cable **il cavo Bowden**

bicycle pump **la pompa (della bicicletta)**

rims **i cerchioni**

repair kit **il kit di riparazione gomme**

hand brake **il freno a mano**

chain guard **il copricatena**

cover **il copertone**

mountain bike **il mountain bike**

nut **il dado**

hub **il mozzo**

wheel **la ruota**

racing bike **la bici da corsa**

taillight **la luce posteriore**

inner tube **il tubo flessibile**

mudguard **il parafango**

spoke **il raggio**

valve **la valvola**

headlight **la luce anteriore**

front wheel fork **la forcella della ruota anteriore**

tools **l'attrezzo**

gear **la ruota dentata**

Another word for "reflector" is *catarifrangente*.

Renting a Bicycle

I would like to rent a bicycle.
Vorrei noleggiare una bicicletta.

Gladly. We have a big selection.
Certo. Abbiamo una grande scelta.

I would like something more sporty.
Vorrei qualcosa di più sportivo.

How is this one?
Cosa ne pensa di questa?

How many gears
does the bicycle
have?
**Quante marce ha
questa bici?**

Twenty-one.
Ventuno.

The proper word for bicycle in Italian is *bicicletta*, but Italians often use the
shortened form *bici*.

Renting a Bicycle

How much does a bicycle cost per day?
Quanto costa una bici al giorno?

That is too expensive.
È troppo caro.

Do I have to leave you a deposit?
Devo lasciare una caparra?

Do you have also special offers for more than one day?
Ha anche offerte speciali per un noleggio di diversi giorni?

Do you also rent ...
Noleggia anche ...
  saddlebags?
  borse porta-attrezzi?
  rain gear?
  ombrelli / protezioni contro la pioggia?
  children's seats?
  seggiolini per bambini?
  children's bicycles?
  biciclette per bambini?
  repair kits?
  kit di riparazione?
  helmets?
  caschi?

Can you show us a scenic route from ... to ...?
Conosce un bell'itinerario da ... a ...?

Can you show me an easier route?
Non conosce un itinerario più comodo?

Do you have information about bicycle routes in the area?
Ha materiale informativo su giri turistici nella zona?

Is there a lot of traffic on this route?
C'è molto traffico su questo tragitto?

We have children with us.
Ci sono anche i bambini.

Is this bicycle route suitable for children?
Questo giro è adatto per i bambini?

I have a flat tire.
Ho una ruota a terra.

Can you lend me your repair kit?
Mi può prestare il Suo kit di riparazione gomme?

I fell off my bike.
Sono caduto.

Do you have some bandages?
Ha delle bende?

Rain protection is of course not limited to the *ombrello*, but can also include an *impermeabile* or raincoat.

Buying Tickets

A ticket to Rome, please.
Un biglietto per Roma per favore.

One-way or round-trip?
Sola andata o andata e ritorno?

Only one way, please.
Sola andata.

When does the next train leave?
Quando parte il prossimo treno?

At 10:28 on platform 3.
Alle 10.28 sul binario 3.

Italians sometimes say *prenotare* instead of *riservare*.

At the Ticket Window

I would like to have a timetable.
Potrei avere un orario?

I would like like to go by train from ... to ...
Vorrei un biglietto ... - ...

When does the next train leave?
Quando parte il prossimo treno?

What does the round trip cost?
Quanto costa il viaggio di andata e ritorno?

Are there special offers for tourists?
Ci sono offerte speciali per i turisti?

There is discount for ...
C'è una riduzione per ...
　children?
　bambini?
　schoolchildren?
　scolari?
　students?
　studenti?
　senior citizens?
　pensionati?
　families?
　famiglie?

I would like to have ...
Vorrei ...
　a place in the sleeping car.
　un posto nel vagone letto.
　a sleeping compartment for ... persons.
　uno scompartimento letti per ... persone.
　a reclining seat.
　una cuccetta.
　a seat in first class.
　un biglietto per la prima classe.

Do I have to reserve a seat?
Devo riservare un posto?

I would like to reserve a window seat.
Vorrei un posto accanto al finestrino.

Is that a nonstop train?
Il treno è un diretto?

Does the train stop at Boston?
Il treno ferma a Boston?

Does the train have a dining car?
Il treno ha un vagone ristorante?

Do I have to change trains?
Devo cambiare treno?

From which track does the train depart?
Da quale binario parte il treno?

Where can I check in my luggage?
Dove posso lasciare i miei bagagli?

Can I take my bicycle?
Posso portare con me la bicicletta?

What does that cost?
Quanto costa?

Written Inquiry

Acqua non potabile
Non-drinking water

Occupato
Occupied

Libero
Vacant

Freno di emergenza
Emergency brake

Uscita
Exit

Toilette
Toilets

The platform at the railroad station is *il binario*.

On the Platform / On the Train

Does the train to Rome leave from this platform?
Il treno per Roma parte da questo binario?

Where does the train to Rome leave?
Da dove parte il treno per Roma?

Is this the train to Rome?
È questo il treno per Roma?

Does the train go via Rome?
Il treno passa per Roma?

Is the train from Rome delayed?
Il treno da Roma è in ritardo?

How long is the delay?
Di quanto è il ritardo?

Excuse me, is this seat still unoccupied?
Scusi, è libero questo posto?

Is this seat occupied?
È occupato questo posto?

That is my seat. I have reserved it.
Questo è il mio posto. L'ho riservato.

Can I ...
Posso ...
  open the window?
  aprire il finestrino?
  close the window?
  chiudere il finestrino?

Is there a smoking compartment?
C'è lo scompartimento fumatori?

Where are we?
Dove siamo?

How long do we stop here?
Per quanto tempo ci fermiamo qui?

Will we arrive on time?
Arriveremo puntuali?

Will I make my connecting train?
Faccio ancora in tempo a prendere la coincidenza?

From which track does my connecting train leave?
Da che binario parte la mia coincidenza?

Where is the dining car?

Dove è il vagone ristorante?

Where can I buy something to drink?
Dove si acquista qualcosa da bere?

Where are the toilets?
Dov'è la toilette?

What You Hear

Il treno per Roma arriva sul binario 3.
The train to Rome is arriving on track 3.

Il treno per Roma atteso sul binario 3 ha dieci minuti di ritardo.
The train to Rome on track 3 is delayed by ten minutes.

Salire per favore!
All aboard!

Già visti i biglietti?
Did someone else get on?

Biglietti per favore.
The tickets, please.

Deve pagare la differenza per il supplemento.
You have to buy the ticket on the train.

Tra pochi minuti saremo a Roma.
In few minutes, we will arrive in Rome.

If a train is behind schedule, you will often hear over the loudspeaker, *Il treno...viaggia con circa...minuti di ritardo.*

Important Vocabulary

departure **la partenza**

compartment **lo scompartimento**

stopover **la sosta**

information **le informazioni**

car-train **il treno navetta**

railway station **la stazione**

platform **il marciapiede**

express train **il (treno) diretto**

railroad **la ferrovia**

last stop **il capolinea**

reduction / discount **la riduzione**

ticket **il biglietto**

ticket counter **la biglietteria**

timetable **l'orario**

family ticket **il biglietto per famiglia**

window seat **il posto accanto al finestrino**

lost-and-found office **l'ufficio oggetti smarriti**

aisle **il corridoio**

baggage **i bagagli**

baggage deposit **il guardaroba**

checkroom **il deposito dei bagagli**

locomotive **la locomotiva**

local traffic **il (treno) locale**

emergency brake **il freno di emergenza**

reservation / reserved seat ticket **il biglietto prenotato**

reservation **la prenotazione**

round-trip ticket **il biglietto di andata e ritorno**

conductor **il bigliettaio / controllore**

sleeping car **il vagone letto**

locker **l'armadietto**

dining car **il vagone ristorante**

commuter train **il treno suburbano**

car number **il numero del vagone**

waiting room **la sala d'attesa**

washroom **il lavatoio**

newsstand **il chiosco**

surcharge **il supplemento**

porter **il facchino**

track **il binario**

group card **il biglietto per gruppo**

sleeper **la carrozza con cuccette**

A sleeping car is known as *un vagone letto* or *una carrozza letto*.

Taking the Bus

I would like to travel by bus for two weeks in this area.
Vorrei visitare questa zona in autobus per due settimane.

Do you any have special offers?
Ha offerte speciali?

Do you give a discount for ...
C'è una riduzione di prezzo per ...
    students?
    studenti?
    students?
    scolari?
    senior citizens?
    pensionati?
    handicapped?
    invalidi?
    groups?
    gruppi?
    families?
    famiglie?

Is it cheaper if I buy a round trip ticket now?
Mi conviene pagare insieme l'andata e il ritorno?

Is it possible to reserve seats?
È possibile riservare dei posti?

On which platform does the bus leave?
Da quale fermata parte l'autobus?

Will the passengers be called for departure?
I passeggeri vengono chiamati all'altoparlante?

Does the bus have ...
L'autobus è dotato di ...
    air conditioning?
    aria condizionata?

    reclining seats?
    cuccette?
    a toilet?
    toilette?

When do I have to be at the bus station?
Quando devo trovarmi alla stazione degli autobus?

Do I have to transfer?
Devo cambiare autobus?

Where / when is the next stop?
Dov' / Quand'è la prossima fermata?

How long does the trip take?
Quanto tempo dura il viaggio?

Where does this bus go to?
Dov'è diretto quest'autobus?

The terminal of a bus or streetcar is *la capolinea*.

Traveling by Boat

Could I have a timetable.
Potrei avere un orario?

When does the next ship leave for Ischia?
Quando parte la prossima nave per Ischia?

I would like to have a ticket to Ischia.
Vorrei un biglietto per Ischia.

How much does the trip cost?
Quanto costa il viaggio?

Are there any special offers for tourists?
Ci sono offerte speciali per i turisti?

Is the ticket also valid for the return trip?
Il biglietto vale anche per il viaggio di ritorno?

I would like to take my car along.
Vorrei portare con me la macchina.

What does that cost?
Quanto costa?

When do we have to board?
Quando dobbiamo imbarcarci?

How long does the crossing take?
Quanto tempo dura il tragitto?

In which harbors do we stop?
In quali porti facciamo scalo?

I would like a round-trip ticket for 11 o'clock.
Vorrei un biglietto per il giro delle 11.00.

On Board

I am looking for cabin No. 12.
Sto cercando la cabina n. 12.

Can I have another cabin?
Posso avere un'altra cabina?

Can I have an outside cabin?
Posso avere una cabina esterna?

How much more does that cost?
Quant'è il supplemento?

Where is my luggage?
Dove sono i miei bagagli?

Where is the dining room?
Dove è la sala da pranzo?

When is the meal served?
A che ora vengono serviti i pasti?

When do we leave?
Quando usciamo?

How long is the stop?
Per quanto tempo ci fermiamo?

Can I go ashore?
È consentito scendere dalla nave?

When do I have to be back?
A che ora devo ritornare?

I am feeling sick.
Mi sento male.

Do you have any medicine for seasickness?
Ha una compressa contro il mal di mare?

The word "boat" is also subject to interpretation in Italian. A motorboat is a *motoscafo*; in Venice the open boats are *battelli*.

deck chair
la sedia sul ponte

lighthouse
il faro

life preserver
il salvagente

life jacket
**il giubbotto di
salvataggio**

anchor **l'àncora**
mooring **l'approdo**
outside cabin **la cabina esterna**
car ferry **l'autotraghetto**
port **babordo**
bow **la prua**
steamer **il piroscafo / vapore**
deck **il ponte**
single cabin **la cabina singola**
ferry **il traghetto**
ticket **il biglietto**
mainland **il continente**
riverboat trip **la gita sul fiume**
freighter **il mercantile**
harbor **il porto**
harbor tour **il giro del porto**

stern **la poppa**
inside cabin **la cabina interna**
yacht **lo yacht**
cabin **la cabina**
quay **la banchina**
berth / cabin **la cabina**
captain **il capitano**
cruise **la crociera**
coast **la costa**
shore excursion **l'escursione a terra**
jetty **la passerella**
reclining seat **la cuccetta**
rubber raft / rubber dinghy
l'aeroscivolante
crew **l'equipaggio**
sailor **il marinaio**
motorboat **il motoscafo**
hurricane **l'uragano**
lifeboat **il battello di salvataggio**
rowing boat **la barca a remi**
round trip **il giro**
swell **il moto
ondoso**
seasickness **il
mal di mare**
sail **la vela**
sailboat **la
barca a vela**
starboard **a
dritta**
steward
l'assistente di bordo
storm **il maltempo**
hydrofoil **l'aliscafo**
wave **l'onda**
double cabin **la cabina doppia**

Since a deck chair on board a boat is usually a chaise lounge, you can also say
sdraio.

Asking for Directions

Excuse me, how do I get to the Colosseum?
Scusi, come si arriva al Colosseo?

Straight ahead, take the second street on the left, then the third on the right.
Prosegua diritto, prenda la seconda strada a sinistra, poi la terza a destra.

The third left?
La terza a sinistra?

No, the second left. There is a gas station, then a supermarket and after that the traffic light.
No, la seconda a sinistra, dove c'è il distributore, poi passa davanti al supermercato e arriva al semaforo.

You mean left at the gas station?
Allora svolto a sinistra al distributore?

No, that is too early. Left at the traffic light.
No, prima deve arrivare al semaforo.

Maybe ten minutes.
Saranno dieci minuti.

Is it far?
È distante?

Ah, thank you. I should be able to find it.
OK, La ringrazio. Vedrò di trovarlo.

If you can't classify a person in Italy according to profession, you should quickly promote him to *dottore*.

What You Hear

Mi spiace, non saprei
I'm sorry, I don't know.

Non sono di queste parti.
I am not from here.

È distante.
It is far.

Non è distante.
It is not far.

Attraversi la strada.
Cross the street.

Non può sbagliarsi.
You cannot miss it.

Chieda ancora una volta.
Ask once again.

Traveling on Foot

Excuse me, can you help me?
Scusi, può aiutarmi?

I am looking for Dante Street.
Cerco Via Dante.

Can you show me that on the map?
Può indicarmela sulla cartina?

How far is it to the Colosseum?
Quanto dista il Colosseo?

traffic light
il semaforo

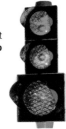

Can I take a bus?
Posso arrivarci in autobus?

Where are the nearest toilets?
Dov'è una toilette nei dintorni?

bridge
il ponte

pedestrian zone
la zona pedonale

alley
il vicolo

building
l'edificio

street number
il numero civico

downtown
il centro urbano

crossing
l'incrocio

park
il parco

square / place
la piazza

street
la strada

Icy roads are *strade ghiacciate*.

Directions

 left
a sinistra

 right
a destra

 straight ahead
diritto

the first left
la prima a sinistra

the second right
la seconda a destra

before
prima

behind
dietro

after
dopo

Instead of saying *cartina* for a road map, you can use *carta stradale*.

Local Traffic

Where is the nearest ...
Dove è la prossima ...
   subway station?
   stazione della metropolitana?
   bus stop?
   fermata dell'autobus?
   streetcar stop?
   fermata del tram?

When does the next bus leave?
Quando parte il prossimo autobus?

When does the last subway train leave?
Quando parte l'ultima metropolitana?

Where can I buy a ticket?
Dove si comprano i biglietti?

Can you help me? I don't know how to use the vending machine.
Può aiutarmi? Non riesco a far funzionare il distributore.

What is this button for?
Che funzione ha questo pulsante?

I would like to go to ... Which ticket must I buy?
Vorrei andare a ... Quale biglietto devo comprare?

Can you give me change for this?
Può cambiarmi la moneta?

How much does a trip cost?
Quanto costa un percorso?

How much does the round trip cost?
Quanto costa il viaggio di andata e di ritorno?

Do you also have ...
Ha anche ...
   multiple ride tickets?
   biglietti per più corse?
   day tickets?
   biglietti giornalieri?
   weekly tickets?
   biglietti settimanali?
   monthly tickets?
   biglietti mensili?
   tourist tickets?
   biglietti per turisti?

How long is this ticket valid?
Per quanto tempo vale questo biglietto?

Can travel as often as I like with this ticket?
Questo biglietto vale per un numero illimitato di corse?

I can get off and then back on again with the same ticket?
Questo biglietto vale per una sola corsa?

Is this ticket also valid for the return trip?
Questo biglietto vale anche per il viaggio di ritorno?

Is this ticket also valid for the bus / the subway?
Questo biglietto vale anche per l'autobus / la metropolitana?

Which line goes to ...?
Qual è la linea per ...?

In which direction do I have to go?
In quale direzione devo andare?

Where do I have to transfer?
Dove devo cambiare?

In Italy a bus, especially a touring coach, is *un pullman*.

What is the name of the next station?
Qual è la prossima stazione?

How many stops are there?
Quante fermate sono in tutto?

Can you please tell me when we reach the stop?
Può avvertirmi quand'è la fermata, per cortesia?

What do I have to do when I want to get off?
Cosa devo fare per scendere?

I did not know that the ticket was not valid here.
Non sapevo che il biglietto non fosse valido su questo mezzo.

I have lost the ticket.
Ho perso il biglietto.

I have left something behind in the bus.
Ho dimenticato qualcosa sull'autobus.

Can you tell me where the lost-and-found office is?
Può dirmi dove si trova l'ufficio oggetti smarriti?

subway
la metropolitana

bus
l'autobus

streetcar
il tram

last stop
il capolinea

driver
il conducente

ticket
il biglietto

ticket vending machine
il distributore di biglietti

timetable
l'orario

stop
la fermata

ticket inspector
il controllore

conductor
il bigliettaio

day ticket
il biglietto giornaliero

one-week ticket
il biglietto settimanale

season ticket
l'abbonamento

When the next train stop is announced over the loudspeaker, you will hear something like, *La prossima fermata è...*

Overnight Accommodations

Where Can One Spend the Night?

Tourism is an important source of income for Italy, and there is a corresponding availability of good overnight accommodations.

Even the less pretentious hotels are generally clean and offer friendly service.

Breakfast is usually not included in the price of a room, and even when it is, the choice is commonly limited to coffee, jelly, and croissants.

Tourists usually go to a neighborhood bar (there is one on practically every corner).

In Italy a bar is a cross between a café and restaurant and is a social meeting place where you can get something to drink and small snacks.

farm
la fattoria

bungalow
il bungalow

campsite
il campeggio

vacation house
appartamenti o case da affittare (per ferie)

vacation apartment
l'appartamento (per villeggiatura)

hotel
l'albergo

youth hostel
l'ostello della gioventù

motel
il motel

private guest house / bed and breakfast
la camera privata

single room
la camera singola

double room
la camera doppia

suite
la suite

breakfast included
la colazione

half board
la mezza pensione

full board / American plan
la pensione completa

Written Inquiry

Camere da affittare
Rooms available / Vacancies

Tutto esaurito
No vacancies

Offerta speciale
Special offer

You can simply say *una singola* or *una doppia* instead of *una camera singola* or *una camera doppia*.

Finding a Room

Is there a good hotel here?
Conosce un buon albergo qui nei dintorni?

How is the hotel?
Com'è (l'albergo)?

I am looking for a room for ...
Cerco una camera per ...
   one night.
   una notte.
   three days.
   tre giorni.
   a week.
   una settimana.

Do you still have rooms available?
Ha ancora camere libere?

What do they cost?
Quanto costano?

Is there a discount for children?
C'è una riduzione per bambini?

That is a little too expensive.
È un po' troppo caro.

Do you have something less expensive?
Non c'è qualcosa di più conveniente?

Do you have a list of private guest houses?
Avrebbe un elenco di alloggi privati?

Where else can I find a vacant room in vicinity?
Dove posso trovare camere libere nei dintorni?

What is the address?
A quale indirizzo?

Can you please write down the address?
Può scrivermi qui l'indirizzo?

How can I get there?
Come ci si arriva?

Is it far?
È distante?

Written Inquiry

Dear Sir / Madam,

We would like to reserve a room for two persons with attached bath, with an ocean view and balcony if possible, from August 7–15.

Please give us the rates for a double room, and also the rates for breakfast, half board and full board.

Sincerely,

Egregi signori,

vorremmo prenotare dal 7 al 15 agosto una camera per due persone con doccia o vasca da bagno, possibilmente con vista sul mare e balcone.

La preghiamo di fornirci l'elenco prezzi per una camera doppia, eventualmente con colazione, metà pensione e pensione completa.

Distinti saluti

Italians have two words for hotel: *hotel* and *albergo*.

Reserving by Phone

Please give me room reservations.
Mi può passare l'ufficio di prenotazione (camere) per favore?

Just a minute, I will connect you.
Un momento, prego.

Grand Hotel, room reservations. May I help you?
Grand Hotel, Prenotazione camere. In cosa posso servirLa?

I would like to have a room for tonight.
Vorrei una camera per questa notte.

About 5 P.M.
Verso le 17.00.

When will you arrive?
Quando arriverà?

We will reserve your room until 6 P.M. If you will be arriving later, please let us know.
Possiamo darLe la camera fino alle 18.00. Se arriva più tardi deve telefonare.

The Italian word for "room" is *camera* or *stanza*; *camera* is always used in booking a hotel reservation.

At the Reception Desk

Good day, I would like a room for one night.
Buon giorno, vorrei una camera per una notte.

We have a double room for 120 euros.
Abbiamo una camera doppia per 120 euro.

That's fine. Can I pay by credit card?
Benissimo. Posso pagare con la carta di credito?

Of course.
Certamente.

Can I look at the room?
Posso vedere la camera?

Of course.
Certo.

Good, I will take it.
Bene, la prendo.

Here are the keys. The room number is 212, on the second floor.
Ecco le chiavi. È la camera n° 212 al secondo piano.

When you check into a hotel, you may simply hear *Ha un documento, per favore?* instead of *Può mostrarmi il Suo passaporto?*

I have reserved a room.
Ho prenotato una camera.

May I look at the room?
Posso vedere la camera?

I will take this room.
La prendo.

I don't like the room.
Non mi piace questa camera.

The room is ...
La camera è ...
  too small.
  troppo piccola.
  too noisy.
  troppo rumorosa.
  too dark.
  troppo buia.

Can I have another room?
Posso avere un'altra camera?

Do you have something ...
Non avrebbe una camera ...
  quieter?
  più tranquilla?
  bigger?
  più grande?
  cheaper?
  più economica?
  with a balcony?
  con balcone?

Do you have non-smoking rooms?
Avete camere per non fumatori?

Do you also have rooms with three beds?
Ha anche camere con tre letti?

Could you put in a third bed?
È possibile aggiungere un terzo letto?

Is there an elevator?
C'è l'ascensore?

Is breakfast included?
La colazione è compresa?

Where can I park my car?
Dove posso lasciare la macchina?

Do you have a garage?
Ha un garage?

I will stay for two nights.
Rimango per due notti.

I don't yet know how long we will stay.
Non abbiamo ancora deciso quanto tempo rimarremo.

Can we still get something to eat in the neighborhood?
Possiamo ancora trovare dei ristoranti aperti nei dintorni?

Please bring the luggage to the room.
Può portarmi le valigie nella camera per favore?

What You Hear

Siamo al completo. È tutto esaurito.
We are full.

Mi dice il nome per favore?
In whose name?

Quanto tempo desidera rimanere?
How long would you like to stay?

Compili il modulo.
Fill in the registration form please.

Può mostrarmi il Suo passaporto?
May I see your passport?

Firmi qui.
Please sign here.

Breakfast is also referred to as *prima colazione*.

Requests and Desires

I would like to extend my stay by one night.
Vorrei prenotare ancora per una notte.

The key for room 212, please.
Mi può dare la chiave per la camera 212 per favore?

I have locked myself out of my room.
Sono rimasto chiuso fuori dalla mia stanza.

I have lost my key.
Ho perso la chiave.

Can you put that into your safe?
Può mettere questo in cassaforte?

Is there any mail for me?
C'è posta per me?

I am expecting a phone call.
Aspetto una telefonata.

Please inform them that I ...
Può lasciar detto che ...
　　will call them back.
　　richiamerò io?
　　will be back in the evening.
　　mi troveranno in serata?

I would like to leave a message for Mr. Smith.
Vorrei lasciare un messaggio per il sig. Smith.

When is breakfast served?
A che ora viene servita la colazione?

Where can one have breakfast?
Dove viene servita la colazione?

Is the hotel open the whole night?
L'hotel rimane aperto tutta la notte?

When must I check out of the room?
Quando devo lasciare libera la camera?

Can you wake me at eight o'clock?
Può svegliarmi alle 8.00?

Can you please bring me a towel?
Mi può portare un asciugamano per favore?

Can I have an extra blanket?
Posso avere un'altra coperta?

Can you get a typewriter for me?
Può procurarmi una macchina per scrivere?

Can I send a fax from here?
Posso usare il Suo fax?

DO
NOT
DISTURB!

When someone asks you, "Did you enjoy yourselves?" you may answer with *Sì, ci è piaciuto molto*.

The Hotel Staff

manager
il direttore

receptionist
il capo ricevimento

bellboy
il fattorino d'albergo

porter
il portinaio

chambermaid
la cameriera

room service
il servizio camere

Complaints

The key doesn't fit.
La chiave non funziona.

The door won't open.
Non riesco ad aprire la porta.

The room has not been made.
La camera non è stata sistemata.

The bathroom is dirty.
Il bagno è sporco.

There are no towels.
Non ci sono asciugamani.

The window doesn't open / close.
Non riesco ad aprire / chiudere la finestra.

Departure

We are leaving tomorrow morning.
Partiamo domani mattina.

We are leaving now.
Partiamo adesso.

I would like the bill.
Potrei avere il conto?

Can I pay by credit card?
Posso pagare con la carta di credito?

I am paying cash.
Pago in contanti.

This does not add up right.
Ha sbagliato il calcolo.

Can I leave my luggage with you for the day?
Posso lasciare qui i bagagli solo per oggi?

Could you call me a taxi?
Può chiamarmi un taxi?

We were very pleased.
Siamo rimasti soddisfatti.

Please get my luggage.
Può prendere i miei bagagli per favore?

Italians use *sistemare* for many things, such as to take care of or look after something, and even to clean up a room.

Accessories

adapter
l'adattatore

child's bed
la culla

ashtray
il posacenere

suitcase
la valigia

iron
il ferro da stiro

pillow
il cuscino

TV
il televisore

refrigerator
il frigorifero

light bulb
la lampadina

sewing kit
l'attrezzatura per il cucito

hand towel
l'asciugamano

lock
la serratura

comb
il pettine

key
la chiave

The abbreviation *TV* is often used for television.

telephone
il telefono

bathroom
la toilette

alarm clock
la sveglia

toothbrush
**lo spazzolino da
denti**

bed **il letto**
blanket **la coperta**
bed sheets **il lenzuolo**
stationery **la carta da lettere**
double bed **il letto doppio**
shower **la doccia**
single bed **il letto singolo**
ice cube **il cubetto di ghiaccio**
electricity **l'elettricità**
floor **il piano**
window **la finestra**
hairdryer **l'asciugacapelli**
breakfast **la colazione**
luggage **i bagagli**
half board **la mezza pensione**
high season **l'alta stagione**
electric blanket **la termocoperta**
heating **il termosifone**
cold water **l'acqua fredda**
babysitting / child care **la sala
ricreazione**

reception desk **la registrazione / la
reception**
elevator **l'ascensore**
bath **il bagno**
bathrobe **l'accappatoio**

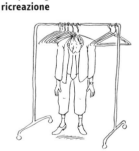

hanger **l'attaccapanni**
wardrobe / closet **il guardaroba**
air conditioning **l'aria condizionata**
lamp **la lampada**
mattress **il materasso**
ocean view **la vista sul mare**
minibar **il minibar**
low season **la bassa stagione**

bath towel **l'asciugamano**
bathtub **la vasca da bagno**
balcony **il balcone**

Italians have several expressions for toilet, including *servizi* and *gabinetto*.

Accessories

night table **il comodino**
off season **la bassa stagione**
wastepaper basket **il cestino**
radio **la radio**
bill **il conto**
reservation **la prenotazione**
restaurant **il ristorante**
reception **la reception**
shutters **la serranda**
quiet **tranquillo**
safe **la cassaforte**
wardrobe / closet **l'armadio**
desk / writing table **la scrivania**

toilet paper **la carta igienica**
door **la porta**
fan / ventilator **il ventilatore**
extension cord **la prolunga**
full board **la pensione completa**
curtain **la tenda**
pre-season **la bassa stagione**
warm water **l'acqua calda**
wash basin **il lavandino**
water **l'acqua**
valuables **gli oggetti di valore**
toothpaste **il dentifricio**
room **la camera**
room number **il numero di camera**
to the street **sulla strada**

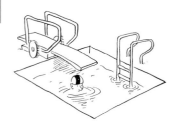

swimming pool **la piscina**
soap **il sapone**
armchair **la poltrona**
mirror **lo specchio**
socket **la presa di corrente**
plug **la spina**
floor **il piano**
plug / stopper **il tappo**
beach **la spiaggia**
chair **la sedia**
terrace **la terrazza**

The Italian word for "swimming pool" is *la piscina*.

Reserving a Vacation Home

vacation apartment
appartamento (per villeggiatura)

vacation house
Casa (di villeggiatura)

We are looking for a vacation apartment for three weeks.
Cerchiamo un appartamento per tre settimane.

We have rented a vacation apartment for three weeks.
Abbiamo affittato un appartamento per tre settimane.

There are four of us.
Siamo in quattro.

We need two bedrooms.
Vogliamo due camere da letto.

We need four beds.
Vogliamo quattro letti.

How many beds are there in the house?
Quanti posti letto sono disponibili?

Where do I pick up the keys?
Dove devo ritirare le chiavi?

Is the vacation apartment completely furnished?
L'appartamento è completamente arredato?

Do we have to bring bed linen?
Dobbiamo portare lenzuola e coperte?

What does it cost to rent bed linen?
Quanto costa affittare lenzuola e coperte?

Does the house have central heating?
L'edificio è dotato di riscaldamento centralizzato?

Does the apartment have a phone?
C'è un telefono nell'appartamento?

Can I make outgoing telephone calls, or only receive incoming calls?
Posso anche fare telefonate o soltanto riceverle?

Is the final cleaning included?
È compresa la pulizia finale?

What does the final cleaning cost?
Quanto costa la pulizia finale?

ocean view
la vista sul mare

"Apartment" can be translated by *appartamento*, but the general term is *alloggio*.

Vacation Home: Practical Matters

Where are the garbage cans / trash cans?
Dove sono i bidoni dell'immondizia?

Do I have to separate the garbage?
Devo provvedere a una raccolta differenziata?

When is the trash / garbage picked up?
A che ora viene ritirata l'immondizia?

Whom should I contact if there are problems?
A chi posso rivolgermi in caso di problemi?

Can you give me the phone number?
Può lasciarmi il numero di telefono?

During our stay, a glass broke.
Si è rotto un bicchiere nel periodo di soggiorno.

How much do I owe you for it?
Quanto Le devo per questo?

The window pane broke.
Si è rotto un vetro della finestra.

Where can I have it repaired?
Dove posso farlo riparare?

Where can one ...
Dov'è che posso ...
 shop?
 fare acquisti?

make a phone call?
telefonare?
do the laundry?
lavare la biancheria?
hang up the laundry?
appendere la biancheria?

The toilet is clogged.
Il WC è intasato.

The heating isn't working.
Il riscaldamento non funziona.

There is no water.
Non c'è acqua.

There is no hot water.
Non c'è acqua calda.

The faucet is dripping.
Il rubinetto gocciola.

→ Also see HOUSEWARES, p. 159; TOOLS, p. 164; CAMPING EQUIPMENT, p. 165.

If you want a laundry, search for a *lavanderia*. If it is dry cleaning service you need, look for a *lavasecco*.

Equipment

 cutlery /
silverware
le posate

 refrigerator
il frigorifero

 TV
il televisore

 light switch
l'interruttore della luce

 gas range
la cucina a gas

frying pan
il tegame

 dishes
le stoviglie

 lock
la serratura

 glass
il bicchiere

key
la chiave

 grill
la griglia

 vacuum cleaner
l'aspirapolvere

 saucepan /
pot
la casseruola

socket
la presa di corrente

A cooking pot can also be designated with the word *pentola*.

chair
la sedia

telephone
il telefono

plate / dish
il piatto

video recorder
**il video-
registratore**

faucet
il rubinetto

bath **il bagno**
balcony **il balcone**
bed **il letto**
hot water heater **lo scaldabagno**
shower **la doccia**
electric range **la cucina elettrica**
window **la finestra**
window pane **il vetro della finestra**
dishwasher **la lavastoviglie**
heat **il riscaldamento**
coffee machine **la macchina del caffè**
chimney **il camino**
coal heating **il riscaldamento a carbone**
kitchen **la cucina**
microwave **il forno a microonde**
radio **la radio**
bedroom **la camera da letto**
terrace **la terrazza**
table **la tavola**
toaster **il tostapane**
door **la porta**
hot water **l'acqua calda**
clothes dryer **l'asciugabiancheria**
washing machine **la lavatrice**
living room **il soggiorno**
central heating **il riscaldamento centralizzato**

Important Vocabulary

departure date **il giorno della partenza**
arrival date **il giorno dell'arrivo**
apartment **l'appartamento**
bungalow **il bungalow**
vacation spot **il residence**
vacation house **la casa di villeggiatura**
vacation apartment **l'appartamento (per villeggiatura)**

garage **il garage**
ocean view **la vista sul mare**
rent **l'affitto**
garbage **l'immondizia**
garbage can **il bidone dell'immondizia**
extra costs **le spese aggiuntive**
power **la corrente**
voltage **la tensione elettrica**
landlord **il locatore**

If you need to say that an apartment is furnished, in addition to the word
arredato you should add *ammobiliato*.

Youth Hostels

Do you still have rooms available?
Ci sono ancora camere libere?

Do you have rooms only for women?
Ci sono anche camere per sole donne?

What is the cost of...
Quanto
an overnight stay?
costa il pernottamento?
bed linen?
costano coperte e lenzuola?
a lockable cabinet?
costa un armadio che si può chiudere a chiave?

Are there any other reasonably priced accomodations?
Ci sono altre possibilità economiche di pernottamento?

Can I use my own sleeping bag?
Posso usare il mio sacco a pelo?

Do you have bed linen?
Ci sono coperte e lenzuola?

Where is ...
Dov'è ...
the washroom?
il lavatoio?
the shower?
la doccia?
the toilet?
la toilette?

Do you have lockers?
Ci sono armadietti?

When do you close in the evening?
A che ora chiude di sera?

Do you close during the day?
È chiuso di giorno?

Is there breakfast in the morning?
Viene servita la colazione?

What does the breakfast cost?
Quanto costa la colazione?

When is breakfast served?
Quando viene servita la colazione?

Is it possible to work in exchange for for the room and breakfast?
Posso pagarmi vitto e alloggio lavorando qui da Lei?

Are there reduced rates for longer stays?
Ci sono prezzi più favorevoli per chi rimane più a lungo?

Where can I leave a message?
Dove posso lasciare un messaggio?

Can I leave a message with you?
Posso lasciare un messaggio presso di Lei?

Can I have mail sent here?
Posso farmi inviare la posta qui?

Has any mail come for me?
C'è posta per me?

Is the area safe at night?
Questa zona è sicura di notte?

Which bus lines go from here ...
Quali linee portano ...
to the railway station?
alla stazione ferroviaria?
to the harbor?
al porto?
to the beach?
alla spiaggia?
to the airport?
all'aeroporto?
downtown?
al centro?

May I have a different room?
Può cambiarmi camera?

May I leave my luggage here until 12 o'clock?
Posso lasciare qui i miei bagagli fino alle 12.00?

Words for "sleeping bag" are *sacco a pelo* and *saccone* (large sack).

At the Campground

Do you still have vacant camping spots?
Ci sono ancora posti liberi?

Do I have to register in advance?
Devo prenotare?

How far in advance?
Quanto tempo prima?

What does it cost per night for ...
Quanto si deve pagare per ogni notte per ...

  a tent?
  una tenda?
  a trailer?
  una roulotte?
  a camper?
  un (auto)caravan?
  one person?
  una persona?
  a car?
  una macchina?
  a cottage?
  un cottage?

We will stay for three days / weeks.
Rimaniamo tre giorni / settimane.

Can you tell me how to get to my camping spot?
Può indicarmi come arrivare al mio posto?

Where are the ...
Dov'è ...
  toilets?
  la toilette?

  washrooms?
  il lavatoio?
  showers?
  la doccia?
  garbage cans?
  il bidone dell'immondizia?

What voltage is used here ?
Quale tensione utilizzate? (220 V)

Is there a grocery store?
C'è un negozio di alimentari?

Are we allowed to light fires?
È permesso accendere un fuoco?

Is there someone on duty at night?
Il campeggio è custodito di notte?

Where can I speak to the ranger?
Dove posso rintracciare la guardia forestale?

Which side is exposed to the wind?
Qual è il lato esposto al vento?

Can you please lend me a tent peg?
Può prestarmi un chiodo di fissaggio per favore?

Where can I rent / exchange gas cylinders?
Dove posso procurarmi / cambiare le bombole del gas?

In the mountains the hut where people take shelter from the tribulations of the weather is called *un rifugio*.

kerosene lamp /
hurricane lamp
**la lampada a
petrolio**

plug
la spina

electrical connection
l'allacciamento elettrico

gas cylinder
la bombola del gas

gas stove
il fornello a gas

tent peg
il chiodo di fissaggio

children's playground
il parcogiochi

grocery store
il negozio di alimentari

rental fee
la tariffa di noleggio

coins
le monete

propane
il gas propano

drinking water
l'acqua potabile

washing machine
la lavatrice

washroom
il lavatoio

water connection
l'allacciamento dell'acqua

camper
l'autocaravan

trailer
la roulotte

tent
la tenda

tent pole
il palo da tenda

→ Also see HOUSEWARES, p. 159;
TOOLS, p. 164; CAMPING EQUIPMENT,
p. 165

A motorhome can be translated as *autocaravan* or *camper*.

On the Farm

tractor
il trattore

harvester
la mietitrebbiatrice

field
il campo

grain
il grano

ear of grain
la spiga

When someone works in agriculture or in the fields, it is said that he or she *lavora nella campagna.*

straw
la paglia

hay
il fieno

horse
il cavallo

donkey
l'asino

pig
il maiale

A cow is often designated with the word *mucca*; the plural is *mucche*.

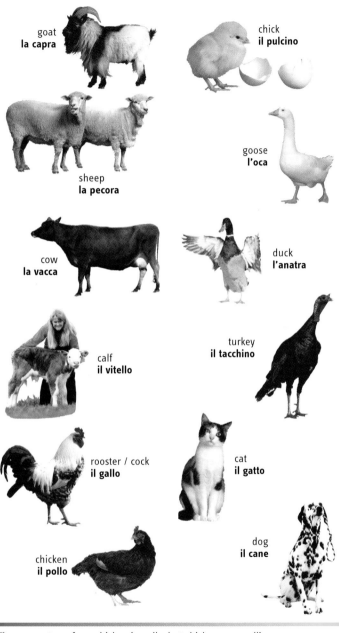

goat
la capra

chick
il pulcino

goose
l'oca

sheep
la pecora

cow
la vacca

duck
l'anatra

calf
il vitello

turkey
il tacchino

rooster / cock
il gallo

cat
il gatto

dog
il cane

chicken
il pollo

The proper term for a chicken is *pollo*, but chickens are *galline*.

Eating and Drinking

Cuisine

Italian cuisine is surely one of the richest in the world. It is noteworthy for its variety, imaginativeness, and (just as importantly) for its nutritive value. The latter can lead to weight problems over time.

People who are used to the philosophy of one-course meals will have to adapt or settle for *un panino* (an open sandwich made with a roll) or *un tramezzino* (a regular sandwich) in one of the many bars that exist even in remote villages. Of course, there's always pizza, pizza everywhere. You may limit yourself to a choice of appetizers in a restaurant and pass up the *primo* (the first course, generally a noodle dish) or the *secondo* (second course, usually a meat dish), not to mention the calorie-rich *dolce* (dessert).

As everywhere in southern Europe, in Italy the midday and evening meals are served hot. The evening meal is the main one, whereas at midday most people are content with *un panino* or a plate of pasta. There is a wide choice among food places, from *pizzerias* to *osterias* and *trattorias* offering simple fare and all the way up to elegant restaurants. Good food, including a bottle of wine, does not come cheap in Italy.

And one thing you should never overlook at a meal is always to get a coupon or a receipt. This is a law in Italy. The server is required to give you a receipt, and you are required to keep it with you. It sometimes happens that Italian tax officials (*guardia di finanza*) check customers when they leave a restaurant. Anyone caught without a receipt for the meal must pay a substantial fine for this "inappropriate tax behavior."

Where to Turn

Ristorante, trattoria, osteria
These are all normal restaurants, although the *ristorante* is often the most elegant.

Spaghetteria
A simple restaurant.

Enoteca
A wine bar, often providing light meals.

Steakhouse
For everything concerning meat.

Paninoteca, spuntinoteca
Simple take-out meals (salads and open sandwiches).

Tavola calda, rosticceria
Snack bars with self-service.

Spuntinoteca
Self-service restaurant with fast-food bar.

Caffé
For breakfast, light meals, and of course all kinds of coffee.

Pasticceria
A pastry shop.

Gelateria
An ice cream parlor.

Autogrill
A restaurant located close to a highway.

Birreria
A pub or bar.

There are many restaurants that are a combination of *Bar e ristorante*, and you can visit them just for something to drink.

Meals

breakfast
la colazione

lunch
il pranzo

dinner
la cena

What You Hear

Ha prenotato?
Do you have a reservation?

Un posto per fumatori o non fumatori?
Smoking or non-smoking?

Desidera un aperitivo?
Would you like a drink before your meal?

Vuole ordinare?
Would you like to order?

I piatti del giorno sono ...
Today's specials are ...

Le consiglio ...
I recommend ...

Mi spiace, quello non ce l'abbiamo.
I'm sorry, we're out of that.

Cosa prende da bere?
What would you like to drink?

Ne gradisce ancora?
Can I give you another?

Va tutto bene?
Is everything okay?

Desidera qualcos'altro?
Would you like anything else?

Il cibo è stato di Suo gradimento?
Did you enjoy your meal?

Meal Times

Breakfast
7 – 9 A.M.

Lunch
12.30 – 2 P.M.

Dinner
7:30 - 10 P.M.

What You Often Need

Where are the restrooms?
Dov'è la toilette?

Can you please pour me another one?
Me ne può versare dell'altro per favore?

Can I please have the menu (again)?
Mi può (ri)portare il menu per cortesia?

May I order.
Potrei ordinare?

Can you bring the wine menu?
Mi può portare il menu dei vini?

No thank you, I'm full / that's all.
No grazie, non prendo altro.

Can I pay by credit card?
Posso pagare con la carta di credito?

Signs and Posters

Piatti pronti
Carryout

Ultima ordinazione alle ...
Last orders at...

Attendere per posti a sedere
Please wait to be seated

Pagare alla cassa
Please pay the cashier

Piatto del giorno
Today's / Daily Special

Most guests don't arrive for the evening meal before 8:30 P.M.; at midday, the greatest crowd begins at 1:00.

In a Restaurant

For Italians, visiting a restaurant involves more than food intake; even if it sounds a little exaggerated, a restaurant is also a catalyst for social interactions, providing the grease, the cement, and the fuel for personal relationships.

In order to meet all these purposes, the participants have to enjoy the food, which explains the good level of meals and service found in so many Italian restaurants.

The purpose of social interaction also justifies the long time that a meal may take. An evening meal with friends or acquaintances, or the Sunday noon meal with the family in a restaurant can go on for two to three hours.

Reservations are recommended, especially on a Saturday evening and for Sunday mid-day.

There is no single recommendation for tipping in Italy. A tip is not necessarily expected—especially when the chef or a member of his family provides the service. Of course you can give a tip to express your satisfaction with the food and the service, but that is not mandatory. If you leave a tip, a sum amounting to five to ten percent is adequate.

In many restaurants you pay at the *cassa*; then you may of course leave a tip on the table. One rule of thumb holds that the better the restaurant, the more likely it is that a tip is expected.

There is no strict dress requirement in good establishments in Italy; in other words, you will be admitted practically everywhere even without jacket and tie.

I am hungry.
Ho appetito.

Can you recommend a good restaurant?
Può consigliarmi un buon ristorante?

I would like something to eat.
Vorrei mangiare qualcosa.

I would just like a bite of something.
Vorrei mangiare un boccone.

I would just like something to drink.
Vorrei solo bere qualcosa.

I would like to have breakfast.
Vorrei fare colazione.

I would like to have dinner.
Vorrei cenare.

I would like to have lunch.
Vorrei pranzare.

Often the waiter will appear before you and say *Dica*, which is equivalent to "May I help you?" or "Fire away."

Ordering

Pardon me!
Scusi!

Yes?
Sì?

Can I please have the menu?
Mi può portare il menu per favore?

Of course. Just a minute.
Certo. Un momento.

Would you like to you order?
Vuole ordinare?

Thanks a lot!
Grazie!

Don't mention it.
Di niente

What do you recommend?
Cosa mi consiglia?

I recommend the day's special.
Le consiglio il piatto del giorno.

Thanks! I would like ...
Grazie! Vorrei ...

If the waiter can't get to you right away, he may call out to you, *Arrivo!*, meaning "I'll be right there."

Making a Reservation

I would like to reserve a table ...
Vorrei prenotare un tavolo ...
for six persons.
per sei persone.
for tonight.
per questa sera.
for 5 P.M.
per le 17.00.

I have reserved a table in the name of Bianchi.
Ho prenotato un tavolo a nome di Bianchi.

I would like a table ...
Vorrei un tavolo ...

by the window.
vicino alla finestra.
in a quiet corner.
in un angolo tranquillo.

Do you have a smoking / non-smoking area?
Vuole un posto per fumatori o non fumatori?

Where can we wait?
Dove possiamo aspettare?

How long will we have to wait until there is a table free?
Quanto tempo dobbiamo aspettare?

Ordering

The menu / beverage menu, please.
Mi può portare il menu per favore?

What do you particularly recommend?
Cosa mi consiglia?

Can we order the beverages right now?
Possiamo ordinare subito da bere?

Do you also have senior citizens' / children's portions?
Ci sono anche porzioni per anziani / bambini?

Are there also vegetarian dishes?
Ci sono anche cibi vegetariani?

Is there any alcohol in this dish?
I cibi contengono sostanze alcoliche?

I am a diabetic.
Io soffro di diabete.

I am not very hungry. Can I have a small portion?
Non ho molta fame. Mi può portare una porzione ridotta?

I will have ...
Io prendo ...

Can you prepare the dish without garlic?
È possibile ordinare cibi senza aglio?

A bottle of wine, please.
Può portare una bottiglia di vino per favore?

You are not likely to find a nonsmoking section in most Italian restaurants.

Paying

I would like the bill, please.
Mi può portare il conto?

I am in a hurry.
Ho fretta.

Is the tip included in the bill?
La mancia è compresa nel conto?

Everything on one bill, please.
Può fare un conto unico?

Separate bills, please.
Può fare conti separati?

Do you take ...
Accettate ...
   credit cards?
   carte di credito?

traveller's checks?
traveller cheque?
checks?
assegni?

I don't think the bill is right.
Credo che il conto sia sbagliato.

I did not have that.
Questo non l'ho preso!

Keep the change.
Tenga il resto.

Praise

The meal was excellent.
Il cibo era eccellente.

I liked it a lot.
Mi è piaciuto molto.

Thank you very much, the service was excellent.
Complimenti per il servizio!

We will recommend you.
Diffonderemo la voce.

Complaints

I didn't order that.
Questo non l'ho ordinato.

The meat is tough.
La carne è dura.

Pardon me! We have been waiting quite a while!
Scusi! É già un po' che aspettiamo!

I am sorry, but I was not pleased with it.
Mi spiace, non sono rimasto soddisfatto.

The service was ...
Il servizio era ...
   sloppy.
   trascurato.
   unfriendly.
   cattivo.

The meal was ...
Il cibo ...
   too salty.
   era troppo salato.
   cold.
   era freddo.

If an Italian restaurant is completely full, the waiter will rarely invite you to wait, for no one knows when the next table will be free.

On the Table

ashtray
il posacenere

cup
la tazza

silverware
le posate

plate
il piatto

fork
la forchetta

beverage **la bibita**
pepper **il pepe**
salt **il sale**
bowl **la scodella**
mustard **la senape**
teaspoon **il cucchiaino**
tablecloth **la tovaglia**
sugar **lo zucchero**

glass
il bicchiere

highchair
il seggiolone

Is Something Missing?

Would you bring me some pepper?
Può portarmi il pepe?

Would you bring me a fork?
Può portarmi una forchetta?

Would you please pass me the sugar?
Può passarmi lo zucchero?

spoon
il cucchiaio

How Was It?

knife
il coltello

The food is ... **Il cibo è ...**
   simple. **semplice.**
   hearty. **sostanzioso.**
   sweet. **dolce.**
   sour. **agro.**
   spicy. **ben condito.**
   very spicy. **molto saporito.**
   hot. **piccante.**
   hellishly hot. **molto piccante.**

napkin
il tovagliolo

If you want only a small serving, say that you want *un assaggio*– a sample, so to speak.

The Menu

A good Italian meal can consist of a practically unlimited number of courses. The courses can also be presented in a number of different ways.

It is entirely up to you if you want to have your meal in the form of appetizers (*antipasti*), or if you wish to have a specific number of appetizers, a first course (*il primo*, usually a noodle dish) followed by a second course (*il secondo*, often meat) and even a dessert (*dolce* or *dessert*). You may also choose a combination of these possibilities.

If you want a menu, you ask for *il menú*. You will often encounter restaurants that offer a *menú turistico* or a *menu a prezzo fisso* (a fixed-price menu).

In small restaurants there are often no menus, and the chef will tell you what he has to offer that day.

It is usual to conclude every meal with an espresso (for that purpose you merely need to ask for *caffè*). You will often be asked if you want *un caffè corretto*, that is, an espresso with a shot of *grappa*, *amaro*, etc., which is either added to the coffee or served separately.

Italy is a wine country, so it is natural to have wine with meals. Local wines, which are served in carafes, can be quite inexpensive.

Of course you can also drink mineral water (*acqua minerale*), or order it in addition to wine. You can order mineral water that's carbonated (*gassata* or *frizzante*) or natural (*naturale* or *senza gas*).

cold appetizers
gli antipasti freddi

hot appetizers
gli antipasti caldi

soups
le zuppe

salads
le insalate

egg dishes
i piatti a base di uova

fish
il pesce

shellfish
i frutti di mare

meat
la carne

poultry
il pollame

side dishes
i contorni

vegetables
la verdura

cheese
il formaggio

dessert
il dessert

soft drinks
le bibite analcoliche

alcoholic beverages
le bibite alcoliche

hot beverages
le bevande calde

For "drink" you can use the word *bevanda* instead of *bibita*.

Breakfast

The only possible weakness in the marvels of Italian cuisine is breakfast.

The average Italian has breakfast standing at the counter of a bar, and breakfast usually consists of a *cappuccino* or a *caffè* (meaning *espresso*) and *una brioche*, a general term that also encompasses such sweets as croissants. Breakfast doesn't amount to any more than this even in many hotels.

You will rarely encounter eggs for breakfast in Italy. Italians don't care much for eggs. Of course, eggs are used for numerous dishes such as omelets, but in general eggs are somewhat alien to Italian cuisine.

Thus, if you prefer a fairly robust breakfast, you should visit the nearest bar, where you will generally find a wide variety of sandwiches.

A cup of coffee.
Una tazza di caffè.

A glass of milk.
Un bicchiere di latte.

A slice of ham.
Una fetta di prosciutto.

When you order a glass of milk, you will usually be asked if you want it *caldo* (warm) or *freddo* (cold).

Drinks

coffee
il caffè

tea
il tè

milk
il latte

orange juice
il succo di arancia

cocoa **il cacao**
herbal tea **la tisana**

 Eggs

fried egg
l'uovo al tegamino

scrambled egg **le uova strapazzate**
poached egg **l'uovo affogato**
bacon and eggs **l'uovo con pancetta affumicata**
ham and eggs **l'uovo con prosciutto**
omelet **l'omelette**

soft-boiled egg
l'uovo à la coque

hard-boiled egg **l'uovo sodo**

Egg dishes are not common in Italian cuisine.

Bread and Rolls

roll
il panino

white bread
pane bianco

whole wheat bread
pane integrale

croissants
il cornetto

toast
il toast

bread **il pane**
wheat **grano**
caraway seed **cumino**
rye **segala**
butter **il burro**
honey **il miele**
crispbread / cracker **il pane croccante di segala**
jam **la marmellata**
syrup **lo sciroppo**
rusks / Zwieback **le fette biscottate**

Miscellaneous

French toast
il pane fritto

fried potatoes / hash browns
le patate arrostite

cornflakes
i cornflakes

oatmeal / porridge
la pappa di avena

cheese
il formaggio

müsli / granola
la pappa di fiocchi d'avena e frutti

fruit
la frutta

pancakes
la frittata

ham
il prosciutto

bacon
il lardo / lo speck

sweetener / sugar substitute
il dolcificante

waffles
i wafer

sausage
la salsiccia / i salumi

frankfurter
la salsiccetta / i wurstel

yogurt
lo yoghurt

sugar
lo zucchero

You will rarely get whole-grain bread in an Italian restaurant; the word for it is *pane nero*.

Appetizers

artichokes **i carciofi**

oysters **le ostriche**

prawn **i gamberetti**

cockles **i cuoretti**

crab cocktail **il cocktail di gamberi**

crab **i granchi**

melon **il melone**

mussels **le cozze**

smoked salmon **il salmone affumicato**

sardines **le sardine**

clams **le vongole**

Soups

soup of the day **la minestra del giorno**

vegetable soup **la minestra di verdura**

noodle soup **la pasta in brodo**

tomato soup **la minestra di pomodori**

chicken broth **il brodo di pollo**

beef broth **il brodo di manzo**

Salads

green salad **l'insalata verde**

mixed salad / tossed salad **l'insalata mista**

potato salad **l'insalata di patate**

garden lettuce salad **la lattuga**

lettuce salad **l'insalata di pomodori**

Salad Dressings

Roquefort dressing **la salsa Roquefort**

vinaigrette dressing **la salsa vinaigrette**

Italian dressing **italiano**

French dressing **francese**

Russian dressing **russo**

Vinegar and Oil

olive oil **l'olio di oliva**

sunflower oil **l'olio di girasole**

balsamic vinegar **l'aceto balsamico**

herb vinegar **l'aceto aromatizzato**

fruit vinegar **l'aceto di frutta**

wine vinegar **l'aceto di vino**

lemon vinegar **l'aceto di limone**

soy sauce **la salsa di soia**

mayonnaise **la maionese**

Italians are no masters of salad dressings. Usually the diners themselves add olive oil and vinegar to their salads.

From Ocean and Lake

eel **l'anguilla**
perch **il pesce persico**
flounder **la passera di mare**
trout **la trota**
golden bream **la dorata**
shark **lo squalo**
pike **il luccio**
herring **l'aringa**
codfish **il merluzzo**
carp **la carpa**
salmon **il salmone**
mackerel **lo sgombro**
ray / skate **la razza**
roe **le uova di pesce**
anchovies **le acciughe**
sardines **le sardine**
haddock **il baccalà**
flounder **la passera di mare**
swordfish **il pesce spada**
sea pike **il merluzzo**
anglerfish **la rana pescatrice**
sole **la sogliola**
turbot **il rombo**
smelt **lo sperlano**
salt cod **lo stoccafisso**
tuna **il tonno**
squid **il calamaro**
wolf perch **la spigola**

lobster
gambero di mare

prawn
gamberetto

crab
il granchio

oyster **l'ostrica**
cockle **il cuoretto**
jacob mussel **le canocchie**
scallop **il pettine**
crab **il granchio**
crayfish **il gambero**
sea crayfish **l'aragosta**
mussel **le cozze**
sea snail **la lumaca di mare**
spider crab **la granseola**
clam **la vongola**

With mussels, you should always make sure they are fresh.

Types of Meat

mutton
il montone

kid
il capretto

veal
il vitello

goat
la capra

rabbit
il coniglio

lamb
l'agnello

beef
il manzo

pork
il maiale

suckling pig
il maialino

Steaks

rare **al sangue**
medium **media (=mediamente cotta)**
well done **ben cotta**

Specialties

Arrosto di vitello di latte Very tender veal, slow-braised in sage butter (Piemont).

Costata alla fiorentina Veal rib steak roasted in oil and served with a side dish of fried potatoes (Tuscany).

Carbonada Veal strips with braised onions (Piemont, Aosta).

Saltimbocca alla romana Veal medallions with sage and ham (Latium).

If you want to say that the food is spicy, you can also say *piccante*.

Cuts of Meat

steak **la bistecca**
round steak **l'ossobuco**
sweetbread **l'animella**
tip **la spalla**
fillet steak **la bistecca di filetto**
neck **il collo**
leg **il garretto**
brain **il cervello**
prime rib **la costola (alta)**
cutlet **la cotoletta**
tripe **la trippa**
liver **il fegato**
loin **il lombo**
loin steak **la lombata**
kidneys **i reni**
chunks **la noce**
spare ribs **la costoletta**
roast beef **il roastbeef**
saddle of lamb / chine of beef **la schiena**
rump steak **la costata di manzo**
ham **il prosciutto**
deep-fried cutlet **la scaloppina**
tail **la coda**
bacon **la pancetta (affumicata)**
tongue **la lingua**
rib steak **la costina**

Ways to Prepare

browned **rosolato**
roast **arrosto**
low cholesterol **povero di colesterolo**
low-fat **poco grasso**
deep-fried **fritto**
for diabetics **per diabetici**
baked **(cotto) al forno**
fried **arrostito**
steamed **cotto a vapore**
stuffed **ripieno**
grilled **cotto alla griglia**
chopped / ground **tritato**
cooked **bollito**
smoked **affumicato**
shaken / stirred **sbattuto**
braised **stufato**

stew **tagliuzzato**
larded **lardellato**
glazed **glassato**
goulash **spezzatino**
meat loaf **polpettone**
low-calorie **povero di calorie**
breaded **impanato**
raw **crudo**
tangy **piccante**

If you can't think of an Italian word for sausage, in an emergency you can also use our word "wurst."

Poultry

duck
l'anatra

chicken
il pollo

goose
l'oca

turkey
il tacchino

pigeon
il piccione

chicken **il galletto**
capon **il cappone**
guinea fowl **la faraona**
young fattened hen **il pollastro da ingrasso**

quail **la quaglia**
grilled chicken **il pollo arrosto**

Wild Game

pheasant
il fagiano

hare
la lepre

stag
il cervo

partridge
la pernice

deer
il capriolo

wild duck
l'anatra selvatica

boar
il cinghiale

Specialties

Cinghiale in agro-dolce Sweet and sour wild boar Specialties browned with various vegetables (onions, carrots, and celery) and cooked in sweet and sour sauce (raisins, chocolate, pine nuts, sugar, and vinegar).

Lepri in salmi Hare.

Anatra arrosto Roast duck wrapped in bacon and roasted in butter.

Balsamic vinegar is used a lot in Italian cuisine, even as a steak sauce.

Potatoes

french fries
le patatine fritte

roasted potatoes **le patate arrostite**

foil-wrapped baked potatoes **le patate al cartoccio**

baked potatoes **le patate cotte al forno**

potatoes au gratin **le patate al gratin**

potato salad **l'insalata di patate**

croquettes **le crocchette**

mashed potatoes **la purea**

pan-fried potatoes **le patate arrostite**

boiled potatoes **le patate salate**

sweet potatoes / yams **le patate dolci**

Noodles

flat noodles **le tagliatelle**

macaroni **i maccheroni**

spaghetti **gli spaghetti**

Rice

wild rice **il riso selvatico**

cooked rice **il riso cucinato**

fried rice **il riso fritto**

whole-grain / brown rice **il riso integrale**

Bread

roll
il panino

black bread
il pane nero

whole wheat bread
il pane integrale

white bread
il pane bianco

corn **il mais**

wheat **il grano**

rye **la segala**

barley **l'orzo**

oats **l'avena**

In Italy you are most likely to encounter either *patatine* (French fries) or *patate fritte* (fried potatoes).

Vegetables

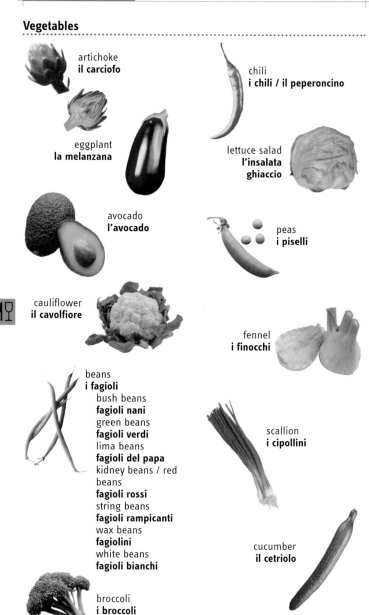

artichoke
il carciofo

chili
i chili / il peperoncino

eggplant
la melanzana

lettuce salad
l'insalata ghiaccio

avocado
l'avocado

peas
i piselli

cauliflower
il cavolfiore

fennel
i finocchi

beans
i fagioli
  bush beans
  fagioli nani
  green beans
  fagioli verdi
  lima beans
  fagioli del papa
  kidney beans / red beans
  fagioli rossi
  string beans
  fagioli rampicanti
  wax beans
  fagiolini
  white beans
  fagioli bianchi

scallion
i cipollini

cucumber
il cetriolo

broccoli
i broccoli

One of the most common soups in Italy is *minestra*; in a slightly thicker form (similar to our stews), it is called *minestrone*.

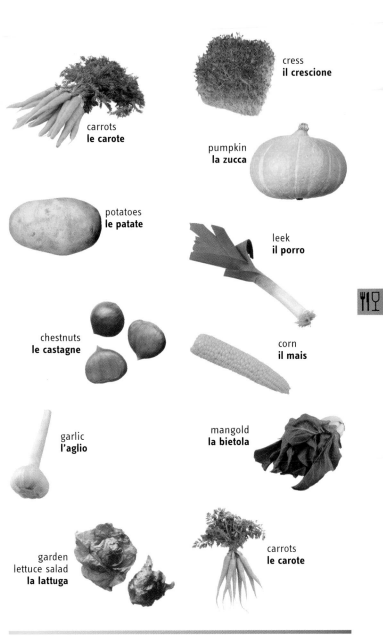

cress
il crescione

carrots
le carote

pumpkin
la zucca

potatoes
le patate

leek
il porro

chestnuts
le castagne

corn
il mais

garlic
l'aglio

mangold
la bietola

garden
lettuce salad
la lattuga

carrots
le carote

A broth is a *consommé*; it has very few vegetables added to it.

Vegetables

okra
okra

radish
il ravanello

pepper
il peperone

brussels sprout
il cavolo di Bruxelles

green peppers / bell peppers
i peperoni

red beets
le rape rosse

mushrooms
i funghi

red cabbage
il cavolo rosso

radishes
i ravanelli

turnips
le rape

In the egg category you need to be concerned only with omelets; you will have to do without the rest of the usual egg dishes in Italy.

zucchini
le zucchine

asparagus
gli asparagi

spinach
gli spinaci

tiny green peas
i piselli dolci

leafy celery
il sedano

onions
le cipolle

tomatoes
i pomodori

watercress **il crescione**
chicory **la cicoria**
endive salad **l'insalata di indivia**
garden salad **l'insalata di campo**
chickpeas **i ceci**
cabbage **il cavolo**
lentils **le lenticchie**
sauerkraut **i crauti**
salsify **le scorzonere**
celery **il sedano**
rutabaga **il navone**

cabbage
il cavolo bianco

savoy cabbage
la verza

Italians call an omelet made with vegetables *una frittata* or *una frittatina*.

Herbs and Spices

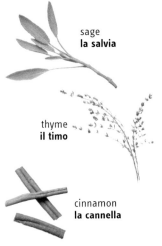

basil
il basilico

sage
la salvia

dill
l'aneto

thyme
il timo

ginger
lo zenzero

cinnamon
la cannella

mint
la menta

oregano
l'origano

parsley
il prezzemolo

rosemary
il rosmarino

vinegar **l'aceto**
tarragon **il dragoncello**
capers **i capperi**
chervil **il cerfoglio**
caraway **il cumino**
bay leaves **le foglie d'alloro**
marjoram **la maggiorana**
horseradish **barbaforte / cren**
nutmeg **la noce moscata**
cloves **i chiodi di garofano**
pepper **il pepe**
saffron **lo zafferano**
salt **il sale**
chive **l'erba cipollina**
mustard **la senape**
vanilla **la vaniglia**
sugar **lo zucchero**

Sun-ripened tomatoes with fresh basil are a special treat in Italy.

Cheese

fresh cheese
il formaggio di crema

grated cheese
il formaggio grattugiato

ewe's-milk cheese
il formaggio pecorino

goat's-milk cheese
il formaggio caprino

Italy doesn't have as many types of cheese as France, but it still offers a rich selection—and not just *mozzarella* and *parmesano*, Italy's leading exports.

In the far northwest of Italy, in the Aosta valley, one specialty is *fontina*, a tasty soft cheese.

In addition there are such cheeses as the blue-mold cheese *gorgonzola*, various grades of *pecorino* (made from sheep's milk), the *taleggio*, which is especially common in Lombardy, and the *grana padano*, a hard cheese that is similar to parmesan.

The real *parmigiano reggiano* comes from the regions of Parma, Modena, Mantua, and Bologna, and it contains milk only from free-ranging animals fed exclusively on green feed. It is generally aged at least 18 months; the *vecchio* is aged up to 24 months, and the *stravecchio*, up to 36 months.

Fruit

pineapple
l'ananas

apple
la mela

apricot
l'albicocca

banana
la banana

pears
le pere

blackberries
le more

strawberries
le fragole

In expressing gratitude for the good food, you can say *Complimenti al cuoco.*

Fruit

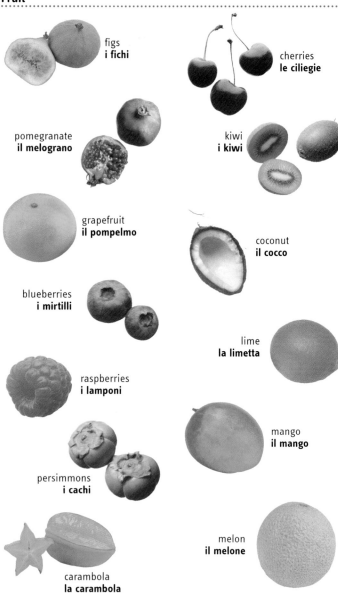

figs
i fichi

cherries
le ciliegie

pomegranate
il melograno

kiwi
i kiwi

grapefruit
il pompelmo

coconut
il cocco

blueberries
i mirtilli

lime
la limetta

raspberries
i lamponi

mango
il mango

persimmons
i cachi

melon
il melone

carambola
la carambola

If you want real orange juice, you must order *un succo*; otherwise, order *una aranciata*.

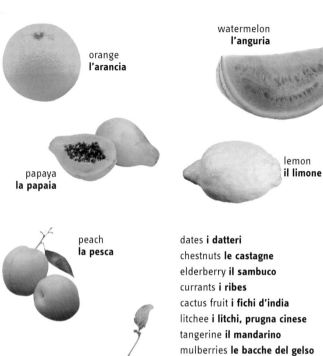

orange
l'arancia

watermelon
l'anguria

papaya
la papaia

lemon
il limone

peach
la pesca

dates **i datteri**
chestnuts **le castagne**
elderberry **il sambuco**
currants **i ribes**
cactus fruit **i fichi d'india**
litchee **i litchi, prugna cinese**
tangerine **il mandarino**
mulberries **le bacche del gelso**
mirabelle / yellow plum **la mirabella**
medlar **le nespole**
passion fruit **la frutta della passione**
cranberries **i mirtilli rossi**
quince **la mela cotogna**
rhubarb **il rabarbaro**
raisins **l'uva passa**
gooseberry **l'uva spina**
tamarind **il tamarindo**

plum
la susina

grapefruit
pomelo

grape
l'uva

Italian does a lot with diminutives; for example, *calzone* is pants, and *calzoncini* is shorts.

Nuts

peanut
le arachidi

pecan nut
le noci di pecan

hazelnut
le nocciole

pistachios
i pistacchi

coconut
la noce di cocco

walnut
le noci

almond
le mandorle

Brazil nuts **le noci del Parà**
pine nuts **i pinoli**
sunflower seeds **i semi di girasole**

Una fetta is what we would call a normal slice of sausage, ham, and so on; *una fettina* is a small slice.

Cakes

apple pie **la crostata di mele**

cheesecake **la torta al formaggio fresco**

blueberry pie **la torta di mirtilli**

carrot nut cake **la torta di noci e di carote**

cherry pie **la torta di ciliegie**

lemon cake **la torta al limone**

fruit tart / pie **la torta di frutta**

cookies **il pasticcino**

chocolate cake **la torta di cioccolato**

vanilla cream pie **la torta alla vaniglia**

cream **la panna**

The combination of cake and coffee served in a café is not very common in Italy. Cake is really used only for dessert, such as a fruit torte or a chocolate cake. Cakes such as a Black Forest cake and other types of cream cakes are mostly unknown.

However, there are an immense variety of very fine sweet pastries available in the *pasticcerie*, the pastry shops, and the pastries are as beautiful as they are delectable. Many people find them to be overly sweet, though.

Desserts

a scoop of ice cream **una pallina di gelato**

assorted ice creams **il gelato misto**

ice cream cone **il cono**

ice cream in a cup **gelato in coppa**

ice cream on a stick **il gelato (da passeggio)**

coffee with ice cream **il caffé gelato**

flavor **il gusto**

with cream **con panna**

vanilla pudding **il budino alla vaniglia**

almond pudding **il budino alle mandorle**

chocolate pudding **il budino al cioccolato**

bread pudding **il budino al pane**

The word *brioche* is often used for *croissant*; however, that's not a real croissant, but rather a variation filled with jelly or chocolate.

Snacks

In Italian a snack is *un spuntino*, and it consists of *un panino* (an open sandwich made on a roll), or a plate of pasta, or the reduced menu in a restaurant that serves lunch.

Italy also has all the known fast-food chains. *Un spuntino* involves essentially everything smaller than the usual menu items and pizza; these small items are known as *piccolezze*.

Pizza

Pizza has been known as an inexpensive snack in Naples for 200 years. Pizza's worldwide conquest began in 1895 when a homesick Neapolitan living in New York opened the first pizzeria. As late as the 1960s the rest of Italy knew of pizza only through hearsay.

Pizza Margherita tomatoes, mozzarella, basil

Pizza alla napolitana tomatoes, mozzarella, anchovies, oregano, olive oil

Pizza calabrese tomatoes, tuna, anchovies, olives, capers

Pizza alle vongole tomatoes, oregano, mussels, parsley, garlic

Pizza quattro stagioni tomatoes, mozzarella, mushrooms, baked ham, artichoke hearts

Pizza al prosciutto tomatoes, mozzarella, baked ham

Pizza con funghi tomatoes, mozzarella, mushrooms, garlic, parsley

Pizza alla siciliana tomatoes, mozzarella, paprika, salami, mushrooms

Pizza alla Pugliese tomatoes, mozzarella, onions

Pizza Romana tomatoes, mozzarella, anchovies, capers, olives

Pizza alla diavola tomatoes, mozzarella, salami, pepperoni

Pilla alla "Re Ferdinando" tomatoes, mozzarella, crab, garlic, parsley

Pizza puttanesca tomatoes, mozzarella, bacon, olives, capers, anchovies

Calzone folded-over pizza with ham, mozzarella, often with ricotta

Pasta is often enriched with *burro salvia* (sage butter).

What Would You Like?

a cup of coffee
una tazza di caffè

a pot of tea
un bricco di tè

a glass of orange juice
un bicchiere di succo di arancia

a bottle of milk
una bottiglia di latte
hot milk
latte caldo
cold milk
latte freddo

a can of coke
una lattina di coca cola

Coffee

coffee **il caffè**
with milk **con latte**

with sugar **con zucchero**
with cream **con panna**
with foamed milk **il cappuccino**
black **nero**
small **ristretto**
medium **normale**
large **allungato**
decaffeinated coffee **il caffè decaffeinato**
espresso **l'espresso**
cappuccino **il cappuccino**
mocha **la moka**

Tea

black tea **il tè nero**
peppermint tea **l'infuso di menta**
fennel tea **il tè al finocchio**
camomile tea **la camomilla**
fruit tea **il tè alla frutta**
herbal tea **la tisana**
flavored tea **il tè aromatico**
unflavored tea **il tè non aromatico**
with lemon **il tè al limone**

Herbal teas are not really an Italian specialty; about the only type you will encounter is *tè di camomilla* (chamomile tea).

Refreshments

mineral water **l'acqua minerale**
carbonated **frizzante**
non-carbonated **naturale**
fruit juice **il succo di frutta**
apple juice **il succo di mela**
orange juice **il succo di arancia**
grape juice **il succo di uva**
tomato juice **il succo di pomodoro**
soda / soft drink **la limonata**

Miscellaneous

cocoa **il cacao**
milk **il latte**
hot / cold chocolate **il cioccolato**

Beer

beer **la birra**
on tap **alla spina**
low alcohol **poco alcolica**
non-alcoholic **analcolica**
bottle **in bottiglia**
can **in lattina**

Liquors

without ice **senza ghiaccio**
with ice **con ghiaccio**
schnapps **grappa / liquore**
herbal schnapps **grappa alle erbe / liquore alle erbe**
liqueur **liquore**
spirits **grappa**

Specialties

Marocchino Coffee with chocolate.
Bicerin alla Cavour Coffee, chocolate, and whipped cream.
Vin brulé Mulled wine.
Elisir china Hot water with Chinese liqueur, orange peels, and sugar.
Nocino Liqueur made from nuts.
Amaretto Almond liqueur.
Limoncello Lemon liqueur.

Generally only checks from an Italian bank are accepted, and then only when the staff recognize the customer.

Wine and Champagne

Can I please see the wine list?
Potrebbe portarmi il menu dei vini?

cork
il tappo

corkscrew
il cavatappi

I would have like to have a bottle of wine.
Vorrei una bottiglia di vino.

What will go best with the meal?
Qual è il miglior vino da tavola?

cooler
il frigorifero

Is this a good year?
È una buona annata (di vino)?

Can I taste the wine?
Posso assaggiare il vino?

The wine tastes like cork.
Il vino sa di sughero.

The wine is too warm.
Il vino è troppo caldo.

Can you please cool the wine?
Le spiace mettermi il vino in fresco?

wine-growing area **l'area coltivabile**
rosé **rosé**
red wine **il vino rosso**
vineyard **la vigna**
vintage **la vendemmia**
wine tasting **l'assaggio del vino**
white wine **il vino bianco**
full-bodied **abboccato**
light **amabile**
fruity **fruttato**
dry **secco**
sweet **dolce**

If you complain about how long you have to wait, you may hear *pazienza*—be patient (the standard Italian apology).

Wine-Producing Regions

Italy is the world's largest wine producer. But the emphasis has always been on quality rather than quantity. The greatest assortment of red wines known beyond the national borders and bearing the DOC designation (*d'origine controllata*) is found in the Piedmont region of northwestern Italy. This is also where *Barolo* comes from. Many people feel that *Barolo* is

designation. Because of the strict regulations concerning origin, many of the best *Chianti* wines bear only the designation *Vino di tavola*, which is normally used to describe common wines.

Like *Chianti*, *Brunello* and the *Vino nobile de Montepulciano* also come from Tuscany; and both are extremely fine, world-class wines. Among white wines, *Chardonnay* is widely available, as are *Pinot grigio* and other types. White wines are more common in the Veneto and Friuli regions, where they are usually fresh and fruity. Even Italian champagne can hold its own against the foreign competition. There's not only *Asti*

the queen of the Italian wines, followed only by *Barbera* and *Barbaresco*.

Some less expensive and less heavy wines that are still very pleasant are the *Dolcetto*, *Grignolino*, *Bonarda*, *Nebbiolo*, and *Freisa*. *Chianti*, almost legendary as the "vacationers' wine," is available not only as an inexpensive mass-produced wine, but also as a very good (and expensive) grade of wine carrying the *Chianti Classico*

Spumante, which is very well known outside Italy, but also many dry sparkling wines (*prosecco*), which we sometimes encounter as fashionable drinks.

When you express gratitude, say either *La ringrazio per...* or simply *Grazie per...*

Shopping

What's Most Important

Do you have toothbrushes?
Mi dà uno spazzolino da denti?

Where do I find a shoe store?
Mi può indicare un negozio di scarpe?

working hours / open hours
orari di apertura

closed
chiuso

I would just like to look around.
Voglio solo guardare.

How much does that cost?
Quanto costa?

That is too expensive for me.
È troppo costoso.

Do you have something cheaper?
Ha qualcosa di più conveniente?

Can I try on the shoes?
Posso provare le scarpe?

That is too big.
Questo numero è troppo grande.

That is too small.
Questo numero è troppo piccolo.

Forget Something?

hairbrush
la spazzola

underwear
la biancheria intima

comb
il pettine

toothbrush
lo spazzolino da denti

band-aid
i cerotti

towel
l'asciugamano

soap
il sapone

pajamas
il pigiama

shoelaces
i lacci delle scarpe

sunblock
la crema da sole

toothpaste
il dentifricio

Business hours are a little chaotic in Italy. On Mondays stores are often open only in the afternoon.

May I help you?
Posso servirLa?

Thanks, I'm just
looking around.
**No, grazie, voglio
soltanto guardare.**

Can I help you?
Posso esserLe utile?

Yes, I would like to have
a pair of pants.
**Sì, vorrei un paio di
pantaloni.**

Here, this is a great
buy.
**Questi sono in
offerta.**

Which size is
that?
Che taglia è?

That is size 38.
**Questa è (di)
taglia trentotto**

Ah, I think that is
too small.
**Oh, allora penso
che siano troppo
piccoli.**

Would you like to try
it on?
Vuole provarli?

Yes. Where are the
changing rooms?
Sì. Dove sono gli spogliatoi?

For "size" you will often hear the word *misura* for shoes and *taglia* for clothes.

What You Often Need

Thanks, that is all.
Basta così, grazie.

I would like to have a pound of cherries.
Vorrei mezzo chilo di ciliegie.

Do you have toothbrushes?
Avete anche spazzolini da denti?

Where are the neckties?
Dove posso trovare le cravatte?

What can you recommend?
Cosa mi consiglia?

Do you have any special offers?
Ci sono offerte speciali?

I have seen a pair of shoes in the display window.
Ho visto un paio di scarpe in vetrina.

I don't want to spend more than ten euros.
Non voglio spendere più di dieci euro.

I like these.
Queste mi piacciono.

I don't like these.
Queste non mi piacciono.

That is not exactly what I want.
Non sono quelle che cercavo.

Can you show me something else?
Ha ancora qualcos'altro da mostrarmi?

What do they cost?
Quanto costano?

Where is the cashier?
Dove è la cassa?

I would like a receipt.
Vorrei una ricevuta.

Can you wrap it for me?
Può impacchettarmele?

Can you deliver that to me in the hotel?
Può spedirmi il pacco in albergo?

Do you deliver to foreign countries too?
Effettua anche consegne all'estero?

I would like to exchange this.
Vorrei cambiare quello che ho acquistato.

I would like to make a complaint.
Ho un problema.

The product is defective.
Il prodotto è difettoso.

I would like my money back.
Vorrei indietro i soldi.

I'll take that.
Prendo queste.

Do you have a shopping bag?
Ha una borsa?

Sometimes you will see the sign *Vendita all'ingrosso.* That means "Wholesale," and you cannot buy anything there without a wholesale license.

What You Hear or Read

Posso aiutarLa?
Can I help you?

È già servito?
Have you already been served / waited on?

Cosa desidera?
What would you like?

Che taglia porta?
What is your size?

Liquidazione, svendita
Sale

Desidera altro?
Will there be something else?

Mi spiace, questo non ce l'abbiamo.
We don't have that, unfortunately.

Sono 10 euro.
That will be 10 euros.

Paga in contanti o con la carta di credito?
Are you paying in cash or by credit card?

Cosa cerca?
Are you looking for something in particular?

In a Department Store

department
il reparto

elevator
l'ascensore

entrance
l'ingresso

cash register / cashier
la cassa

customer service
il servizio clienti

emergency exit
l'uscita di emergenza

escalator
la scala mobile

floor
il piano

toilets
la toilette

stairways
gli scalini

exit
l'uscita

If you encounter the question *Dove gli fa male?*, it means *Where does it hurt?*

Shops

souvenir shop **il negozio di souvenirs**

antique store **l'antiquariato**

drugstore **la farmacia**

bakery **la panetteria**

florist **il fioraio**

bookstore **la libreria**

computer store **il negozio di computer**

drugstore **la farmacia**

shopping center **il centro commerciale**

retail sale **la vendita al dettaglio**

hardware **il negozio di ferramenta**

electrical appliances store **il negozio di elettrodomestici**

bike shop **il ciclista**

delicatessen **la gastronomia**

fish store **il pescivendolo**

flea market **il mercato delle pulci**

photo store **il fotografo**

hairdresser **il parrucchiere**

fresh produce stand **la frutta e verdura**

household merchandise **il negozio di casalinghi**

jeweler **la gioielleria**

department store **il grande magazzino**

clothing store **l'abbigliamento**

pastry shop **la pasticceria**

cosmetics store **l'istituto di bellezza**

art gallery **la galleria d'arte**

arts and crafts **l'artigianato artistico**

notions **la merceria**

grocery store **gli alimentari**

leather goods **la pelletteria**

market **il mercato**

butcher **la macelleria**

creamery / dairy **il caseificio**

furniture **i mobili**

music store **dischi e musica**

fruit stand **la frutta e verdura**

optician **l'ottico**

perfumery **la profumeria**

furrier **la pellicceria**

pawnbroker **monte di pietà, monte dei pegni**

health food store **i prodotti dietetici**

cleaning / dry cleaning **la lavanderia**

travel agency **l'agenzia di viaggi**

record store **dischi e musica**

tailor **la sartoria**

stationery **la cartoleria**

shoe store **le scarpe**

shoemaker **il calzolaio**

second-hand store **secondamano**

toy store **i giocattoli**

liquor store **vini e liquori**

sporting goods store **gli articoli sportivi**

fabric store **i tessuti**

supermarket **il supermercato**

candy **i dolciumi**

tobacco store **la tabaccheria**

pet shop **gli animali**

second-hand dealer **le anticaglie**

watchmaker **l'orologeria / orefice**

laundromat **la lavanderia a gettone**

wine store **vini e liquori**

newsagent **l'edicola**

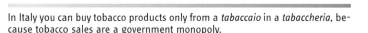

In Italy you can buy tobacco products only from a *tabaccaio* in a *tabaccheria*, because tobacco sales are a government monopoly.

Colors

 black
nero

 green
verde

 white
bianco

 blue
blu

 gray
grigio

 pink
rosa

red
rosso

 orange
arancio

yellow
giallo

 purple
viola

Designs

colored / colorful
a colori

checkered
a quadretti

mottled
mélange

printed / patterned
a fantasia

knotted
bouclé

light
chiaro

dark
scuro

high-contrast
molto contrastato

low-contrast
poco contrastato

matte / dull
opaco

glossy / shiny
brillante

polka-dotted
a pois

 vertically striped
a strisce longitudinali

 diagonally striped
a strisce trasversali

 black-and-white
in bianco e nero

With the color blue you will think of the poetic word *azure*, which bears a resemblance to the Italian word *azzurro* (light- or sky-blue).

At the Market

Cherries, beautiful cherries!
Ciliegie, ottime ciliegie!

They look nice.
Queste sono belle.

Would you like a taste?
Vuole assaggiarle?

Mm, delicious. Give me one pound.
Mh, delizioso. Me ne dia mezzo chilo.

What is that?
Cos'è quello?

Okra.
Scorzonere.

How do you prepare it?
Come si cucinano?

You cook it like a vegetable.
Come verdura.

The expression "That's all" is *Basta così*.

Foods

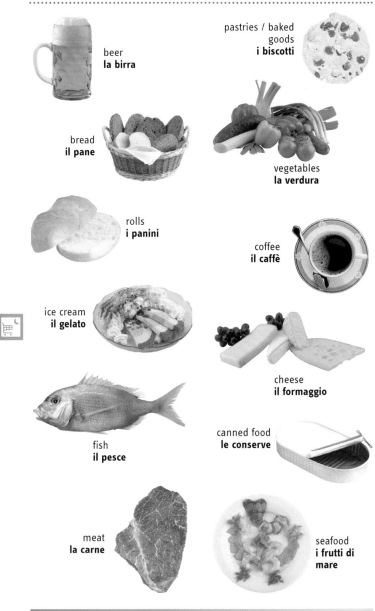

beer
la birra

pastries / baked goods
i biscotti

bread
il pane

vegetables
la verdura

rolls
i panini

coffee
il caffè

ice cream
il gelato

cheese
il formaggio

fish
il pesce

canned food
le conserve

meat
la carne

seafood
i frutti di mare

Sour cream is relatively unknown in Italy, and if you ask for it you may get some strange looks.

organic foods **i prodotti biologici**

butter **il burro**

vinegar **l'aceto**

beverages **le bibite**

spices **le spezie**

semolina **il semolino**

honey **il miele**

cake **la torta**

margarine **la margarina**

jam **la marmellata**

mayonnaise **la maionese**

flour **la farina**

milk products / dairy products **i latticini**

oil **l'olio**

chocolates **i cioccolatini**

rice **il riso**

salt **il sale**

sour cream **la panna acida**

whipped cream **la panna montata**

chocolate **il cioccolato**

mustard **la senape**

candies **i dolciumi**

yogurt **lo yoghurt**

sugar **lo zucchero**

nuts
le noci

fruit
la frutta

salad
l'insalata

tea
il tè

→ Also see FISH AND SHELLFISH,
p. 117; TYPES OF MEAT, p.118;
POULTRY, p. 120; VEGETABLES, p. 122;
FRUITS, p. 127; and NUTS, p. 130

wine
il vino

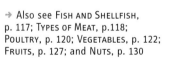

noodles
la pasta

sausages
i salumi

Speaking in general terms of sausage, the word is *salumi* (*salami* is just one type).

shopping basket
il cestino per gli acquisti

shopping cart
i carrelli per la spesa

shopping bag
la borsa

Quantities

100 grams
100 grammi

a pound
mezzo chilo

a kilo
un chilo

a piece
un pezzo

a slice
una fetta

a liter
un litro

a packet
un pacchetto

a bottle
una bottiglia

a can
una lattina / una scatola / un barattolo

a glassful / a glass of ...
un bicchiere

Sales Conversations

I would like to have some butter.
Vorrei del burro.

Do you have flour, too?
Ha anche della farina?

A bit more, please.
Ancora un po' per favore.

Can I taste it?
Posso assaggiarne?

Some more?
Ne vuole ancora?

Anything else?
Desidera altro? / Prende altro?

Thanks, that is all.
Basta così, grazie.

Instead of 100 grams, in Italy 125 grams is more common; it's known as *un etto*

Drugs and Cosmetics

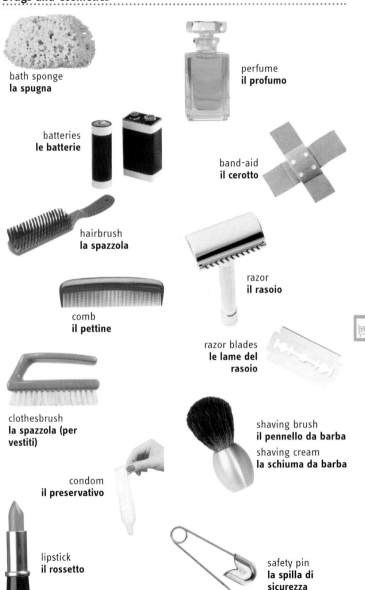

bath sponge
la spugna

perfume
il profumo

batteries
le batterie

band-aid
il cerotto

hairbrush
la spazzola

razor
il rasoio

comb
il pettine

razor blades
le lame del rasoio

clothesbrush
la spazzola (per vestiti)

shaving brush
il pennello da barba

shaving cream
la schiuma da barba

condom
il preservativo

lipstick
il rossetto

safety pin
la spilla di sicurezza

A battery for radios and flashlights is known as *una pila*.

Drugs and Cosmetics

suntan lotion
la crema da sole

mirror
lo specchio

matches
i fiammiferi

bandages
le bende

toothbrush
lo spazzolino da denti

eyeshadow **l'ombretto**

mouthwash **il collutorio**

nail file **la limetta da unghie**

nail polish **lo smalto (per unghie)**

nail polish remover **l'acetone (per unghie)**

nail scissors **le forbicine (per unghie)**

concealer **la matita**

eyebrow pencil **la matita per le sopracciglia**

sanitary napkins **gli assorbenti**

deodorant **il deodorante**

disinfectant **il disinfettante**

stain-remover **lo smacchiatore**

shampoo **lo shampoo**

hand cream **la crema per mani**

insect repellent **l'insetticida**

body lotion **il latte per il corpo**

tissues / kleenex **i fazzoletti di carta**

tweezers **la pinzetta**

powder **la polvere**

cleaners / cleaning products **il detersivo**

rouge **il rouge**

sponge **la spugna**

soap **il sapone**

scrubbing brush **la spazzola per bagno**

dishwashing liquid **il detersivo (per piatti)**

tampons **i tamponi**

tissues / kleenex **i fazzoletti**

toilet paper **la carta igienica**

face cloths **lo strofinaccio per lavare**

laundry detergent (powder) **il detersivo**

cotton **il cotone, bambagia**

mascara **il rimmel**

toothpaste **il dentifricio**

dental floss **il filo interdentale**

Washcloths are nonexistent in Italy.

For Children and Babies

ball
la palla

sand pail
il secchiello

kite
l'aquilone

nipple
il succhietto

shovel
la paletta

bottle
il biberon

pacifier
il succhietto

watering can
l'annaffiatoio

child's bed
il letto per bambini / la culla

swimming ring
il salvagente

toy
il giocattolo

balloon
il palloncino

baby cream **la crema per bambini**

swimming trunks **i calzoncini da bagno**

infant food / baby food **il cibo per neonati**

water wings **i braccioli**

swimming goggles **gli occhiali da sub**

diapers **i pannolini**

portable crib
il letto da viaggio

In some parts of Italy, mosquitoes can be a real nuisance during the summer. An *insetticida* (*...contro le zanzare*) can be helpful in warding them off.

Tobacco Products

ashtray
il posacenere

lighter
l'accendino

pipe
la pipa

matches
i fiammiferi

cigarettes
le sigarette
filtered
con filtro
unfiltered
senza filtro

cigarillos
i sigari

cigars
i sigari

pipe accessories
lo scovolino

pipe filter
il filtro per pipa

pipe cleaner
lo scovolino

tobacco
il tabacco

cigarette case
l'astuccio delle sigarette

cigarette holder
il bocchino per sigarette

What Would You Like?

a box of cigarettes
una scatola di sigarette

a pack of cigarettes
una stecca di sigarette

a packet of tobacco
una confezione di tabacco

a can of tobacco
un pacchetto di tabacco

ten cigarillos
dieci sigari

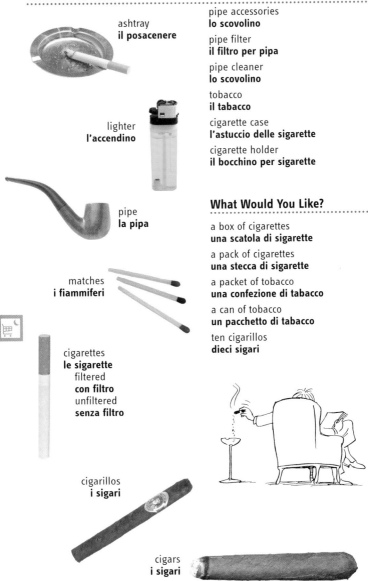

Italians don't make a distinction between "cigar" and "cigarillo." To make yourself understood, you can say *sigaro piccolo* for cigarillo.

Clothing

I am looking for a skirt.
Vorrei una gonna.

I looking for something to go with it.
Poi vorrei qualcosa da abbinare alla gonna.

Can I try that on?
Posso provarlo?

I'll take that.
Lo prendo.

I don't like that.
Questo non mi piace.

The color doesn't look good on me /
The color doesn't suit me.
Il colore non mi piace.

Where is the changing room? /
dressing room?
Dove è lo spogliatoio?

Do you have a mirror?
Ha un specchio?

The sleeves are too long.
Le maniche sono troppo lunghe.

Can you alter it?
Può modificarlo?

How long will the alteration take?
Quanto ci vorrà per averlo?

What You Hear

Che taglia ha?
What is your size?

Vuole provarlo?
Would you like to try it on?

Vuole che lo modificarlo?
Should we alter it?

Di che colore lo vuole?
Which color?

Sizes

I wear size 38. **La mia taglia è trentotto**

small **piccola**

medium **media**

large **grande**

extra large **molto grande**

Do you have a larger / smaller one?
Lo avete anche più grande / più piccolo?

That fits well. **Mi va bene.**

That doesn't fit. **Non mi va bene.**

That is too ... **È troppo ...**
  small. **piccolo.**
  big. **grande.**
  tight / narrow. **stretto.**
  loose / wide. **largo.**
  short. **corto.**
  long. **lungo.**

The terms *saldi* and *saldissimi* are often used to announce the end-of-summer sales in Italy.

Articles of Clothing

swimsuit
il costume da bagno

hat
il cappello

trunks
i calzoncini da bagno

tie
la cravatta

bikini
il bikini

cap
il berretto

bowtie
la (cravatta) a farfalla

scarf
la sciarpa

gloves
i guanti

baseball cap / cap with visor
il berretto

Size Conversions

Men's Suits		Women's Clothing		Men's Shirts	
Europe	**USA**	**Europe**	**USA**	**Europe**	**USA**
46	36	38	10	36	14
48	38	40	12	37	14 $\frac{1}{2}$
50	40	42	14	38	15
52	42	44	16	39/40	15 $\frac{1}{2}$
54	44	46	18	41	16
56	46	48	20	42	16 $\frac{1}{2}$
58	48			43	17
60	50			44	17 $\frac{1}{2}$
				45	18

If you can't recall the longer term for "a pair of pants" (*un paio*...), you can use the shorter *un pantalone*.

umbrella
l'ombrello

handkerchief
il fazzoletto

socks
i calzini

underpants
le mutande

windbreaker / parka **la giacca a vento**
suit **l'abito**
bathrobe **l'accappatoio**
blazer **il blazer**
blouse **la camicetta**
brassiere / bra **il reggiseno**

belt **la cintura**
scarf **la sciarpa**
shirt **la camicia**
pants **i pantaloni**
suspenders **le bretelle**

jacket **la giacca**
suit jacket **la giacchetta / giacca**
dress **il vestito**
outfit **il tailleur**
coat **il cappotto**
housecoat **la vestaglia**
nightshirt **la camicia da notte**
sweater / pullover **il pullover**
raincoat **l'impermeabile**
skirt **la gonna**
pajamas **il pigiama**
apron **il grembiule**
shorts **i pantaloncini**
panties **le mutandine**
stockings **le calze**
tights **i collant**
t-shirt **la t-shirt**
undershirt **la canottiera**
slip / petticoat **la sottogonna**
vest **il gilet**

Maglia is another word for sweater. A sweatshirt is known as *una canottiera*.

Sewing

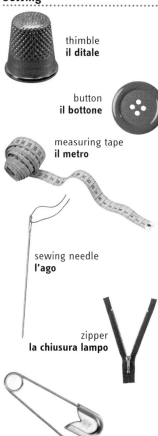

thimble
il ditale

button
il bottone

measuring tape
il metro

sewing needle
l'ago

zipper
la chiusura lampo

safety pin
la spilla di sicurezza

sleeves **le maniche**
thread **il filo**
elastic **l'elastico**
collar **il colletto**
cuffs **i polsini**
pin **lo spillo**

Fabrics

What material is this made from?
Di che materiale è fatto?

I would like something in cotton.
Vorrei qualcosa di cotone.

Is that machine-washable?
Si può lavare in lavatrice?

Can one put this in the dryer?
Lo si può mettere nell'asciugatrice?

Does that shrink when washed?
Si restringe lavandolo?

wrinkle-free / no ironing
da non stirare

lining
fodera

cambric / batiste **batista**
cotton **cotone**
corduroy **vellutino**
felt **feltro**
flannel **flanella**
terry towelling **spugna**
worsted **tessuto pettinato**
crepe **crespo**
synthetic fiber **fibra sintetica**
leather **cuoio**
linen **lino**
microfiber **microfibra**
poplin **popeline**
velvet **velluto**
satin **raso**
silk **la seta**
wool **lana**

A literal translation of *chiusura lampo* (zipper) is *lightning closure*.

Leather Goods

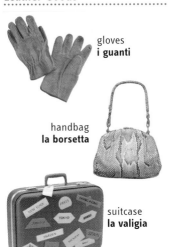

gloves
i guanti

handbag
la borsetta

suitcase
la valigia

tote bag
la borsa da viaggio

Dry Cleaning, Laundromat

Please clean this garment.
Porto a far lavare questo vestito.

Which type of cleaning do you prefer?
Che tipo di pulizia desidera?

I would like ...
Vorrei una ...
  dry-cleaning.
  pulizia a secco.
  gentle cleaning.
  pulizia delicata.
  thorough cleaning.
  pulizia completa.

What will that cost?
Quanto costa?

How long will it take?
Quanto tempo ci vorrà?

When can I pick it up again?
Quando posso passare a ritirarlo?

Can you send me the garment?
Può spedirmi il vestito?

Here is my address.
Le do il mio indirizzo.

briefcase **la borsa portadocumenti**
wallet / billfold **il portafoglio**
purse **il portamonete**
belt **la cintura**
artificial leather **la similpelle**
leather jacket **la giacca di pelle**
leather coat **il cappotto di pelle**
shoulder bag **la borsa a tracolla**
suede **la pelle di daino**

washing machine **la lavatrice**
dryer **l'asciugatrice**
spin-dryer **la centrifuga**
coins **le monete / i gettoni**
rinse **risciacquare**
spin-dry **centrifugare**
hot wash **lavare a 90 gradi**
delicate / gentle wash **ciclo delicato**
laundry **la lavanderia**
colored laundry **capi colorati**
hot-water wash **bucato lavabile a 90 gradi**

You can say *lavaggio a secco* instead of *pulizia a secco*.

Shoes

I wear size 7.
Porto il trentasette.

The shoes pinch.
Le scarpe mi fanno male.

The shoes are ...
Le scarpe sono ...
  too narrow.
  troppo strette.
  too wide.
  troppo larghe.
  too small.
  troppo piccole.
  too big.
  troppo grandi.

Shoes with a...
Scarpe ...
  flat heel.
  con tacco basso.
  high heel.
  con tacco alto.

Can you resole the shoes?
Può risuolarmi le scarpe?

I need new heels.
Vorrei rifare il tacco.

When will the shoes be ready?
Per quando sono pronte le scarpe?

heel **il tacco**

bath slippers **le scarpe / ciabatte da spiaggia**

rubber boots **gli stivali di gomma**

slippers **le pantofole**

children's shoes **le scarpe per bambini**

sandals **i sandali**

shoelaces **i lacci delle scarpe**

shoe brush **la spazzola per scarpe**

shoe polish **il lucido per scarpe**

shoes **le scarpe**

soles **le suole**

boots **gli stivali**

track shoes **le scarpe da ginnastica**

leather soles **le suole in pelle**

rubber soles **le suole in gomma**

walking shoes / hiking boots **gli scarponcini**

climbing boots **le scarpe da montagna**

Where Does It Pinch?

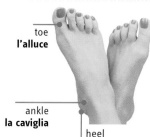

toe
l'alluce

ankle
la caviglia

heel
il tallone

Size Conversions

Men's Shoes		Women's Shoes	
Europe	**USA**	**Europe**	**USA**
39	6 ½	36	5 ½
40	7 ½	37	6
41	8 ½	38	7
42	9	39	7 ½
43	10	40	8 ½
44	10 ½	41	9
45	11		
46	11 ½		

Ski boots are also known as *scarponi*.

In the Sporting Goods Shop

swimsuit / bathing suit
il costume da bagno

golf clubs
la mazza da golf

golf bag
la borsa da golf

trunks
i calzoncini da bagno

ball
la palla

dumbbell
il manubrio

basketball
pallacanestro

backpack / knapsack
lo zaino

bikini
il bikini

snorkel
il tubo respiratore

soccer ball
il pallone

fins
le pinne

golf ball
la pallina da golf

sun umbrella / parasol
l'ombrellone

The simplest word in Italian for "expensive" is *caro*, which is also used in a figurative sense, e.g., *caro amico*.

In the Sporting Goods Shop

diving goggles /
diving mask
**gli occhiali da
sub**

tennis ball
la palla da tennis

tennis racket
**la racchetta da
tennis**

ping-pong ball
la pallina da ping-pong

ping-pong rackets /
paddles
la racchetta da ping-pong

walking shoes / hiking boots
gli scarponcini

fishing rod
la canna da pesca

bathing cap
la cuffia

hiking boots / climbing boots
le scarpe da montagna

shuttlecock
la palla da volano

badminton rackets
la racchetta da volano

inline skates / rollerblades
il pattinatore su roller-blade

thermal mattress
il materassino termico

air mattress
il materassino

sleeping bag
il sacco a pelo

ice skates
i pattini sul ghiaccio

water wings
i braccioli

skateboard
lo skateboard

tennis shoes / sneakers
le scarpe da tennis

track shoes / sneakers
le scarpe da ginnastica

→ Also see TYPES OF SPORTS, p. 179;
AT THE BEACH, p. 183; WATER SPORTS,
p. 186; DIVING, p. 187; HIKING AND
CLIMBING, p. 191

Under tax law there is a difference between a receipt (*una ricevuta*) and a bill
(*una fattura*). Usually all you'll need is a receipt.

Housewares

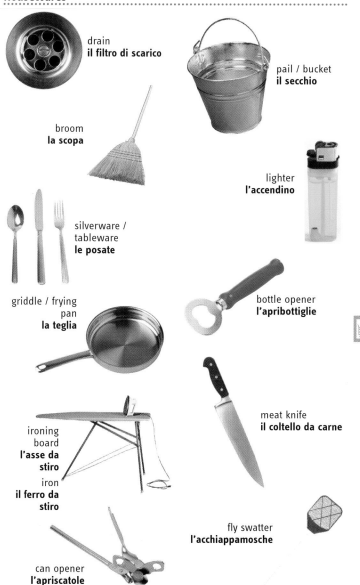

drain
il filtro di scarico

pail / bucket
il secchio

broom
la scopa

lighter
l'accendino

silverware /
tableware
le posate

griddle / frying
pan
la teglia

bottle opener
l'apribottiglie

ironing
board
**l'asse da
stiro**

iron
**il ferro da
stiro**

meat knife
il coltello da carne

fly swatter
l'acchiappamosche

can opener
l'apriscatole

Should you need to use a knife for fish, it is known as *un coltello da pesce*.

Housewares

hairdryer
il fon

brush
la scopetta

dishes
le stoviglie
dishrack
lo scolapiatti

coffee mill /
coffee grinder
**il macinino del
caffè**

mug
la brocca

watering can
l'annaffiatoio

dustpan
la pattumiera

glass
il bicchiere

candle
la candela

light bulb
la lampadina

candlestick
il candeliere

The hairdryer is less frequently (but correctly) referred to as *asciugacapelli*.

chain
la catena

ladder
la scala

clothes brush
la spazzola per abiti

magnet
il magnete / la calamita

saucepan /
pot
la casseruola

knive
il coltello

corkscrew
il cavatappi

creamer /
milk jug
il bricco per il latte

kitchen sponge
la spugna

kerosene lamp /
hurricane lamp
la lampada a petrolio

insulated bag
la borsa termica

cleaning rag
lo straccio

You use a *cavatappi* to pull a cork; but "to pull the cork" is *stappare*.

Housewares

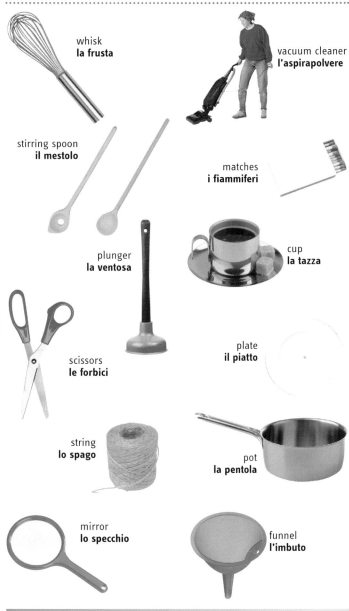

whisk
la frusta

vacuum cleaner
l'aspirapolvere

stirring spoon
il mestolo

matches
i fiammiferi

plunger
la ventosa

cup
la tazza

scissors
le forbici

plate
il piatto

string
lo spago

pot
la pentola

mirror
lo specchio

funnel
l'imbuto

A cigarette lighter is an *accendisigari*, but the term *accendino* has become popular, especially for disposable lighters.

padlock
il lucchetto

water hose
il tubo dell'acqua

scales
la bilancia

rolling pin
il matterello

hot water bottle /
bed warmer
**la borsa dell'acqua
calda**

lemon
squeezer
**lo
spremiagrumi**

clothes pins
**le mollette (per la
biancheria)**

laundry basket
**il cesto della
biancheria**

trash bags **il sacchetto
dell'immondizia**

aluminum foil **la carta stagnola**

cup **la tazza**

twine **lo spago**

plastic wrap **il sacchetto per alimenti**

paper napkins **i tovaglioli di carta**

plastic bags **la borsa di plastica**

scrubbing brush **la spazzola**

flashlight **la torcia**

pocket knife / jacknife **il coltellino da
tasca**

immersion heater **il bollitore a
immersione**

thermos **il termos**

fan / ventilator **il ventilatore**

clothes rack **lo stendibiancheria**

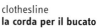

clothesline
la corda per il bucato

La bilancia is "the scale," and it should not be confused with *il bilancio*, the balance sheet.

Tools

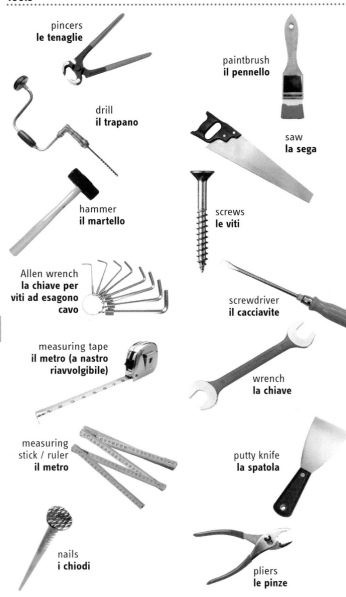

pincers
le tenaglie

paintbrush
il pennello

drill
il trapano

saw
la sega

hammer
il martello

screws
le viti

Allen wrench
**la chiave per
viti ad esagono
cavo**

screwdriver
il cacciavite

measuring tape
**il metro (a nastro
riavvolgibile)**

wrench
la chiave

measuring
stick / ruler
il metro

putty knife
la spatola

nails
i chiodi

pliers
le pinze

A wrench in Italian is precisely the same word as a normal key: *una chiave*.

Camping Equipment

grill
la griglia

butane gas
il gas butano

gas stove
il fornello a gas

cooler
la borsa frigo

hammock
l'amaca

tent pegs
i chiodi di fissaggio

charcoal
il carbone

deck chair
**la sedia a
sdraio**

folding chair
la sedia ripiegabile

folding table
il tavolo ripiegabile

air mattress
il materassino

air pump
la pompa

mosquito net
la rete per zanzare

propane
il gas propano

sleeping bag
il sacco a pelo

water jug
la tanica di acqua

kerosene lamp /
hurricane lamp
**la lampada a
petrolio**

tent
la tenda

tent pole
il palo da tenda

string
la corda

→ Also see IN THE CAMPGROUND,
p. 100

If something is not working, you can say quickly and painlessly *non va*; that will get the meaning across to the other person.

The Bookshop

Where can I find a bookstore? **Dove posso trovare una libreria?**

Do you also have books in English? **Avete anche libri in inglese?**

I am looking for a novel. **(Io) cerco un romanzo.**

postcards **le cartoline (illustrate)**

illustrated book / coffee-table book **il volume illustrato**

picture book **il libro illustrato**

stamps **i francobolli**

writing paper **la carta da lettere**

technical book **il libro specialistico**

wrapping paper / gift wrap **la carta da regalo**

children's book **il libro per bambini**

cookbook **il libro di cucina**

mystery / detective novel **il giallo**

map **la cartina**

short novel / novella **la novella**

guidebook **la guida**

nonfiction **la saggistica**

science fiction **la fantascienza**

map of the city **la pianta della città**

dictionary **il dizionario**

magazine **la rivista**

newspaper **il giornale**

calendar **il calendario**

Writing Implements

pencil
la matita

paper clips
le graffette

color pen
la matita colorata

fountain pen
la penna

ruler
il righello

notepad
il blocco note

The opposite of *chiuso*, closed, is *aperto*, open.

notebook
il quaderno di appunti

twine
lo spago

pencil sharpener
il temperino

labels
le etichette

felt tip pen
il pennarello

paper clips
i fermagli

glue
la colla

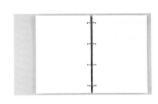

thumbtacks
i chiodini

ballpoint pen
la biro

eraser
la gomma

stationery
la carta da scrivere

stationery / office supplies
gli articoli di cancelleria

cellophane
il nastro adesivo (schotch)

loose-leaf notebook
il raccoglitore (ad anelli)

scissors
le forbici

pocket calculator
la calcolatrice tascabile

string
la corda

playing cards
le carte (da gioco)

ink
l'inchiostro

Both a fountain pen and a ballpoint pen are known as *penna*.

Painting Supplies

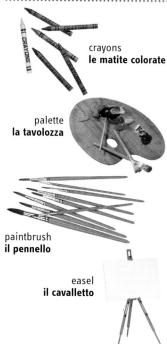

crayons
le matite colorate

palette
la tavolozza

paintbrush
il pennello

easel
il cavalletto

watercolors **gli acquerelli**

watercolor paper **la carta per acquerelli**

fixative **il fissatore**

canvas stretcher / frame **la cornice con cunei agli angoli**

charcoal pencils **i carboncini**

chalk / crayon **il gesso**

canvas **la tela**

watercolor crayons / chalk **i pastelli**

oil paints **i colori ad olio**

oil pastels **i gessetti**

pastels **le tinte pastello**

watercolors **i colori ad acquerello**

sketch pad **il blocco da disegno**

In the Photography Shop

I am looking for a ...
Io cerco ...
single-lens reflex camera.
una macchina fotografica reflex.
35-mm camera.
un apparecchio fotografico per formato ventiquattro per trentasei.

I would like to spend about 100 euros.
Non voglio spendere più di 100 euro.

Is the guarantee valid internationally?
La garanzia è valida a livello internazionale?

I need passport pictures.
Vorrei una foto passaporto.

What Is Broken?

Something is wrong with my camera.
La mia macchina fotografica non funziona bene.

The film is jammed.
La pellicola si inceppa.

Can you repair it?
Può ripararla?

How much will it cost?
Cosa mi costerà?

How long will it take?
Quanto tempo ci vorrà?

exposure meter / light meter
esposimetro

distance meter
telemetro

shutter
otturatore

You can also say *foto tessera* for "passport photo"; this applies to practically all photos in passport-photo format.

Accessories

film
la pellicola

lens
l'obiettivo

battery
la batteria

flashbulb
il flash

camera bag
la borsa delle fotografie

automatic shutter release / self-timer
il cavo dell'autoscatto

lens shade
lo schermo parasole

tripod
il treppiede

telephoto lens
il teleobiettivo

uv-filter
il filtro UV

wide-angle lens
l'obiettivo grandangolare

zoom lens
l'obiettivo zoom

Films

I would like ...
Vorrei ...
    black and white film.
    una pellicola in bianco e nero.
    color-negative film.
    una pellicola a colori.
    slide film / transparency film.
    una pellicola per diapositive.

100 / 200 / 400 ASA.
Con 100 / 200 / 400 ASA.

36 exposures.
Con trentasei foto.

daylight film.
pellicola per luce solare.

artificial-light film.
pellicola per luce artificiale.

Can you put the film into the camera?
Può mettermi la pellicola nella macchina fotografica?

developing
lo sviluppo

printing
la copia

format
il formato

slide frames
il telaietto per diapositive

If you forget the word *pellicola* for film, you can also say *film*.

Developing Film

Could you develop
this film, please?
**Mi può sviluppare
questa pellicola?**

Do you also want a
print of each
picture?
**Vuole anche una
copia delle foto?**

Yes, size 4 by 6.
**Sì, in formato
dieci per
quindici**

Glossy or matt?
Lucido o opaco?

Glossy. When can I pick
up the pictures?
**Lucido. Quando posso
passare a ritirare le foto?**

The day after tomorrow.
Dopodomani.

You can also avoid the word "film" entirely by using the word for "roll": *rulli-
no.*

Video Cameras

I would like to buy a video camera.
Vorrei una telecamera.

It should not cost more than 300 euros.
Non vorrei spendere più di 300 euro.

Does the camera have a worldwide guarantee?
La garanzia della macchina fotografica è valida a livello mondiale?

Is this a discontinued model?
È un modello di fine serie?

Is this the most current model from this company?
È il modello più attuale della ditta?

I would like ...
Vorrei ...
  a film for my video camera.
  una pellicola.
  batteries for my video camera.
  delle batterie.
  a charger for my video camera.
  un caricatore.
  a halogen light for my video camera.
  una luce alogena per videocamera.

Camcorders, DVD

VCR
il videoregistratore

video cassette
la cassetta per videoregistratore

DVD player
il lettore DVD

Note that even though you can say *videocamera* in other countries, the Italians have settled on *telecamera*.

Electronic Devices

adapter
l'adattatore

plug
la spina

battery
la batteria

alarm clock
la sveglia

iron
il ferro da stiro

razor
il rasoio

flashlight
la torcia

extension cord
la prolunga

hair dryer
il fon

light bulb
la lampadina

fuse
il fusibile

socket
la presa (di corrente)

Concerning wall sockets, three-pronged plugs are still used in Italy, so you'll need an adaptor.

Stereo

diskman
il Diskman

remote control
il telecomando

headphones
le cuffie

speakers
l'altoparlante

CD player
il lettore CD

DVD player
il lettore DVD

stereo system
l'impianto Hifi

cassette recorder
il registratore

MD player
il lettore MD

radio
la radio

record player
il giradischi

walkman
il Walkman

Computer

screen
lo schermo

keyboard
la tastiera

RAM **la memoria di lavoro**

operating system **il sistema operativo**

CD-burner **il masterizzatore**

CD-ROM drive **il drive per CD-ROM**

hard disk **harddisk**

graphics card **la scheda grafica**

laser printer **la stampante laser**

speakers **l'altoparlante**

modem **il modem**

network cable **il cavo di rete**

network card **la scheda di rete**

paper **la carta**

processor **il processore**

scanner **lo scanner**

sound card **la scheda audio**

control unit **l'unità di comando**

electrical cord **il cavo di alimentazione**

inkjet printer **la stampante a getto d'inchiostro**

toner **il toner**

extension cord **la prolunga**

video card **la scheda video**

You can also use the word "CPU" (pronounced as in English) for the main component of a computer.

At the Optician's

My frames are
broken.
**Si è rotta la
montatura.**

No problem, I can solder
that.
**Non è grave, posso
saldarla.**

Can I wait for it?
Può farmelo subito?

I'm sorry, it won't be
ready until tomorrow.
**No, mi spiace, posso
farglielo per domani
mattina.**

Don't you have an extra pair of glasses?
Non ha occhiali di ricambio?

The best choice for "broken" or "out of order" is *rotto*.

earpiece
la stanghetta

glass
il vetro

frame
la montatura

The glass is broken.
Si è rotto il vetro.

sunglasses
gli occhiali da sole

binoculars
il cannocchiale

My glasses are broken.
Si sono rotti gli occhiali.

Can you repair it?
Si possono riparare?

How long will it take?
Quanto tempo ci vorrà?

Can I wait for it?
Può farmelo subito?

magnifying glass
la lente di ingrandimento

contact lenses
lenti a contatto
  hard lenses
  lenti dure
  soft lenses
  lenti morbide

vision
il grado visivo

near-sighted
miope

far-sighted
presbite

glasses case
la custodia (per occhiali)

cleaner
il prodotto per la pulizia (degli occhiali)

If no specific quantity is intended, Italian often uses what is known as the partitive article: *delle batterie.*

At the Watchmaker's

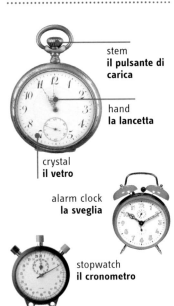

stem
il pulsante di carica

hand
la lancetta

crystal
il vetro

alarm clock
la sveglia

stopwatch
il cronometro

My watch / clock isn't working.
Il mio orologio non funziona più.

My watch / clock is fast.
Il mio orologio è avanti.

My watch / clock is slow.
Il mio orologio è indietro.

Can you repair it?
Si può riparare?

How long will it take?
Quanto tempo ci vorrà?

wristband
il cinturino

wristwatch
l'orologio da polso

pocket watch
l'orologio da tasca

wall clock
l'orologio a parete

waterproof
resistente all'acqua

Jeweler

I am looking for a gift. **Vorrei fare un regalo.**

It is for a man / a woman. **È per un uomo / una donna.**

Do you have something less expensive? **Non c'è qualcosa di più economico?**

What material is that? **Di che materiale è?**

What kind of stone is that? **Che pietra è?**

pendant **il ciondolo**

badge / pin **lo spillo**

bracelet **il braccialetto**

brooch **la spilla**

necklace **la collana**

tie pin **il fermacravatta**

cufflinks **i gemelli**

pearl necklace / string of pearls **la collana di perle**

ring **l'anello**

earrings **gli orecchini**

amethyst **l'ametista**

amber **l'ambra**

diamond **il diamante**

high-grade steel **l'acciaio legato**

ivory **l'avorio**

gold **l'oro**
goldplate(d) **placcato in oro**

coral **il corallo**

copper **il rame**

onyx **l'onice**

pearl **la perla**

platinum **il platino**

ruby **il rubino**

sapphire **lo zaffiro**

silver **l'argento**
silverplate(d) **placcato in argento**

emerald **lo smeraldo**

If you are speaking of gemstones, you might want to complement *pietra* with *preziosa*.

Hair Stylist

hairspray
la lacca

elastic
l'elastico per capelli

hairpins
le forcine

barrette
il fermaglio

hairspray
la lacca

hair conditioner
il lavaggio / balsamo

shampoo
lo shampoo

curler
il bigodino

hair dye / hair color
la tinta per riflessi

color rinse / tint
riflesso

hairbrush
la spazzola

comb
il pettine

perm
permanente

sideburns
basette

curls
ricci

center part
la riga in mezzo

part
la riga di lato

mustache
baffi

dandruff
forfora

strands
ciocche

wig
la parrucca

eyebrow
sopracciglia

beard
barba

If you cannot recall the right word for "hairspray" (*la lacca*), you can also say *spray*, but it's pronounced more like the English word "spry."

How Would You Like It?

Are you free, or do I have to make an appointment?
Ha tempo adesso o devo prendere un appuntamento?

A wash and set, please.
Vorrei una messa in piega.

Please color my hair.
Vorrei fare la tinta.

I want my hair to stay long.
Voglio tenere i capelli lunghi.

Please cut off only the ends.
Vorrei solo spuntarli.

Cut off a little more.
Me li tagli un po' più corti.

My ears should stay covered.
Me li tagli sotto le orecchie.

That's fine.
Così va bene.

Would you please trim my beard too?
Vorrei spuntare la barba

A shave, please.
Vorrei fare la barba

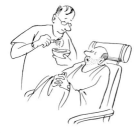

color
fare la tinta

blow-dry
asciugare al fon

set
fare la messa in piega

wash
lavare i capelli

tint
fare i riflessi

tease / back-comb
cotonatura

Which Hair Stylist?

modern
(taglio) moderno

very short
(taglio) molto corto

sporty
(taglio) sportivo

Italians always refer to a hairstyle as *un taglio*.

Beach, Sports, and Nature

What's Happening?

fishing
la pesca con l'amo

darts
le freccette

baseball
il baseball

hang-gliding
il deltaplano

basketball
la pallacanestro

ice hockey
l'hockey sul ghiaccio

billiards
il biliardo

boxing
la boxe, pugilato

If you tend to forget the term for fishing, *pescare all'amo*, you can use *pescare* and everybody will understand..

soccer
il calcio

athletics / track and field
l'atletica leggera

golf
il golf

cycling
il ciclismo

hot-air balloon
la mongolfiera

rugby
il rugby

inline skating /
rollerblading
**il pattinaggio su
roller-blade**

chess
gli scacchi

jogging
il footing

judo
lo judo

The word "basketball" will be understood in Italy even if you can't remember
the proper term, *pallacanestro*.

skiing
gli sci

snowboard
lo snowboard

diving
**l'immersione
subacquea**

tennis
il tennis

ping-pong / table
tennis
il ping-pong

windsurfing
il windsurf

aerobics **l'aerobica**

car racing **la corsa automobilistica**

badminton **il volano**

mountaineering / mountain
climbing **l'alpinismo**

ice-skating **il pattinaggio sul
ghiaccio**

sky diving / parachute jumping **il
paracadutismo**

badminton **il volano**

gymnastics **la ginnastica**

handball **la pallamano**

canoeing **il canottaggio**

karate **il karatè**

bowling **i birilli**

mountaineering / mountain
climbing / rock climbing **l'alpinismo**

cricket **il cricket**

horse racing **la corsa dei cavalli**

bicycle racing **la gara ciclistica**

regatta **la regata**

riding / horseback riding
l'equitazione

wrestling **la lotta libera**

rowing **il canottaggio**

swimming pool **la piscina**

sailing **la vela**

squash **lo squash**

beach **la spiaggia**

surfing **il surf**

gymnastics **la ginnastica**

volleyball **la pallavolo**

hiking **l'escursionismo**

water polo **la pallanuoto**

waterskiing **lo sci nautico**

→ Also see IN THE SPORTING GOODS
SHOP, p. 157

Mountain climbing is a form of *alpinismo*, but the more precise term is *scalare*.
A mountain climber is *un scalatore*.

Renting

I would like to rent a tennis racquet.
Vorrei noleggiare una racchetta da tennis.

What does it cost ...
Quanto costa ...
　per hour?
　all'ora?
　per day?
　al giorno?
　per week?
　alla settimana?

That is too expensive.
È troppo caro.

Must I leave a deposit?
Devo lasciare una caparra?

Instruction

I would like to take a tennis course.
Vorrei frequentare un corso di tennis.

Are there sailing courses here?
Si tengono corsi di vela in questa zona?

I have never been diving.
Non ho mai fatto immersioni.

I am a beginner.
Sono principiante.

I am advanced.
Sono esperto.

Creative Vacations

cooking course **il corso di cucina**

painting course **il corso di pittura**

language course **il corso di lingua**

dance **il ballo**

theater **il teatro**

At the Beach

Where is the nearest beach?
Può indicarmi la spiaggia più vicina?

Where can I rent a sun umbrella?
Dove posso noleggiare un ombrellone?

What does a place on the beach cost per day?
Quanto costa un posto in spiaggia al giorno?

I am looking for a nudist beach.
Cerco una spiaggia per nudisti.

Is it high or low tide?
C'è l'alta marea o la bassa marea?

How deep is the water?
Quanto è profonda l'acqua?

How warm is the water?
È calda l'acqua?

Are there any dangerous currents?
Ci sono correnti pericolose?

Is there a lifeguard on the beach?
La spiaggia è controllata?

What do the flags mean?
Cosa significano le bandiere?

Notices and Signs

Divieto di balneazione
No swimming

Avviso di tempesta
Storm warning

Pericolo!
Danger!

Spiaggia senza bagnino (non vigilata)
Swimming at your own risk.

Solo per nuotatori
Only for swimmers

Vietato tuffarsi
Diving prohibited.

Correnti pericolose!
Dangerous current!

Spiaggia privata
Private beach

A horse track is *un ippodromo*.

At the Beach

swimsuit
il costume da bagno

fins
le pinne

trunks /
swimming trunks
i calzoncini da bagno

crab
il gambero

bathing shoes
le scarpe / ciabatte da spiaggia

beach chair
la sedia a sdraio

bath towel
il telo da bagno

motorboat
il motoscafo

ball
la palla

bikini
il bikini

A dramatic expression for "heatstroke" is *un colpo di sole* (a hit from the sun).

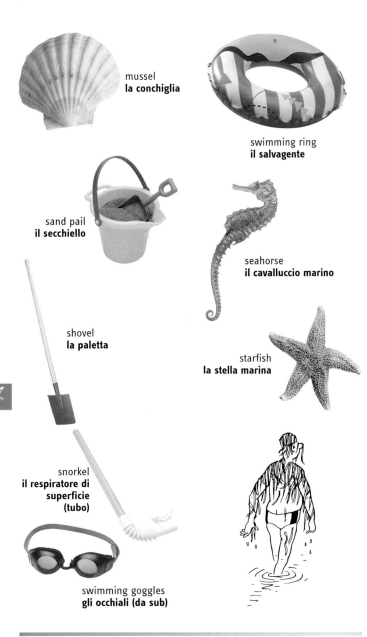

mussel
la conchiglia

swimming ring
il salvagente

sand pail
il secchiello

seahorse
il cavalluccio marino

shovel
la paletta

starfish
la stella marina

snorkel
il respiratore di superficie (tubo)

swimming goggles
gli occhiali (da sub)

A fishing lure is *un galleggiante* (a float).

sunglasses
gli occhiali da sole

suntan lotion
la crema solare

sunburn
la scottatura

sunstroke
l'insolazione

sun umbrella
l'ombrellone

diving goggles / mask
la maschera da sub

water polo
la pallanuoto

seaweed **le alghe**
beach cabin / cabana **la cabina**
boat **la barca**
boat rental **il noleggio imbarcazioni**
surf **la risacca**
dune **la duna**
low tide **la bassa marea**
shuttlecock **il palla da volano**
rocky shoreline **la scogliera**
river **il fiume**
high tide **l'alta marea**
pebble beach **la spiaggia di ghiaia**
air mattress **il materassino**
sea **il mare**
non-swimmers **non nuotatore**
canoe **la canoa**
jellyfish **la medusa**
life guard / beach patrol **il bagnino**
rowboat **la barca a remi**
sand **la sabbia**
sandy beach **la spiaggia di sabbia**
shadow **l'ombra**
swimmer **il nuotatore**
water wings **i braccioli**
sea / ocean **il mare**
beach shoes **le scarpe / ciabatte da spiaggia**
beach towel **il telo da spiaggia**
current **la corrente**
surfboard **la tavola da surf**
pedal boat **il pedalò**
pollution **la sporcizia**
waterski **lo sci nautico**
wave **l'onda**

The tiller is *la barra*, and *le pinne* in Italian means "the fins."

Indoor and Outdoor Swimming Pools

I would like two entrance tickets, please.
Mi dà due biglietti per favore?

Is there also a weekly pass / multiple-entry pass?
Ci sono anche biglietti settimanali o biglietti multipli?

Is there is a discount for ...
C'è una riduzione per ...

children?
bambini?

teenagers?
ragazzi?

students?
studenti?

the handicapped?
invalidi?

senior citizens?
anziani?

groups?
gruppi?

Where are the changing cabins?
Dove sono gli spogliatoi?

Do you have lockers?
Gli armadietti si possono chiudere a chiave?

Is the use of the sauna included in the price?
Il servizio sauna è compreso nel prezzo?

Does everyone have to wear a bathing cap?
L'uso della cuffia è obbligatorio?

Is there also a restaurant at the swimming pool?
C'è anche un ristorante qui vicino?

What the water temperature today?
Qual è la temperatura dell'acqua oggi?

Are there days when the water is heated?
Ci sono dei giorni prestabiliti in cui l'acqua è più calda?

How do you purify the water, with chlorine or ozone?
L'acqua viene pulita con il cloro o con l'ozono?

Do you use salt water or fresh water?
Usate acqua di mare o acqua dolce?

Water Sports

kayak **il caiacco**

canoe **la canoa**

motorboat **il motoscafo**

paddle **la pagaia**

canoe **la canoa**

oar **il remo**

rowboat **la barca a remi**

rubber dinghy **il canotto gonfiabile**

diving **l'immersione**

pedal boat **il pedalò**

waterskiing **lo sci nautico**

surfing **il surf**

windsurfing **il windsurf**

Wind Surfing

sail **la vela**

mast **l'albero**

boom **la boma da surf**

surfboard **la tavola da surf**

centerboard **la deriva principale**

auxiliary board **la deriva secondaria**

foot strap **la cinghia per i piedi**

To be seasick in Italian is *sofrire il mal di mare* (to suffer the evil of the sea).

Diving

I would like to go deep-sea diving.
Vorrei fare immersioni in profondità.

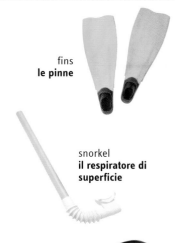

fins
le pinne

snorkel
il respiratore di superficie

I would like go cave-diving.
Vorrei fare escursioni speleologiche.

I have diving certification.
Ho un brevetto da sub.

I would like to get a diving certificate.
Vorrei conseguire un brevetto da sub.

diving mask / face mask
gli occhiali da sub

How much does it cost to get a diving certificate?
Quanto costa conseguire un brevetto da sub?

How long does it take to get a diving certificate?
Quanto tempo ci vorrà per conseguire un brevetto da sub?

Will this diving certificate accepted internationally?
Il brevetto è valido a livello mondiale?

weight belts **la cintura di piombo**

decometer **il decometro**

compressed-air bottles **le bottiglie ad aria compressa**

wetsuit **la tuta subaquea**

diving clock **l'orologio subacqueo**

depth gauge **il misuratore di profondità**

The air tanks for diving are often referred to as *cilindri*.

Sailing

I have a Class B sailing license.
Ho la patente nautica classe B.

I would like get a sailing license.
Vorrei conseguire una patente nautica.

Do you also organize sailing trips that last several days?
Ci sono anche regate di vela di più giorni?

What does that cost?
Quanto costa?

When can we cast off?
Quando possiamo imbarcarci?

Have any other people put down their names?
Ci sono già degli iscritti?

I would like to sail in offshore waters.
Vorrei praticare vela nelle acque costiere.

I am interested in sailing in the open sea.
Vorrei praticare vela in alto mare.

knot
il nodo

paddle
la pagaia

life preserver
il salvagente

life jacket
il giubbetto di salvataggio

The centerboard of a sailboat goes by the peculiar term *la deriva*, which really means *adrift*.

mast
l'albero

mainsail
la vela maestra

jib
la vela di prua / il fiocco

main boom
la boma

forecastle
la galloccia

tiller
la barra del timone

stern
la poppa

bow
la prua

rudder
il timone

main sheet
la scotta principale

centerboard
la deriva

anchor **l'àncora**
port **a babordo, a sinistra**
leeward **il sottovento**
lighthouse **il faro**
windward **il sopravento**
motor **il motore**
starboard **a tribordo, a dritta**
rigging **l'attrezzatura**

yawl **lo iole**
cruiser **l'incrociatore**
trawler **il cutter**
schooner **lo schooner**
yacht **lo yacht**

You speak to the shipping agent (*agente marittimo*) at the shipping office (*agenzia di navigazione*) to send your parcel (*pacco*).

Fishing

I would like to go fishing.
Vorrei pescare.

Do I need a fishing license?
Devo essere in possesso di una licenza di pesca?

What does the license cost per day / per week?
Quanto costa la licenza al giorno / alla settimana?

Where can I get a license?
A chi devo rivolgermi per ottenere la licenza?

I am interested in deep-sea fishing.
Vorrei pescare in alto mare.

What does it cost to take part in a fishing tournament?
Quanto costa partecipare ad una battuta di pesca?

Whom should I contact?
A chi posso rivolgermi?

Can we sail to other fishing grounds too?
Possiamo pescare anche in altre zone?

I am particularly interested in catching ...
Io sono interessato a pescare ...

hook.
l'amo.

bait.
l'esca.

Which types of fish can be caught?
Quali tipi di pesce si possono pescare?

fishing rod **la canna da pesca**
fishing line **la lenza**
fishing rod **la canna da pesca**
weights / sinker **il piombino**
float **il galleggiante**

→ Also see FISH AND SHELLFISH, p. 117

In Italian the sinker is *il piombino* (*il piombo* is *lead*).

Hiking

Do you have a hiking map?
Ha una cartina?

Are the trails well marked?
C'è una buona segnaletica per i percorsi?

Is the route easy / difficult?
Questo percorso è facile / difficile?

Is the route suitable for children?
Questo percorso è anche adatto per bambini?

Approximately what altitude is that?
Che altitudine è all'incirca?

Where do I have to register for the hike?
Dove si tengono le iscrizioni all'escursione?

Is there anything special to watch out for on the hike?
Occorre prestare attenzione a qualcosa in particolare durante l'escursione?

About how long will take me to go to ...?
Quanto tempo ci si impiega per arrivare a ...?

Is the water drinkable?
L'acqua è potabile?

In this area, am I allowed to ...
In questa zona è possibile ...
    spend the night in a tent?
    pernottare in tenda?
    light a fire?
    accendere un fuoco?

Do I need any special permission for this area?
Devo avere un permesso speciale per fare escursioni in questa zona?

Where do I get permission?
Dove posso ritirare il permesso?

Is that the right way to ...?
Vado bene per ...?

Can you show me the way on the map?
Può indicarmi la strada sulla cartina?

I got lost.
Mi sono perso.

How much farther is it to ...?
Quanto dista ancora ...?

Climbing

I am looking for climbing possibilities in the area.
Sto cercando dei percorsi per scalatori in questa zona.

Where can I rent the necessary equipment?
Dove posso noleggiare l'attrezzatura necessaria?

Are there guides?
Ci sono delle guide?

How much does a guide cost per day?
Quanto costa una guida al giorno?

Are there any guides who speak English?
Ci sono delle guide che parlano inglese?

For altitude, you can use the common word *altezza* instead of *altitudine*.

Equipment

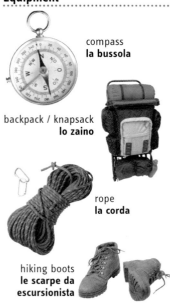

compass
la bussola

backpack / knapsack
lo zaino

rope
la corda

hiking boots
le scarpe da escursionista

water bottle
la bottiglia dell'acqua

reflective blankets **la copertura in alluminio**

helmet **il casco**

snaphook / clip **la carabina**

climbing belt **la cintura per scalatori**

climbing boots **le scarpe per scalatori**

emergency kit **il kit di pronto intervento**

crampons **il rampone**

flashlight **la torcia**

tent **la tenda**

Important Vocabulary

descent **la discesa**

ascent **la salita**

brook **il ruscello**

mountain **la montagna**

mountain hut **la baita di montagna**

mountain peak **la cima della montagna**

bridge **il ponte**

field **il campo**

footpath **il sentiero**

gradient **il dislivello**

high-altitude hiking **l'escursione ad alta quota**

cave **la caverna**

hill **la collina**

canal **il canale**

climbing path **la mulattiera**

climbing track **la via per scalatori**

cliff **la rupe**

nature park **il parco naturale**

national park **il parco nazionale**

pass **il passo, valico**

mountain spring **la fonte**

degree of difficulty **il grado di difficoltà**

lake **il lago**

cable railway **la funivia**

one-day hike **l'escursione giornaliera**

valley **la valle**

pond **lo stagno**

footpath **il sentiero**

waterfall **la cascata**

vineyard **la vigna, vigneto**

meadow **il prato**

The word *mulattiera* for "climbing trail" comes from the time when cargo was carried into the mountains on the backs of mules.

Nature

maple
l'acero

tree
l'albero

beech
il faggio

oak
la quercia

hibiscus
l'ibisco

chestnut
il castagno

lily
il giglio

lime tree
il tiglio

laurel
l'alloro

daisy
la margherita

narcissus
il narciso

carnation
il garofano

orchid
l'orchidea

rose
la rosa

sunflower
il girasole

pine cone
il cono d'abete

Almost all trees are masculine in Italian, e.g., *il castagno*; however the fruits are feminine, as with *la castagna*.

Winter Sports

I would like to go skiing.
Vorrei sciare.

I would like to like to learn skiing.
Mi piacerebbe imparare a sciare.

Do you have deep-snow runs?
Ci sono dei fuori-pista?

I am a beginner.
Sono principiante.

I am an experienced skier.
Sono uno sciatore esperto.

Can you recommend a ski instructor?
Può consigliarmi un istruttore di sci?

Where can I rent / buy ski equipment?
Dove posso noleggiare / acquistare l'attrezzatura da sci?

What are the current snow / skiing conditions?
In che condizioni si trova la neve?

How difficult are the ski runs?
Qual è il grado di difficoltà delle piste?

downhill skiing **la discesa**

binding **l'attacco / aggancio (degli sci)**

cross-country skiing **lo sci di fondo**

ski lift **lo skilift**

ski trail **la pista**

sled **la slitta**

ice skate **i pattini sul ghiaccio**

skis **gli sci**

ski instructor **l'istruttore di sci**

ski pass **lo ski-pass**

ski boots **lo scarpone da sci**

ski pole **il bastoncino da sci**

snowboard **lo snowboard**

wax **la cera**

cable railway **la funivia**

chair lift **la seggiovia**

Spectator Sports

Is there a soccer game this week?
C'è una partita di calcio questa settimana?

Where do I get tickets?
Dove si comprano i biglietti?

I would like to buy a ticket for the game of ... against ...
Vorrei acquistare un biglietto per la partita ... - ...

What is the admission fee?
Quanto costa il biglietto?

Which teams are playing?
Quali squadre giocano?

What is the score?
A che punto è la partita?

A tie / draw.
Pareggio.

Four to one for Milan.
quattro a uno per il Milan.

Milan has won.
Il Milan ha vinto.

Milan has lost.
Il Milan ha perso.

Can you please explain the rules to me?
Può spiegarmi le regole del gioco?

referee
l'arbitro

win
la vittoria

loss / defeat
la sconfitta

Italians make an easy distinction between beginner and advanced by saying *principiante* and *non principiante*.

Culture and Entertainment

At the Tourist Office

Excuse me, could I get some information?
Scusi, potrei avere un'informazione?

I am looking for the tourist office.
Sto cercando l'ufficio turistico.

Please may I have ...
Può darmi ...
    a map.
    una cartina.
    a subway map.
    una cartina della metropolitana.
    brochures.
    dei depliant.

Do you have information on ...
Può darmi informazioni su ...
    events?
    spettacoli?
    city tours?
    giri turistici della città?
    sights?
    attrazioni?
    restaurants?
    ristoranti?
    hotels?
    alberghi?

I would like a calendar of events.
Vorrei un calendario degli spettacoli.

Are there any particularly interesting events this week?
Ci sono spettacoli particolarmente interessanti questa settimana?

What are the main sights?
Quali sono le principali attrazioni?

I would like to see ...
Vorrei visitare ...

I am particularly interested in art.
Mi interessa soprattutto l'arte.

Are there guided tours in English there?
Ci sono guide che parlano inglese?

What does a city tour cost?
Quanto costa un giro turistico della città?

When does it begin?
Quando si parte?

What is included in the price?
Cos'è incluso nel prezzo?

When will we be back?
Quando si ritorna?

Can you get tickets for me?
Può procurarmi dei biglietti?

In many places the tourist bureau is referred to as *il proloco*.

What Is There?

old city **il centro storico**

antiques **i pezzi d'antiquariato**

archaeology **l'archeologia**

architecture **l'architettura**

excavations **gli scavi**

exhibition **l'esposizione**

building **l'edificio**

library **la biblioteca**

sculpture **la scultura**

botany **la botanica**

botanical gardens **il giardino botanico**

bridge **il ponte**

castle **il castello**

well **la fontana**

monument **il monumento**

shopping center **centro commerciale**

factory **la fabbrica**

fortress **la fortezza**

flea market **il mercato delle pulci**

graveyard / cemetary **il cimitero**

gallery **la galleria**

garden **il giardino**

birthplace **la casa natale**

painting **il quadro, dipinto**

geology **la geologia**

history **la storia**

glass painting **la pittura su vetro**

grave **la tomba**

dock **il porticciolo**

caves **le caverne**

city center **il centro città**

ceramics **la ceramica**

cliff **la rupe**

concert hall **sala concerti**

art **l'arte**

art gallery **la galleria d'arte**

handicrafts **l'artigianato**

landscape **il panorama**

literature **la letteratura**

painting **la pittura**

market **il mercato**

fair **la fiera**

furniture **i mobili**

fashion **la moda**

coins **le monete**

museum **il museo**

music **la musica**

national park **il parco nazionale**

reservation / sanctuary **il parco nazionale**

opera **l'opera**

park **il parco**

planetarium **il planetario**

town hall **il municipio**

religion **la religione**

reservation **la riserva naturale**

ruins **la rovina**

canyon **il canyon**

lake **il lago**

stadium **lo stadio**

statue **la statua**

dam / barrage **la diga**

wetland / swamp **la regione paludosa**

theater **il teatro**

pottery **la ceramica**

tower **la torre**

remains / ruins **le rovine**

university **l'università**

ornithology **l'ornitologia**

volcano **il vulcano**

economy / finance **l'economia**

skyscraper **il grattacielo**

desert **il deserto**

zoo **lo zoo**

The word *castello* means both "castle" and "fortress" in Italian.

Churches and Monasteries

abbey **l'abbazia**
altar **l'altare**
arch **l'arco**
choir **il coro**
Christian **cristiano**
Christianity **il cristianesimo**
cathedral **il duomo**
choir loft **la galleria**
windows **la finestra**
wing **l'ala**
frieze **il fregio**

dome **la cupola**
nave **la navata**
mass **la messa**
Middle Ages **il medioevo**
medieval **medievale**
center nave **la navata centrale**
Muslim **il musulmano**

priest **il sacerdote**
bell **la campana**
Gothic **il gotico**
church service **la messa**
Jew **l'ebreo**
pulpit **il pulpito**
chapel **la cappella**
cathedral **la cattedrale**
Catholic **il cattolico**
church **la chiesa**
steeple **il campanile**
convent **il convento**
denomination **la confessione**
cross **la croce**
cloisters **il chiostro**
crypt **la cripta**

pilgrim **il pellegrino**
main entrance **il portale**
Protestant **il protestante**
transept **la navata trasversale**
relief **il rilievo**
religion **la religione**
romanesque **il romanico**
rosette **il rosone**
sacristy **la sagrestia**
sarcophagus **il sarcofago**
side aisle **la navata laterale**
synagogue **la sinagoga**
font **il fonte battesimale**
temple **il tempio**
tower **la torre**
mural **la pittura murale**

A general term for priest is *sacerdote;* a parish priest is *un parroco.*

In the Museum

When is the museum open?
A che ora apre il museo?

What does admission cost?
Quanto costa l'ingresso?

How much does a guided tour cost?
Quanto costa una guida?

Two admission tickets for adults.
Due biglietti per adulti.

Three admission tickets for children.
Tre biglietti per bambini.

Is there an English-language catalog?
Ha un catalogo in inglese?

Can I take photographs?
Si possono fare foto?

Is there is a discount for ...
C'è una riduzione per ...
  children?
  bambini?
  groups?
  gruppi?
  senior citizens?
  anziani?
  students?
  studenti?
  handicapped?
  invalidi?

What is the name of the ...
Come si chiama ...
  architect?
  l'architetto?
  artist?
  l'artista?
  founder?
  il fondatore?

Who has done ...
Di chi è ...
  the painting?
  il dipinto?
  the sculpture?
  la scultura?
  the music?
  il brano musicale?

the exhibition?
  la mostra?

Do you have a poster / postcard of ... ?
Avete poster / cartoline di ... ?

Notices and Signs

Vietato scattare fotografie
No Photography

Guardaroba
Cloakroom

Chiuso
Closed

Armadietti
Lockers

Toilette
Toilets

Chiuso per restauri
Closed for Renovation

What's It Like?

amusing **divertente**

impressive **impressionante**

astonishing **stupefacente**

magnificent **meraviglioso**

ugly **brutto**

splendid **splendido**

pretty **bello**

romantic **romantico**

dreadful **spaventoso**

strange / unusual **strano**

great **bellissimo**

uncanny **misterioso**

If you want to see some archaeological sites, ask for the *scavi*, the excavations.

What Is There?

ballet **il balletto**

discotheque / disco **la discoteca**

festival **il festival**

film **il film**

folklore **il folclore**

jazz concert **il concerto jazz**

cabaret **il cabaret**

concert **il concerto**

musical **il musical**

nightclub **il nightclub**

opera **l'opera**

operetta **l'operetta**

procession **la processione**

casino **il casinò**

theater **il teatro**

parade **il corteo**

circus **il circo**

What You Hear or Read

Mi spiace, è tutto esaurito.
I'm sorry, we are sold out.

Il Suo biglietto per favore.
Your ticket, please.

Questo è il Suo posto.
Here is your seat.

guardaroba
cloakroom

toilette
toilets

uscita
exit

Information

What is playing at the theater tonight?
Cosa danno stasera a teatro?

Can you recommend a play?
Quale spettacolo mi consiglia?

What is playing at the cinema today?
Cosa c'è oggi al cinema?

I would like to see a good musical.
Vorrei vedere un bel musical.

Where is ...
Dov'è ...
the cinema / movie theater?
il cinema?
the theater?
il teatro?
the concert hall?
il salone concerti?
the opera?
l'opera?

When does the performance begin?
A che ora inizia lo spettacolo?

How long is the show?
Quanto dura lo spettacolo?

When does the show end?
A che ora finisce lo spettacolo?

Where is the cloakroom, please?
Dove è il guardaroba?

How long is the intermission?
Quanto tempo dura la pausa?

Is evening attire necessary?
Ci vuole l'abito di gala?

A *casinò* with the stress on the *ò* is a gambling establishment; a *casino,* on the other hand, is a house of ill repute.

Theater and Concerts

What type of play is this?
Di che genere è lo spettacolo?
  comedy
  commedia
  tragedy
  tragedia
  drama
  dramma

Who is the playwright?
Di chi è lo spettacolo?

Who is the producer?
Chi ha messo in scena lo spettacolo?

Who plays the leading role?
Chi è il protagonista?

Who are ...
Chi sono ...
  the actors?
  gli attori?
  the singers?
  i cantanti?
  the dancers?
  i ballerini?

Who is ...
Chi è ...
  the director?
  il regista?
  the choreographer?
  il coreografo?
  the conductor?
  il direttore d'orchestra?
  the author?
  l'autore?
  the set designer?
  lo scenografo?
  the orchestra?
  l'orchestra?
  the composer?
  il compositore?

Can I rent binoculars?
Posso noleggiare un binocolo?

Buying Tickets

Do you still have tickets for today?
Ci sono ancora biglietti per oggi?

Do you have also discounted tickets?
Ci sono biglietti ridotti?

How much does a seat cost in a ...
Quanto costa un posto ...
  lower price range?
  a prezzo basso?
  expensive price range?
  a prezzo elevato?

I would like a seat ...
Vorrei un posto ...
  in the orchestra.
  in platea.
  in the gallery.
  in galleria.
  in the balcony.
  in balconata.
  in the middle.
  nel mezzo.
  with a good view.
  con una buona visuale.
  in the box.
  in palco.

I would like to reserve three tickets.
Vorrei prenotare tre posti.

Discos and Nightclubs

Where is something going on here in the evening?
Dove ci si può divertire?

Is there a discotheque / disco here?
C'è una discoteca nei dintorni?

What does one wear?
Come bisogna vestirsi?

Are there young / older people there?
C'è un pubblico giovane o vecchio?

Would you like to dance?
Le va di ballare?

May I invite you?
Posso invitarLa?

Can I take you home?
Posso accompagnarLa a casa?

A nightclub is often designated as *nite* in Italian.

Offices and Institutions

Offices and Institutions

bank **la banca**

library **la biblioteca**

embassy **l'ambasciata**

mayor's office **l'ufficio del sindaco**

immigration authority **l'ufficio stranieri**

fire department **i vigili del fuoco**

lost and found **l'ufficio oggetti smarriti**

consulate **il consolato**

hospital **l'ospedale**

police **la polizia**

police station **il commissariato di polizia**

post office **la posta**

town hall **il municipio**

environmental protection agency **l'ufficio protezione ambientale**

Where can I find the nearest police station?
Può indicarmi il commissariato di polizia più vicino?

When does the bank open?
A che ora apre la banca?

When are you open?
Da che ora è aperto?

Are you also open on Saturdays?
È aperto anche il sabato?

closed
chiuso

I am looking for ...
(Io) cerco ...

The Right Address

sig.ra Emanuela Rossi
Via Dante 3
10100 - Torino

The mayor's office, the town hall, or the municipal office in smaller towns is *il municipio*.

At the Post Office Counter

Where is the nearest post office?
Può indicarmi l'ufficio postale più vicino?

When is it open?
Quali sono gli orari di apertura (al pubblico)?

Where is the nearest mailbox?
Può indicarmi la buca delle lettere più vicina?

What color is it?
Di che colore è?

How much does a letter cost ...
Quanto costa spedire una lettera ...
    to the United States / Canada?
    negli Stati Uniti / nel Canadà?
    to Austria?
    in Austria?
    to Switzerland?
    in Svizzera?

How long does a letter take to ... ?
In quanto tempo arriva una lettera in ... ?

Please give me a ... cent stamp.
Mi può dare un francobollo da ... cent.

Can you help me fill this out?
Può aiutarmi a compilare?

Next-day delivery, please.
Può inoltrarla domani, per favore?

Can I send a fax from here?
Posso spedire un fax da qui?

Can I insure this parcel?
Posso assicurare questo pacco?

sender **il mittente**
address **l'indirizzo**
stamp **il francobollo**
printed matter **la stampa**
express mail **l'espresso**
registered mail **la raccomandata**
recipient **il destinatario**
acknowledgment **la ricevuta**
fax **il fax**
charge **la tariffa**
money order **il vaglia**
weight **il peso**
airmail **la posta aerea**
COD **il contrassegno**
small parcel **il pacchetto**
parcel **il pacco**
postage **l'affrancatura**
remittance **il vaglia**
postcard **la cartolina**
general delivery **il fermo posta**
zip code **il codice postale**
counters **lo sportello**
telegram **il telegramma**
telex **il telex**
insurance **l'assicurazione**
customs declaration **la dichiarazione doganale**

Telegrams

I would like to send a telegram.
Vorrei spedire un telegramma.

How much does it cost per word?
Quanto costa la parola?

Will the telegram arrive today?
Il telegramma arriva entro oggi?

Picking Up Mail

Is there any mail for me?
C'è posta per me?

My name is ...
Mi chiamo ...

Your ID, please.
Posso avere la Sua carta d'identità per favore?

You will encounter the abbreviation PT for "post office" (*Posta e Telegrafo* or, more recently, *Poste e Telecomunicazioni*).

The Bank

Where is the nearest bank?
Può indicarmi la banca più vicina?

I would like to cash a traveler's check.
Vorrei riscuotere un travel cheque.

What is the exchange rate today?
Com'è oggi il cambio?

I would like to withdraw 400 euros with my credit card.
Vorrei prelevare quatrocento euro con la carta di credito.

I am having problems with your automatic teller. Would you please help me?
Non riesco a far funzionare il distributore automatico di banconote. Mi può aiutare per favore?

The automatic teller has taken my credit card.
Il distributore ha inghiottito la mia carta di credito.

I would like to make a transfer.
Vorrei fare un vaglia.

I would like to open an account.
Vorrei aprire un conto.

My credit card was stolen.
Mi hanno rubato la carta di credito.

I would like to have my card stopped.
Vorrei bloccare la mia carta di credito.

All common credit cards and EC cards are accepted in Italy. Using your personal identification number you can even use them to withdraw money from a *bancomat*. You can pay using a credit card in most stores in large cities, but that's less common at gas stations and in the countryside.

Italy is part of the European Union and uses the euro currency. Thus the coins are 1, 2, 5, 10, 20, and 50 cents, plus 1 and 2 euros. The bills are 5, 10, 20, 50, 100, 200, and 500 euros. It is a good idea to keep some small denominations on hand if you use a taxi.

cash **i contanti**

PIN (personal identification number) **il numero segreto**

remittance **il vaglia**

automatic teller (ATM) **il distributore automatico di banconote / bancomat**

money exchange **il cambio di valuta**

cash register / cashier **la cassa**

change **gli spiccioli**

credit card **la carta di credito**

coins **le monete**

working hours **gli orari di apertura**

traveler's checks **i travel cheque**

counter **lo sportello**

check **l'assegno**

bills / notes **le banconote**

transfer **il bonifico**

currency **la valuta**

exchange rate **il cambio**

exchange bureau **il cambiavalute**

Italian banks are closed on Saturday, but post offices are open until noon on that day.

Help! Thief!

My car was broken into.
Mi hanno forzato la serratura della macchina.

Where did it happen?
Dov'è successo?

There in the parking lot.
Al parcheggio.

When did it happen?
Quando è successo?

Between 11 A.M. and one o'clock.
Tra le undici e le tredici.

What was stolen?
Cosa Le hanno rubato?

All our luggage.
Tutti i nostri bagagli.

Your ID, please.
Posso avere il Suo passaporto per favore?

That was also stolen.
Mi hanno rubato anche quello.

If you have to turn to the police for any reason, the first ones you speak to are generally the *carabinieri*.

At the Police Station

Help!
Aiuto!

Where is the nearest police station?
Può indicarmi il commissariato di polizia più vicino?

I would like to do make a complaint.
Devo fare una denuncia.

I would like to report an accident.
Devo denunciare un incidente.

Does anyone here speak English?
C'è qualcuno che parla inglese?

I don't understand you.
Non La capisco.

I would like a lawyer.
Ho bisogno di un avvocato.

I need an interpreter.
Ho bisogno di un interprete.

Please inform my consulate.
Si metta in contatto con il mio consolato.

Please inform me of my rights.
Mi può spiegare quali sono i miei diritti?

I need a report for my insurance.
Ho bisogno di un certificato per la mia assicurazione.

I am not responsible.
Non sono responsabile dell'incidente.

What Happened?

I have lost my wallet.
Ho perso il portafoglio.

My money has been stolen.
Mi hanno rubato i soldi.

I have been cheated.
Sono stato imbrogliato.

I have been molested.
Sono stato molestato.

I have been robbed.
Sono stato rapinato.

I have been attacked / mugged.
Sono stato aggredito.

My son is missing.
Ho perso mio figlio.

I have been raped.
Sono stata violentata.

My car was broken into.
Hanno forzato la serratura della mia macchina.

The police is *la Polizia di Stato, la Polizia Stradale*, etc.

What Was Stolen?

ID **la carta di identità**

car **la macchina**

car documents **i documenti della macchina**

wallet **il portafoglio**

camera **la macchina fotografica**

purse **il portafoglio**

luggage **i bagagli**

handbag **la borsetta**

credit card **la carta di credito**

check **l'assegno**

watch **l'orologio**

Lost and Found

Where is the lost and found office?
Mi può indicare l'ufficio oggetti smarriti?

I have lost my clock.
Ho perso l'orologio.

I have left my handbag somewhere.
Ho perso la borsetta.

Has a suitcase been handed to you?
Avete trovato una valigia?

Would you please get in touch with me?
Mi terrà informato?

Here is my address.
Questo è il mio indirizzo.

Important Vocabulary

lawyer **l'avvocato**

complaint **la denuncia**

statement **la dichiarazione**

right to remain silent **il diritto di astensione dalla testimonianza**

swindler / cheat **l'imbroglione**

thief **il ladro**

theft **il furto**

prison **la prigione**

legal proceedings **l'udienza**

marriage fraud **il responsabile di truffa con promessa di matrimonio**

report **il verbale**

trial **il processo**

drugs **la droga**

judge **il giudice**

district attorney **il pubblico ministero**

pickpocket **il borsaiolo**

mugging **l'aggressione**

crime **il crimine**

rape **lo stupro**

arrest **l'arresto**

The word *stupro*, from the verb *stuprare* (past participle *stuprato*) is normally used for "rape."

Health

First Aid

I fell down.
Sono caduto.

I was hit by a car.
Sono stato investito.

I was attacked.
Sono stato aggredito.

I need a doctor.
Ho bisogno di un dottore.

Call an ambulance please.
Per favore chiami un'ambulanza.

I have injured my arm.
Sono ferito ad un braccio.

I cannot move my leg.
Non riesco a muovere la gamba.

I have broken my arm.
Ho un braccio rotto.

I am bleeding.
Sto perdendo sangue.

My blood type is ...
Il mio gruppo sanguigno è ...

I have ...
Soffro di ...
  asthma.
  asma.
  diabetes.
  diabete.
  hypertension.
  pressione alta.
  low blood pressure.
  pressione bassa.

AIDS.
AIDS.

I am allergic to ...
Sono allergico ...
  mites.
  agli acari.
  dust.
  alla polvere.
  animal fur.
  al pelo degli animali.
  grass.
  all'erba.
  pollen.
  al polline.

I am allergic to penicillin.
Sono allergico alla penicillina.

I am pregnant.
Sono incinta.

What You Hear

Si è fatto male? / Posso aiutarLa?
Are you hurt? / Can I help you?

Devo chiamare un'ambulanza?
Should I call an ambulance?

Resti lì sdraiato.
Just lie there quietly.

Vado a cercare aiuto.
I will get help!

Tra poco arriverà il dottore.
Help is on the way.

Ha perso i sensi / conoscenza.
You were unconscious.

A *visita* is usually a social occasion, but with respect to a doctor, it also means an examination.

Drugstore

Where is the nearest drugstore?
Può indicarmi la farmacia più vicina?

I need some medicine for diarrhea.
Ho bisogno di un medicinale contro la diarrea.

I need some bandages.
Vorrei delle bende.

Can I wait for it?
Posso ritirarle subito?

This medication is only on prescription.
Per questo medicinale ci vuole la ricetta / prescrizione del medico.

How do I take the medicine?
Come devo assumere il medicinale?

thermometer
il termometro

condoms
i preservativi

band-aids
i cerotti

hot-water bottle
la borsa dell'acqua calda

laxative **il lassativo**

eye drops **il collirio**

sedative / tranquilizer **il sedativo, tranquillante**

ointment for burns **la pomata per bruciature**

disinfectant **il disinfettante**

disposable needles / syringes **la siringa usa-e-getta**

throat lozenges / cough drops **le pastiglie per mal di gola**

cough syrup **lo sciroppo per la tosse**

ointment for insect bites **un farmaco per le punture d'insetti**

carbon tablets **l'astringente**

tablets for headache **le pastiglie per mal di testa**

tablets for poor circulation **le medicine per la circolazione**

ear drops **le gocce per le orecchie**

sleeping pills **i sonniferi**

painkillers **gli antidolorifici, analgesici**

pregnancy test **il test di gravidanza**

cotton **il cotone, l'ovatta**

Taking Medications

uso esterno **external use**

uso interno **internal use**

diluire in acqua **dissolve in water**

a digiuno **on an empty stomach**

assumere per via orale **let it melt in the mouth**

assumere per via orale senza masticare **swallow without chewing**

prima / dopo i pasti **before / after meals**

due volte al giorno **twice daily**

ogni tre ore **every three hours**

In Italy vitamins are considered useful in building up the body and are referred to as *ricostituenti* ("reconstituents").

The Human Body

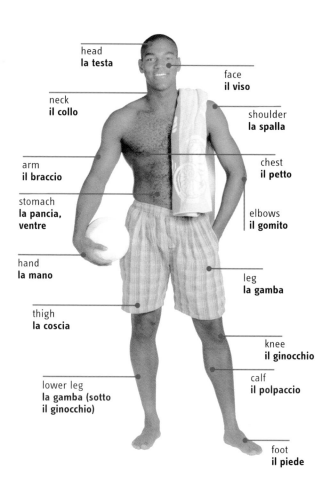

head
la testa

face
il viso

neck
il collo

shoulder
la spalla

arm
il braccio

chest
il petto

stomach
**la pancia,
ventre**

elbows
il gomito

hand
la mano

leg
la gamba

thigh
la coscia

knee
il ginocchio

calf
il polpaccio

lower leg
**la gamba (sotto
il ginocchio)**

foot
il piede

A lady's bust is *il seno* or *il petto*; the anatomical term is *torace* (thorax).

The Human Body

eyebrows
le sopracciglia

eyelid
la palpebra

eye
l'occhio

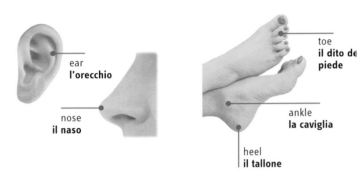

ear
l'orecchio

nose
il naso

toe
**il dito de
piede**

ankle
la caviglia

heel
il tallone

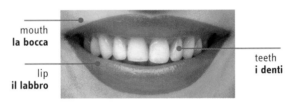

mouth
la bocca

lip
il labbro

teeth
i denti

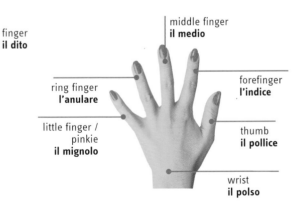

finger
il dito

middle finger
il medio

ring finger
l'anulare

forefinger
l'indice

little finger /
pinkie
il mignolo

thumb
il pollice

wrist
il polso

In addition to *viso* for face, there is also the designation *faccia*.

Parts of the Body

artery **l'arteria**

bladder **la vescica**

appendix **l'appendice**

blood **il sangue**

bronchial tubes **i bronchi**

intestine **l'intestino**

gallbladder **la cistifellea**

brain **il cervello**

joint **l'articolazione**

skin **la pelle**

heart **il cuore**

hip **l'anca**

jaws **la mascella**

bones **le ossa**

liver **il fegato**

lung **il polmone**

stomach **lo stomaco**

tonsils **le tonsille**

muscle **il muscolo**

nape of the neck **la nuca**

nerve **il nervo**

kidneys **i reni**

rib **la costola**

back **la schiena**

collarbone **la clavicola**

tendon **il tendine**

vein **la vena**

spinal column **la spina dorsale**

tongue **la lingua**

At the Doctor's

Is there a doctor here?
C'è un dottore?

What are the office hours?
Quand'è l'orario di visita?

Can I come immediately?
Posso venire subito?

Can the doctor come to me?
Può dire al dottore di venire da me?

I have a pain.
Sto male.

I feel weak.
Mi sento debole.

I feel ...
Sto / Ho ...
  sick.
  male.
  dizzy.
  le vertigini.

I have a cough.
Ho la tosse.

I (regularly) take high blood pressure medicine.
Prendo regolarmente dei medicinali per la pressione alta.

The name of the medication is ...
Il nome del medicinale è ...

Can you prescribe some medicine for me?
Può prescrivermi una medicina?

Do I need a prescription for it?
Ho bisogno della ricetta per questa medicina?

I have insurance.
Sono in possesso di una polizza contro le malattie.

Here is my international insurance card.
Questa è la mia tessera sanitaria, valida a livello internazionale.

Please give me the bill and a copy of your report.
Mi può dare la fattura e una copia del referto medico.

Ossa is the plural of "bone," whereas "the bone" is *l'osso.*

What the Doctor Says

Dove ha male?
Where does it hurt?

Ha dei dolori?
Are you feeling any pain?

Da quanto tempo?
For how long?

Quante volte si verificano i dolori?
How often?

Dove Le fa male?
Where does it hurt?

Sente dolore?
Does this hurt?

Si spogli.
Please undress.

Inspiri profondamente.
Take a deep breath.

Apra la bocca.
Open your mouth.

Tiri fuori la lingua.
Stick out your tongue.

Tossisca.
Cough.

Ancora.
Once again.

Lei fuma?
Do you smoke?

Beve alcolici?
Do you drink alcohol?

È allergico?
Do you have any allergies?

Prende regolarmente dei medicinali?
Do you take any medication regularly?

Prende la pillola?
Are you taking the pill?

Le prescrivo qualcosa.
I will prescribe something for you.

Le faccio un'iniezione.
I will give you a shot.

Ha un certificato di vaccinazione?
Do you have an vaccination certificate?

Bisogna cucire la ferita / Dare dei punti.
The wound must be stitched.

Deve fare delle radiografie.
You must have an X-ray.

Le prescrivo una visita specialistica.
You must see a specialist.

Deve essere operato.
You must have an operation.

Deve rimanere a letto per alcuni giorni.
You must stay in bed a few days.

Ritorni domani.
Come back tomorrow.

Non è niente di grave.
It is nothing serious.

Non ha niente.
There is nothing wrong with you.

Specialists

surgeon
il chirurgo

gynecologist
il ginecologo

ear, nose, and throat specialist
l'otorinolaringoiatra

internist
l'internista

pediatrician
il pediatra

psychiatrist
lo psichiatra

urologist
l'urologo

If you want to say "I have caught a cold," you say *Ho preso un raffreddore* or *Mi sono raffreddato.*

Illnesses

allergy **l'allergia**

angina **l'angina**

rash **l'eruzione cutanea**

lump / swelling **il bernoccolo; gonfiore**

bite **il morso**

boil **il foruncolo**

stomachache **il mal di pancia**

flatulence **la flatulenza**

inflammation of the bladder **la cistite**

appendicitis **l'appendicite**

hemorrhage **l'ematoma**

high blood pressure **l'ipertensione, la pressione alta**

bleeding **l'emorragia**

burn **l'ustione**

bronchitis **la bronchite**

diabetes **il diabete**

diptheria **la difterite**

diarrhea **la diarrea**

inflammation **l'infiammazione**

cold **il raffreddore**

fever **la febbre**

concussion **il trauma cranico**

jaundice **l'itterizia**

ulcer **l'ulcera**

flu **l'influenza**

sore throat **il mal di gola**

heart problems **il male al cuore**

heart attack **l'attacco cardiaco, infarto**

lumbago **la lombaggine, il colpo della strega**

cough **la tosse**

infection **l'infezione**

insect bite **la puntura d'insetto**

sciatica **la sciatica**

whooping cough **la pertosse**

fracture **la frattura (ossea)**

headache **il mal di testa**

cancer **il cancro**

circulatory disorder **i disturbi circolatori**

paralysis **la paralisi**

pneumonia **la polmonite**

stomachache **il mal di stomaco**

tonsillitis **la tonsillite**

measles **il morbillo**

migraine **l'emicrania**

mumps **gli orecchioni**

nosebleed **l'emoraggia nasale**

smallpox **il vaiolo**

bruise **la contusione**

rheumatism **il reumatismo**

German measles **la rosolia**

backache **il mal di schiena**

salmonella **la salmonella**

cut **il taglio**

head cold **il raffreddore**

chills **i brividi di freddo**

swelling **il gonfiore**

stitch in the side **le fitte ai fianchi**

heartburn **il bruciore di stomaco**

sunburn **la scottatura**

sunstroke **l'insolazione**

tetanus **il tetano**

nausea **la nausea**

burn **l'ustione**

poisoning **l'avvelenamento**

injury **la ferita**

sprain **la slogatura**

constipation **la costipazione**

viral illness **la malattia virale**

chickenpox **la varicella**

wound **la ferita**

strain **il stiramento, strappo**

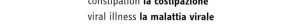

The most common word for stroke is *ictus*.

What's the Matter?

I have cut myself.
Mi sono tagliato.

I have been bitten.
Sono stato morsicato.

I have something in my eye.
Ho qualcosa nell'occhio.

My child has fallen down.
Mio figlio è caduto.

My ankle is swollen.
Ho la caviglia gonfia.

I have vomited.
Ho vomitato.

At the Gynecologist's

È incinta?
Are you pregnant?

Prende la pillola?
Are you taking the pill? / Are you on the pill?

Quando ha avuto l'ultimo ciclo?
When was your last period?

I am having my period.
Ho le mestruazioni.

I have not had a period for two months.
Sono due mesi che non ho più le mestruazioni.

I think I am pregnant.
Penso di essere incinta.

I am pregnant.
Sono incinta.

I have menstrual problems.
Ho disturbi mestruali.

I take the pill. / I'm on the pill.
Prendo la pillola.

swab **lo striscio**

abortion **l'aborto**

inflammation of the bladder
l'infiammazione alla vescica / la cistite

breast **il seno**

fallopian tubes **l'ovaia**

miscarriage **l'aborto spontaneo**

uterus **l'utero**

condom **il preservativo**

cramp **il crampo**

vaginitis **la vaginite**

pregnancy **la gravidanza**

intrauterine device **la spirale**

vagina **la vagina**

"My child" can of course also be a daughter, in which case it is *mia figlia.*

At the Dentist's

Is there a dentist here?
C'è un dentista nei dintorni?

I need an appointment urgently.
Ho bisogno di un appuntamento urgente.

I have toothache.
Ho mal di denti.

A filling has fallen out.
Ho perso un'otturazione.

A tooth is broken.
Ho un dente rotto.

My denture has broken.
Ho la dentiera rotta.

I would like a local anesthetic.
Vorrei un'anestesia.

Adesso può risciacquare.
Rinse please.

Devo otturare il dente.
I will fill your tooth.

Per ora Le faccio un'otturazione provvisoria.
I'm only treating it temporarily.

Vuole che Le faccia un'iniezione?
Would you like a shot?

Bisogna togliere il dente.
I have to remove / pull the tooth.

abscess **l'ascesso**

(local) anesthetic **l'anestesia**

inflammation **l'infiammazione**

denture **la dentiera**

dental surgeon **l'ortodontista**

crown **la capsula**

nerve **il nervo**

filling **l'otturazione**

wisdom tooth **il dente del giudizio**

root canal work **il trattamento della radice**

(dental) bridge **il ponte**

gum **la gengiva**

toothache **il mal di denti**

braces **l'apparecchio per i denti**

root (of the tooth) **la radice del dente**

The natural teeth are *la dentatura*, in contrast to *la dentiera*, false teeth.

In the Hospital

Does anybody speak English here?
C'è qualcuno che parla inglese qui?

Please speak more slowly.
Può parlare più lentamente per favore?

I would like to be flown home.
Vorrei essere rimpatriato.

I have repatriation insurance.
Ho un'assicurazione per il rimpatrio.

What do I have?
Che cos'ho?

Do I have to have an operation?
Devo essere operato?

How long do I have to stay in the hospital?
Quanto tempo devo rimanere in ospedale?

Can you please give me a pain killer?
Può darmi un analgesico?

Please inform my family.
Può informare la mia famiglia per favore?

bed **il letto**

bedpan **la padella**

blood transfusion **la trasfusione di sangue**

surgeon **il chirurgo**

call button **il campananello**

male nurse **l'infermiere**

nurse **l'infermiera**

anesthesia **l'anestesia**

operation **l'operazione**

wheelchair **la sedia a rotelle**

injection **l'iniezione**

Another word for *anesthesia* is *narcosi*.

Business Travel

At the Reception Desk

I have made an appointment with Mr. Pavone.
Ho preso un appuntamento con il sig. Pavone.

Mr. Pavone is expecting me.
Sono atteso dal sig. Pavone.

Would you please tell him I'm here.
Può annunciarmi per favore?

Here is my card.
EccoLe la mia carta da visita.

I am sorry, I am somewhat late.
Mi spiace, sono un po' in ritardo.

At the Conference Table

...sends his regards to you.
Devo riferirLe i saluti di ...

Our company would be pleased to offer you the following.
La nostra ditta vorrebbe farLe questa offerta.

Is that your final offer?
È la Sua ultima offerta?

I'm sorry, that's our limit.
Mi spiace, di più non possiamo fare.

I think there is a misunderstanding.
Credo che ci sia un equivoco.

That is an interesting suggestion.
È una proposta interessante.

Can you explain that in more detail?
Può spiegarmela più in dettaglio?

What exactly are you thinking of?
Che cosa intende precisamente?

Let's summarize once again.
Riassumiamo.

Let me put it like this.
Permetta che riassuma con le mie parole.

Would you excuse me a moment?
Vuole scusarmi un momento?

I must discuss this with my company first.
Devo prima parlarne con la mia ditta.

We will think it over.
Ci penseremo su.

We will check that.
Controlleremo.

Can I phone you?
Posso fare una telefonata?

Could we make another appointment for tomorrow?
Potremmo fissare un altro appuntamento per domani?

We will stay in phone contact.
Rimaniamo in contatto per telefono.

Thank you for the constructive discussion.
La ringrazio per la conversazione costruttiva.

I am very pleased with our negotiations.
Sono molto soddisfatto di queste trattative.

To our successful cooperation.
Facciamo un brindisi al nostro successo.

Facciamo un brindisi is what people usually say in proposing a toast.

Important Vocabulary

conclusion / finalization **la stipulazione**

shares **le azioni**

offer **l'offerta**

investment **la partecipazione**

import limitations / restrictions **le restrizioni all'importazione**

purchase price **il prezzo di acquisto**

euro **l'euro**

European Union **l'Unione Europea**

freight charges **le spese di trasporto**

guarantee **la garanzia**

business partners **il partner (commerciale)**

business meeting **appuntamento di lavoro**

law **la legge**

profit **il guadagno**

liability **la responsabilità**

trade agreements **l'accordo (commerciale)**

profit margin **il margine (commerciale)**

manufacturer **il fabbricante**

fees **la parcella**

import **l'importazione**

colleague **il collega**

conditions **le condizioni**

conference **la conferenza**

cooperation **la cooperazione**

expenses / costs **le spese**

retail / selling price **il prezzo (di vendita) al consumatore**

supplier **il fornitore**

licensing fee **la tassa di licenza**

marketing **il marketing**

value-added tax **l'IVA (imposta sul valore aggiunto)**

coworker / employee **il dipendente**

price **il prezzo**

protocol **il protocollo**

commission **la commissione**

discount / rebate **lo sconto**

invoice **il conto**

tax **la tassa**

price per piece **il prezzo per unità**

agenda **l'ordine del giorno**

percentages / royalties **le quote di utile**

transportation costs **le spese di trasporto**

takeover **l'accettazione**

negotiation **la trattativa**

loss **la perdita**

insurance **l'assicurazione**

representative / agent **il rappresentante**

business card **la carta da visita**

chairman **il superiore**

customs regulations **le norme doganali**

A calling card is also referred to as *un biglietto di visita*.

Corporate Structure

Corp. (Corporation)
SRL (società a responsabilità limitata)

Inc. (Incorporated)
società per azioni (S.p.A.)

board of trustees
il collegio sindacale

chairman of the board
il presidente del collegio sindacale

advisory board
il comitato consultivo

board of directors
il consiglio di amministrazione

advertising / marketing manager
il direttore dell'ufficio pubblicità

sales manager
il direttore delle vendite

secretary
il segretario / la segretaria

assistant
l'assistente

chief executive officer (CEO), president
l'amministratore delegato

board member
il membro consigliere

general manager
il direttore esecutivo

executive vice president
il direttore centrale

divison manager
il capo reparto

department manager
il capo settore

general manager
il procuratore principale

authorized officer
il procuratore

Trattative are concrete negotiations; for a conversation you can also use the word *discorso*.

Contracts

enclosure **il supplemento**

order **l'incarico / l'ordine**

security **la cauzione**

proprietary reservation **la riserva di proprietà**

place of fulfillment of contract **il luogo di adempimento**

deadline **il termine**

guarantee **la garanzia**

court of jurisdiction **il foro competente**

business conditions **le condizioni di transazione**

liability **le responsabilità**

purchase contract **il contratto di**

acquisto

delivery terms **le condizioni di consegna**

time of delivery **il termine di consegna**

paragraph **il paragrafo**

appointment **il termine**

signature **la firma**

agreement **l'accordo**

contract **il contratto**

penalty **la pena convenzionale**

right of preemption **il diritto di prelazione**

payment terms **le condizioni di pagamento**

Trade Fairs

I am looking for the stall of the company ...
Sto cercando lo stand della ditta ...

We deal in ...
Noi commerciamo con ...

We produce ...
Noi produciamo ...

Here is my card.
EccoLe la mia carta da visita.

Can I give you a brochure?
Posso lasciarLe un depliant?

Can I show it to you?
Posso illustrarglielo brevemente?

Can you send me an offer?
Può inviarmi un'offerta?

Do you have a catalog?
Ha un catalogo?

Can I arrange a final date?
Posso stabilire un termine?

exit **l'uscita**

exhibitor **l'espositore**

ID card **la carta d'identità**

entrance **l'ingresso**

invitation **l'invito**

technical visitors **i visitatori specializzati**

aisle **il corridoio**

hall **il padiglione**

catalog **il catalogo**

brand **la marca**

name badge **la targhetta**

press conference **la conferenza stampa**

brochure **il depliant**

stall / stand **lo stand**

floor **il piano**

trademark **il marchio di fabbrica**

Instead of *ditta* for "company," the term *azienda* is often used. The latter has the connotation of the English "enterprise" or "venture."

Glossary

English - Italian

A

a little un po'
a, an un, una
abbey abbazia (f)
abortion aborto (m)
abscess ascesso (m)
accident incidente (m)
acknowledgment accusa (f)
acquaintance conoscente (m)
actor attore (m)
actress attrice (f)
ad inserzione publicitaria (f)
adapter adattatore (m)
address indirizzo (m)
administration amministrazione (f)
aerobics aerobica (f)
afterward dopo
again ancora
agent sensale (m)
agreement accordo (m)
air aria (f)
air conditioning climatizzatore (m)
air mattress materassino (m)
air pump pompa (f)
airmail posta aerea (f)
airport aeroporto (m)
aisle corridoio (m)
aisle seat posto sul corridoio (m)
alarm clock sveglia (f)
all tutt-i/-e
Allen wrench chiave per viti ad esagono cavo (f)
allergy allergia (f)
alley vicolo (m)
almond mandorle (f)
altar altare (m)
alter modificare
although benchè
aluminum foil carta stagnola (f)
alumna diplomata (f)
amazing sorprendente
ambulance ambulanza (f)
amusing divertente
anchor àncora (f)
anchovies acciughe (f)
and e
anesthesia anestesia (f)
anesthetic anestesia (f)

angina angina (m)
anglerfish rana pescatrice (f)
angry arrabbiato
ankle caviglia (f)
annoyed stressato
answering machine segreteria telefonica (f)
antique store antiquariato (m)
antiques pezzi d'antiquariato (m)
apartment appartamento (m)
appendicitis appendicite (f)
appendix appendice (f), supplemento (m)
apple mela (f)
apple flan crostata di mele (f)
apple juice succo di mela (m)
apple pie torta di mela (f)
appointment termine (m), appuntamento (m)
apricot albicocca (f)
April aprile (m)
apron grembiule (m)
archaeology archeologia (f)
architect architetto (m)
architecture architettura (f)
area code prefisso (m)
arm braccio (m)
armchair poltrona (f)
army esercito (m)
arrest arresto (m)
arrival entrata (f)
arrival time orario di arrivo (m)
art arte (f)
art gallery galleria d'arte (f)
artery arteria (f)
artichokes carciofi (m)
artificial leather similpelle (f)
artist artista (m/f)
arts and crafts artigianato artistico (m)
as come
ascent salita (f)
ashtray posacenere (m)
ask chiedere
asparagus asparagi (m)

asthma asma (f)
at night di notte
at noon a mezzogiorno
ATM bancomat (m)
August agosto (m)
aunt zia (f)
author scrittore (m), autore (m)
authorized officer procuratore (m)
automatic shutter release cavo dell'autoscatto (m)
autumn autunno (m)
avocado avocado (m)
awesome meraviglioso

B

baby cream crema per bambini (f)
baby food cibo per neonati (m)
backache mal di schiena (m)
backfire accensione difettosa (f)
backpack zaino (m)
backyard cortile posteriore (m)
bacon speck (m)
bad cattivo
badminton volano (m)
badminton racket racchetta da volano (f)
baggage bagagli (m)
baggage carts carrello portabagagli (m)
baggage claim consegna dei bagagli (f)
baggage deposit guardaroba (m)
bait esca (f)
baked (cotto) al forno
baked goods biscotti (m)
baker panettiere (m)
bakery panetteria (f)
balcony balcone (m)
ball palla (f)
ballet balletto (m)
balloon palloncino (m)
ballpoint pen biro (f)
balsamic vinegar aceto balsamico (m)
banana banana (f)
bandage bende (f)
band-aid cerotti (m)
bank banca (f)

barley orzo (m)
barrette fermaglio (m)
baseball baseball (m)
baseball cap berretto (m)
basil basilico (m)
basketball pallacanestro (f)
bath bagno (m)
bath slippers ciabatte da spiaggia (f)
bath sponge spugna (f)
bath towel asciugamano (m)
bathing cap cuffia (f)
bathrobe accappatoio (m)
bathtub vasca da bagno (f)
batiste batista (f)
battery batteria (f)
bayleaves foglie d'alloro (f)
beach spiaggia (f)
beach towel telo da spiaggia (m)
beans fagioli (m)
beard barba (f)
beautiful bello
because perchè
bed letto (m)
bed sheets lenzuolo (m)
bedpan padella (f)
bedroom camera da letto (f)
beech faggio (m)
beef manzo (m)
beef broth brodo di manzo (m)
beer birra (f)
before prima
beginner principiante (m)
believe credere
bell campana (f)
bellboy cameriere (m)
belt cintura (f)
berth cabina (f)
beverage bibita (f)
bicycle pump pompa (della bicicletta) (f)
bicycle racing gara ciclistica (f)
bicycle store ciclista (m)
bikini bikini (m)
bill conto (m)
billboard cartellone (m)
billfold portafoglio (m)
billiards biliardo (m)
billion miliardo (m)
binoculars cannocchiale (m)
biologist biologo (m)
birthplace casa natale (f)
bite morso (m)

black nero
black bread pane nero (m)
black tea tè nero (m)
black-and-white in bianco e nero
blackberries more (f)
bladder vescica (f)
blanket coperta (f)
blazer blazer (m)
bleeding emorragia (f)
blinker frecce (f)
blood sangue (m)
blood transfusion trasfusione di sangue (f)
blood type gruppo sanguigno (m)
blouse camicetta (f)
blow-dry asciugare al fon
blue blu
blueberries mirtilli (m)
bluefish spigola (f)
boar cinghiale (m)
board of trustees collegio sindacale (m)
boarding pass imbarco (m)
boat barca (f)
boat rental noleggio imbarcazioni (m)
body lotion latte per il corpo (m)
boil foruncolo (m)
bones ossa (f)
bookkeeper contabile (m)
bookseller libraio (m)
bookstore libreria (f)
bootlegger contrabbandiere di liquori (m)
boots stivali (m)
botanical gardens giardino botanico (m)
botany botanica (f)
bottle bottiglia (f)
bottle opener apribottiglie (m)
bow prua (f)
bowl scodella (f)
bowling birilli (m)
bowtie (cravatta) a farfalla (f)
boxing boxe (f)
bra reggiseno (m)
bracelet braccialetto (m)
braces apparecchio per i denti (m)
brain cervello (m)
braised stufato
brake frenare, freno
brake cable fune freno (f)
brake fluid liquido dei freni (m)

brake light stop (luci freno) (m)
brake lining guarnizione del freno (f)
brand marca (f)
Brazil nuts noci del Parà
bread pane (m)
breaded impanato
break rompere
breakdown assistance assistenza meccanica (f)
breakfast colazione (f)
breast petto (m)
bridge ponte (m)
briefcase borsa portadocumenti (f)
broccoli broccoli (m)
brochure depliant (m)
bronchial tubes bronchi (m)
bronchitis bronchite (f)
brooch spilla (f)
brook ruscello (m)
broom scopa (f)
brother fratello (m)
browned rosolato
bruise contusione (f)
brussel sprouts cavolo di Bruxelles (m)
buck capriolo (m)
bucket secchio (m)
building edificio (m)
bumper paraurti (m)
bungalow bungalow (m)
burn ustione (f)
bush beans fagioli nani (m)
business card carta da visita (f)
business meeting appuntamento di lavoro (m)
business partners partner (commerciale) (m)
businessman commerciante (m), imprenditore (m)
busy signal tono (di) occupato (m)
butane gas gas butano (m)
butcher macellaio (m)
butter burro (m)
button bottone (m)
buy comprare

C...............................
cabana cabina (f)
cabaret cabaret (m)
cabbage cavolo (m), cavolo bianco (m)
cabin cabina (f)
cable railway funivia (f)

cables cavo (m)
cactus fruit fichi d'india (m)
cake torta (f)
calendar calendario (m)
calf vitello (m), polpaccio (m)
call button campanello (m)
camera macchina fotografica (f)
camera bag borsa delle fotografie (f)
camper autocaravan (m)
campsite campeggio (m)
can lattina (m), potere
can opener apriscatole (m)
canal canale (m)
cancer cancro (m)
candies dolciumi (m)
candle candela (f)
candlestick candeliere (m)
candy confetto (m)
canned food conserve (f)
canoe canoa (f)
canoeing canottaggio (m)
canvas tela (f)
canyon canyon (m)
cap berretto (m)
capers capperi (m)
capon cappone (m)
cappuccino cappuccino (m)
captain capitano (m)
car macchina (f)
car documents documenti della macchina (m)
car ferry autotraghetto (m)
car mechanic meccanico per automobili (m)
car number numero del vagone (m)
car racing corsa automobilistica (f)
carambola carambola (f)
caraway seed bread cumino (m)
carburetor carburatore (m)
card telephone telefono a scheda (m)
carnation garofano (m)
carp carpa (f)
carpenter falegname (m), carpentiere (m)
carrots carote (f)
car-train treno navetta (m)
cash payment pagamento in contanti (m)
cash register cassa (f)
casino casinò (m)
cassette player Walkman (m)

cassette recorder registratore (m)
castle castello (m)
cat gatto (m)
catalog catalogo (m)
catfish pesce gatto (m)
cathedral cattedrale (f), duomo (m)
Catholic cattolico (m)
cauliflower cavolfiore (m)
cave caverna (f)
CD burner masterizzatore (m)
CD player lettore CD (m), giradischi (m)
CD-ROM drive drive per CD-ROM (m)
celery sedano (m)
cell phone cellulare (m)
cemetery cimitero (m)
center nave navata centrale (f)
center part riga in mezzo (f)
centimeter centimetro (m)
central heating riscaldamento centralizzato (m)
ceramics ceramica (f)
chain catena (f)
chain guard copricatena (m)
chair sedia (f)
chairlift seggiovia (f)
chairman superiore (m)
chalk gesso (m)
chambermaid cameriera (f)
change modificare, spiccioli (m)
chapel cappella (f)
charcoal carbone (m)
charcoal pencils carboncini (m)
charge tariffa (f)
cheap economico
cheat ingannare
check assegno (m)
checkered a quadretti
checkroom deposito dei bagagli (m)
cheese formaggio (m)
chemist chimico (m)
chemistry chimica (f)
cherry ciliegie (f)
chervil cerfoglio (m)
chess scacchi (m)
chestnut castagno (m)
chestnuts castagne (f)
chick pulcino (m)
chicken galletto (m), pollo (f)

chicken broth brodo di pollo (m)
chickenpox varicella (f)
chickpeas ceci (m)
chicory cicoria (f)
child care sala ricreazione (f)
children bambini (m)
children's book libro per bambini (m)
children's playground parcogiochi (m)
children's shoes scarpe per bambini (f)
child's bed culla (f)
chili peperoncino (m)
chills brividi di freddo (m)
chimney camino (m)
chimney sweep spazzacamino (m)
chive erba cipollina (f)
chocolate cioccolato (m)
chocolates cioccolatini (m)
choir coro (m)
choir loft galleria (f)
chopped tritato
Christian cristiano (m)
Christianity cristianesimo (m)
Christmas Natale (m)
church chiesa (f)
church service messa (f)
cigarette holder bocchino per sigarette (m)
cigarettes sigarette (f)
cigarillos sigari (m)
cigars sigari (m)
cinema cinema (m)
cinnamon cannella (f)
circulatory disorder disturbi circolatori (m)
circus circo (m)
citizens' initiative comitato civico (m)
city map pianta della città (f)
civil servant impiegato (m)
clam vongola (f)
cleaning products detersivo (m)
cleaning rag straccio (m)
clearing schiarita (f)
cliff rupe (f)
climbing belt cintura per scalatori (m)
climbing boots scarpe da montagna (f), scarpe per scalatori (f)
climbing path mulattiera (f)
cloakroom guardaroba (m)

cloister chiostro (m), convento (m)
closed chiuso
clothes brush spazzola (per vestiti) (f)
clothes dryer asciugabiancheria (f)
clothes racks stendibiancheria (m)
clothesline corda per il bucato (f)
clothespins mollette (per la biancheria) (f)
clothing store abbigliamento (m)
clouds nubi (f)
cloudy nuvoloso
clove chiodi di garofano (m)
clutch frizione (f)
coal heating riscaldamento a carbone (m)
coalition coalizione (f)
coast costa (f)
coat cappotto (m)
cock gallo (m)
cockle cuoretto (m)
cocoa cacao (m)
coconut cocco (m)
COD contrassegno (m)
codfish merluzzo (m)
coffee caffè (m)
coffee grinder macinino del caffè (m)
coffee machine macchina del caffè (f)
coffee with ice cream caffé gelato (m)
coins monete (f)
cold freddo, raffreddore
collar colletto (m)
collarbone clavicola (f)
colleague collega (m)
collect call chiamata a carico del destinatario (f)
college università (f)
color fare la tinta
color pen matita colorata (f)
color rinse riflesso (m)
colored laundry capi colorati (m)
colorful, colored a colori
comb pettine (m)
come venire
comedy commedia (f)
commission commissione (f)
commuter train treno suburbano (m)
compartment scompartimento (m)

compass bussola (f)
complaint denuncia (f)
compressed-air bottles bottiglie ad aria compressa (f)
computer expert esperto EDP (m)
computer store negozio di computer (m)
concealer matita (f)
concert concerto (m)
concert hall sala concerti (m)
concussion trauma cranico (m)
condom preservativo (m)
condominium condominio (m)
conductor controllore (m)
conference conferenza (f)
confession confessione (f)
connecting flight volo di coincidenza (m)
constipation costipazione (f)
constitution costituzione (f)
construction worker lavoratore edile (m)
consulate consolato (m)
contact lenses lenti a contatto (f)
contract contratto (m)
convention asamblea (f), convegno (m)
cook cuoco (m)
cookbook libro di cucina (m)
cooked bollito
cookies pasticcino (m)
cooking course corso di cucina (m)
coolant acqua di raffreddamento (f)
cooler frigorifero (m)
cooperation cooperazione (f)
copper rame (m)
corduroy vellutino (m)
corks tappo (m)
corkscrew cavatappi (m)
corn mais (m)
cosmetics store istituto di bellezza (m)
costs spese (f)
cotton cotone (m)
cough tosse (f)
cough drops pastiglie per mal di gola (f)
cough syrup sciroppo per la tosse (m)
counter sportello (m)
country road strada provinciale (f)

county contea (f)
course corso (m)
cousin cugino (m), cugina (m)
cover copertone (m)
cow vacca (f)
crab granchio (m), gambero (m)
crab cocktail cocktail di gamberi (m)
cracker pane croccante di segala (m)
craftsperson artigiano (m)
cramp crampo (m)
crampons rampone (m)
cranberries mirtilli rossi (m)
crawfish aragosta (f)
crayon matite colorate (f), pastello (m)
cream panna (f)
credit card carta di credito (f)
crepe crespo (m)
cress crescione (m)
crew equipaggio (m)
crime crimine (m)
croissant cornetto (m)
croquettes crocchette (f)
cross croce (f)
cross-country skiing sci di fondo (m)
crossroad incrocio (m)
crossroads crocicchio (m)
crosswalk zona pedonale (f)
crown capsula (f)
cruise crociera (f)
crypt cripta (f)
cucumber cetriolo (m)
cufflinks gemelli (m)
cuffs polsini (m)
culture cultura (f)
cup tazza (f)
curd cagliata (f)
curler bigodino (m)
curls ricci (m)
currants ribes (m)
currency valuta (f)
current corrente (f)
curtain tenda (f)
customer service servizio clienti (m)
customs dogana (f)
customs check controllo doganale (m)
customs declaration dichiarazione doganale (f)
customs regulations norme doganali (f)
cute destro

cutlery posata (f)
cutlet cotoletta (f)
cycling ciclismo (m)
cylinder head testata cilindri (f)

D

daily quotidiano
dairy caseificio (m)
dairy products latticini (m)
daisy margherita (f)
dam diga (f)
dance ballo (m)
dandruff forfora (m)
dark scuro
darling amore (m)
darts freccette (f)
date data (f)
date of arrival arrivo (m)
date of departure giorno della partenza (m)
dates datteri (m)
daughter figlia (f)
daughter-in-law nuora (f)
day giorno (m)
day after tomorrow dopodomani
day before yesterday l'altro ieri
day ticket biglietto giornaliero (m)
deadline termine (m)
deceive ingannare
December dicembre (m)
deck ponte (m)
deck chair sedia sul ponte (f), sedia a sdraio (f)
decorator decoratore (m)
deep profondo
deep-fried fritto
deep-fried cutlet scaloppina (f)
deer capriolo (m)
defeat sconfitta (f)
degree of difficulty grado di difficoltà (m)
delay ritardo (m)
delicate wash ciclo delicato (m)
delicatessen gastronomia (f)
delivery terms condizioni di consegna (f)
democracy democrazia (f)
dental bridge ponte (m)
dental floss filo interdentale (m)
dental surgeon ortodontista (m)
dental technician odontotecnico (m)
dentist dentista (m)

denture dentiera (f)
deodorant deodorante (m)
department reparto (m)
department head capo (di) reparto (m)
department store grande magazzino (m)
departure uscita (f), partenza (f)
departure time orario di decollo (m)
deposit caparra (f)
depressed depresso
depth meter misuratore di profondità (m)
descent discesa (f)
desert deserto (m)
desk scrivania (f)
dessert dessert (m)
diabetes diabete (m)
diagonally striped a strisce trasversali
dial tone signale libero (m)
diamond diamante (m)
diapers pannolini (m)
diarrhea diarrea (f)
dictionary dizionario (m)
diesel Diesel (m)
dill aneto (m)
dining car vagone ristorante (m)
dinner cena (f)
diphteria difterite (f)
direct dialling interno (m)
disco, discotheque discoteca (f)
discount sconto (m), riduzione (f)
dish piatto (m)
dishes stoviglie (f)
dishrack scolapiatti (m)
dishwasher lavastoviglie (f)
dishwashing liquid detersivo (per piatti) (m)
disinfectant disinfettante (m)
diskman Diskman (m)
disposable needles siringa usa-e-getta (f)
distance meter telemetro (m)
distributor distributore (m)
district attorney pubblico ministero (m)
diving immersione (m)
diving clock orologio subacqueo (m)
diving license brevetto da sub (m)

do fare
doctor medico (m)
doctor's assistant assistente del medico (f)
dog cane (m)
dome cupola (f)
donkey asino (m)
door porta (f)
door handle maniglia (della porta) (f)
double bed letto doppio (m)
double cabin cabina doppia (f)
double room camera doppia (f)
downhill skiing discesa (f)
downtown centro urbano (m)
dozen dozzina (f)
drain filtro di scarico (m)
drama dramma (m)
dreadful spaventoso
dress vestito (m)
drill trapano (m)
drink bere
drinking water acqua potabile (f)
driver conducente (m)
drizzle pioviggine (f)
drug droga (f)
druggist droghiere (m)
drugstore farmacia (f)
drum brake freno a tamburo (m)
dry secco
dry cleaning lavanderia (f)
dry goods mercerie (f)
dry-cleaning pulizia a secco (f)
dryer asciugatrice (f)
duck anatra (f)
dull opaco
dumbbell manubrio (m)
dune duna (f)
during the day durante la giornata
dustpan pattumiera (f)
dutiable soggetto a dazio doganale
duty-free esente da dazio doganale
DVD player lettore DVD (m)
dynamo dinamo (f)

E

each ogni
ear orecchio (m)
ear drops gocce per le orecchie

ear of grain spiga (f)
ear, nose, and throat specialist otorinolaringoiatra (m)
earlier prima
early primo
earrings orecchini (m)
easel cavalletto (m)
Easter Pasqua (f)
eat mangiare
economy economia (f)
eel anguilla (f)
egg dishes piatti a base di uova (m)
eggplant melanzana (f)
elastic elastico per capelli (m), elastico (m)
elbows gomito (m)
elderberries sambuco (m)
elections elezioni (f)
electric blanket termocoperta (f)
electric heating riscaldamento elettrico (m)
electric range cucina elettrica (f)
electrical appliances store negozio di elettrodomestici (m)
electrical connection allacciamento elettrico (m)
electrical cord cavo di alimentazione (m)
electrician elettricista (m)
electricity elettricità (f)
elevator ascensore (m)
embassy ambasciata (f)
emergency chiamata di emergenza (f)
emergency brake freno di emergenza (m)
emergency exit uscita di emergenza (f)
emergency flashers impianto lampeggio emergenza (m)
employee dipendente (m), impiegato (m)
empty vuoto
enclosure allegato (m)
engineer ingegnere (m)
England Inghilterra (f)
enough abbastanza
entrance ingresso (m)
envelope busta (f)
eraser gomma (f)
escalator scala mobile (f)
espresso espresso (m)
event spettacolo (m)
ewe's-milk cheese formaggio pecorino (m)

excavations scavi (m)
excellent eccellente
excess baggage (pacco di consegna) sovraccarico (m)
exchange bureau cambiavalute (m)
exchange rate cambio (m)
exhaust scarico (m)
exhibition esposizione (f)
exhibitor espositore (m/f)
exit uscita (f)
expensive caro
export esportazione (f)
express mail espresso (m)
express train (treno) diretto (m)
extension cord prolunga (f)
external esterno
extra costs spese aggiuntive (f)
eye occhio (m)
eye shadow ombretto (m)
eyebrow sopracciglia (f)
eyebrow pencil matita per le sopracciglia (f)
eyelid palpebra (f)

F

fabric store tessuti (m)
face viso (m)
face cloths strofinaccio per lavare (m)
factory fabbrica (f)
fair fiera (f)
fall cadere
fall in love innamorarsi
fallopian tubes ovaia (f)
family ticket biglietto per famiglia (m)
fan ventilatore (m)
fantastic fantastico
far distante
farm fattoria (f)
farmer agricoltore (m)
far-sighted presbite
fashion moda (f)
fast rapido
father padre (m)
father-in-law suocero (m)
faucet rubinetto (m)
fax fax (m)
February febbraio (m)
feel sentire
fees parcella (f)
felt feltro (m)
felt tip pen pennarello (m)
fender parafango (m)
fennel finocchi (m)
ferry traghetto (m)

festival festival (m)
fever febbre (f)
fiancé fidanzato (m)
fiancée fidanzata (f)
field campo (m)
figs fichi (m)
fillet steak bistecca di filetto (f)
filling otturazione (f)
film pellicola (f)
find trovare
finger dito (m)
fins pinne (f)
fire fuoco (m)
fire department vigili del fuoco (m)
first primo
fish pesce (m)
fish store pescivendolo (m)
fishing pesca con l'amo (f)
fishing license licenza di pesca (f)
fishing line lenza (f)
fishing rod canna da pesca (f)
fixative fissatore (m)
flannel flanella (f)
flashbulb flash (m)
flashlight torcia (f)
flat noodles tagliatelle (f)
flatulence flatulenza (f)
flavor gusto (m)
flea market mercato delle pulci (m)
flight volo (m)
flight number numero del volo (m)
flight schedule orario (dei voli) (m)
float galleggiante (m)
flood inondazione (f)
floor piano (m)
florist fioraio (m)
flounder passera di mare (f)
flour farina (f)
flu influenza (f)
fly swatter acchiappamosche (m)
fog nebbia (f)
folding chair sedia ripiegabile (f)
folding table tavolo ripiegabile (m)
folklore folclore (m)
font fonte battesimale (m)
foot piede (m)
footpath sentiero (m), marciapiede (m)
for per

forefinger indice (m)
foreigner straniero (m)
forget dimenticare
fork forchetta (f)
format formato (m)
fortress fortezza (f)
fountain pen penna (f)
fracture frattura (ossea) (f)
freight charges spese di trasporto (f)
freighter mercantile (m)
french fries patatine fritte (f)
fresh cheese formaggio di crema (m)
fresh produce stand frutta e verdura (f)
Friday venerdì (m)
fried arrostito
fried egg uovo al tegamino (m)
fried potatoes patate arrostite (f)
friend amico (m)
frieze fregio (m)
front axle assale anteriore (m)
front wheel fork forcella ruota anteriore (f)
frost gelo (m)
fruit frutta (f)
fruit juice succo di frutta (m)
fruit stand frutta e verdura (f)
fruit tea tè alla frutta (m)
fruity fruttato
frustrated frustrato
frying pan tegame (m), teglia (f)
fuel gauge spia serbatoio (f)
fuel injector pump iniettore (m)
full al completo
full board pensione completa (f)
full-bodied abboccato
funnel imbuto (m)
furniture mobili (m)
furrier pellicceria (f)

G
gallbladder cistifellea (f)
gallery galleria (f)
garage garage (m)
garbage immondizia (f)
garbage can bidone dell'immondizia (f)
garden giardino (m)
garden lettuce salad lattuga (f)

gardener giardiniere (m)
garlic aglio (m)
gas benzina (f)
gas can tanica di benzina (f)
gas cylinder bombola del gas (f)
gas pedal acceleratore (m)
gas pump distributore (m)
gas range cucina a gas (f)
gas station distributore di benzina (m)
gas stove fornello a gas (m)
gash taglio (m)
gaskets guarnizione (f)
gate uscita (il cancello) (f)
gear ruota dentata (f)
gears cambio (m)
gearshift innesto marce (m)
gearshift lever leva del cambio (f)
general delivery il fermo posta
geology geologia (f)
German measles rosolia (f)
get ricevere
gift regalo (m)
gift wrap carta da regalo (f)
ginger zenzero (m)
give dare
glass bicchiere (m)
glass painting pittura su vetro (f)
glasses case custodia (per occhiali) (f)
glazed glassato
glazier vetraio (f)
glossy glossario (m)
glove compartment vano posaoggetti (m)
gloves guanti (m)
glue colla (f)
go andare
goat capra (f)
goat's milk cheese formaggio caprino (m)
gold oro (m)
golden bream dorata (f)
golden perch persico dorato (f)
golf golf (m)
golf bag borsa da golf (f)
golf ball pallina da golf (f)
golf clubs mazza da golf (f)
good buon
Good Friday Venerdì santo (m)

goose oca (f)
gooseberry uva spina (f)
gorgeous magnifico
Gothic gotico (m)
goulash spezzatino (m)
government governo (m)
gradient dislivello (m)
grain grano (m)
gram grammo (m)
grandfather nonno (m)
grandmother nonna (f)
grandson nipote (m)
grape uva (f)
grape juice succo di uva (m)
grapefruit pompelmo (m)
graphics card scheda grafica (f)
grave tomba (f)
graveyard cimitero (m)
gray grigio
grayling temolo (m)
great eccellente
green verde
green beans fagioli verdi (m)
green pepper peperoni (m)
green salad insalata verde (f)
greeting formula di saluto (f)
grill griglia (f)
grilled cotto alla griglia
grilled chicken pollo arrosto (m)
grocery store negozio di alimentari (m)
ground tritato
group card biglietto per gruppo (m)
guarantee garanzia (f)
guidebook guida (f)
guinea fowl faraona (f)
gum gengiva (f)
gym shoes scarpe da ginnastica (f)
gymnastics ginnastica (f)
gynecologist ginecologo (m)

H
haddock baccalà (m)
hail grandine (f)
hair capelli (m)
hair dye tinta per riflessi (f)
hair spray laca (f)
hairbrush spazzola (f)
hairdresser parrucchiere (m)

hairdryer asciugacapelli (m)
hairpins forcine (f)
hairspray lacca (f)
half metà (f), mezzo ()
half board mezza pensione (f)
halibut ippoglosso (m)
hall padiglione (m)
ham prosciutto (m)
hammer martello (m)
hammock amaca (f)
hand mano (f)
hand baggage bagaglio a mano (m)
hand brake freno a mano (m)
hand cream crema per mani (f)
hand towel asciugamano (m)
handbag borsetta (f)
handball pallamano (f)
handicrafts artigianato (m)
handlebars manubrio (m)
hands lancetta (f)
hanger attaccapanni (m)
hang-gliding deltaplano (m)
harbor porto (m)
harbor tour giro del porto (m)
hard disk harddisk (m)
hard-boiled egg uovo sodo (f)
hardware store negozio di ferramenta (m)
hare lepre (f)
harvester mietitrebbiatrice (f)
hash browns patate arrostite (f)
hat cappello (m)
have avere
hay fieno (m)
hay fever raffreddore da fieno (m)
hazelnut nocciole (f)
hazy nebbioso
head testa (f)
head cold raffreddore (m)
headache mal di testa (m)
headache tablets pastiglie per mal di testa (f)
headlight luce anteriore (f), fari (m)
headlight flasher lampeggiatore (m)
headphones cuffie (f)
healer guaritore (m)
health food store prodotti dietetici (m)
hear sentire

heart cuore (m)
heart attack infarto (m)
heart problems male al cuore (m)
heartburn bruciore di stomaco (m)
heat calore (m)
heater riscaldamento (m)
heating termosifone (m)
heel tacco (m), tallone (m)
Hello! Buon giorno!
helmet casco (m)
help aiutare, aiuto
hemorrhage ematoma (m)
herbal tea tisana (f)
here qui
herring aringa (f)
hibiscus ibisco (m)
high alto
high blood pressure pressione alta (f)
high season alta stagione (f)
high tide acqua alta (f), alta marea (f)
highchair seggiolone (m)
high-contrast molto contrastato
hiking fare escusioni
hiking boots scarponcini (m)
hill collina (f)
hillbilly montanaro rustico (m)
hip anca (m)
history storia (f)
homemaker casalingo (m)
honey miele (m)
hood cofano (m)
hooker prostituta (f)
horn clacson (m)
horse cavallo (m)
horse racing corsa dei cavalli (f)
horseback riding equitazione (f)
horseradish cren (m)
hose tubo dell'acqua (m)
hospital ospedale (m)
hot caldo
hot water acqua calda (f)
hot water bottle borsa dell'acqua calda (f)
hot water heater scaldabagno (m)
hot-air balloon mongolfiera (f)
hotel albergo (m)
hotelier albergatore (m)
hot-water wash bucato lavabile a 90 gradi (m)
hour ora (f)

hourly ogni ora
housecoat vestaglia (f)
household merchandise negozio di casalinghi (m)
housewife casalinga (f)
how long quanto tempo
how much quanto
hub mozzo (m)
humidity umidità (f)
hunger fame (f)
hurricane uragano (m)
husband marito (m)
hydrofoil aliscafo (m)

I . . . .

ice ghiaccio (m)
ice cream gelato (m)
ice cream cone cono (m)
ice cube cubetto di ghiaccio (m)
ice hockey hockey sul ghiaccio (m)
ice skates pattini sul ghiaccio (m)
ice skating pattinaggio sul ghiaccio (m)
if se
ignition accensione (f)
illustrated book volume illustrato (m)
immersion heater bollitore a immersione (m)
immigration immigrazione (m)
immigration authority ufficio stranieri (m)
import importazione (f), importare ()
impressive impressionante
in in
in the afternoon di pomeriggio
in the evening di sera
in the morning di mattina
industry industria (f)
infection infezione (f)
inflammation infiammazione (f)
inflammation of the bladder infiammazione alla vescica (f)
information informazioni (f)
injection iniezione (f)
injure ferire
injury ferita (f)
ink inchiostro (m)
inkjet printer stampante a getto d'inchiostro (f)
inline skates pattinatore su roller-blade (m)

inner tube tubo flessibile (m)
insect bite puntura d'insetto (f)
insect repellent insetticida (m)
inside interno
inside cabin cabina interna (f)
insulated bag borsa termica (f)
insulated box borsa frigo (f)
insurance assicurazione (f)
intermission pausa (f)
internal interno
internist internista (m)
interpreter interprete (m)
intestine intestino (m)
intrauterine device spirale (f)
introduce presentare
investment partecipazione (f)
invitation invito (m)
invoice conto (m)
iron ferro da stiro (m)
ironing board asse da stiro (f)
Italian-American Italo-americano (m)
Italy Italia (f)

J
jack martinetto (m)
jacket giacca (f)
jacknife coltellino da tasca (m)
jacob mussel canocchie (f)
jam marmellata (f)
January gennaio (m)
jaundice itterizia (f)
jaws mascella (f)
jazz jazz (m)
jellyfish medusa (f)
jetty passerella (f)
Jew ebreo (m)
jeweler gioielliere (m)
jogging footing (m)
joint articolazione (f)
journalist giornalista (m)
judge giudice (m)
judo judo (m)
July luglio (m)
jumper cables cavo per avviamento con cavi ponte (m)
June giugno (m)

K
karate karatè (m)
kayak caiacco (m)

kerosene lamp lampada a petrolio (f)
key chiave (f)
keyboard tastiera (f)
kid capretto (m)
kidney beans fagioli rossi (m)
kidneys reni (m)
kilo chilo (m)
kilometer chilometro (m)
kingdom monarchia (f)
kitchen cucina (f)
kitchen sponge spugna (f)
kitchenette cucinetta (f)
kite aquilone (m)
kiwi kiwi (m)
knees ginocchio (m)
knife coltello (m)
knots nodo (m)
knotted bouclé
know sapere

L
labels etichette (f)
ladder scala (f)
lake lago (m)
lamb agnello (m)
lamp lampada (f)
landing atterraggio (m)
landlord locatore (m)
landscape panorama (m)
language course corso di lingua (m)
larded lardellato
large grande
laser printer stampante laser (f)
last stop capolinea (f)
late tardi
later più tardi
laundromat lavanderia a gettone (f)
laundry basket cesto della biancheria (m)
laundry detergent *(powder)* detersivo (m)
laurel alloro (m)
law giurisprudenza (f), legge (f)
lawyer dottore in legge (m), avvocato (m)
laxative lassativo (m)
leafy celery sedano (m)
leather cuoio (m)
leather coat cappotto di pelle (f)
leather goods pelletteria (f)
leather jacket giacca di pelle (f)
leather soles suole in pelle (f)

leek porro (m)
leeward sottovento (m)
left sinistra
leg gamba (f), garretto (m)
legal proceedings udienza (f)
lemon limone (m)
lemon squeezer spremiagrumi (m)
lens obiettivo (m)
lens shade schermo parasole (m)
lentils lenticchie (f)
let lasciare
letter lettera (f)
letterhead intestazione (f)
liability responsabilità (f)
library biblioteca (f)
licensing fees tassa di licenza (f)
life guard bagnino (m)
life jacket giubbetto di salvataggio (m)
life preserver salvagente (m)
lifeboat battello di salvataggio (m)
light chiaro, amabile
light bulb lampadina (f)
light meter esposimetro (m)
light switch interruttore della luce (m)
lighter accendino (m)
lighthouse faro (m)
lightning lampo (m)
like come, piacere
lily giglio (m)
lime limetta (f)
lime tree tiglio (m)
linen lino (m)
lip labbro (m)
lipstick rossetto (m)
liqueur liquore (m)
liquor store vini & liquori
listen ascoltare
liter litro (m)
literature letteratura (f)
little piccolo
liver fegato (m)
living room soggiorno (m)
lobster gambero di mare (m)
local call (comunicazione) urbana (f)
lock serratura (f)
locker armadietto (m)
locking system fusibile (m)
locksmith fabbro (m)
locomotive locomotiva (f)
loin lombo (m)

loin steak lombata (f)
long lungo
long-distance call (comunicazione) interurbana (f)
look for cercare
loose-leaf notebook raccoglitore (ad anelli) (m)
loss perdita (f)
lost-and-found office ufficio oggetti smarriti (m)
low basso
low cholesterol povero di colesterolo
low season bassa stagione (f)
low tide bassa marea (f)
low-calorie povero di calorie
low-contrast poco contrastato
lower leg gamba (sotto il ginocchio) (f)
low-fat poco grasso
luggage bagagli (m)
lumbago colpo della strega (m)
lump bernoccolo (m)
lunch pranzo (m)
lung polmone (m)

M

macaroni maccheroni (m)
mackerel sgombro (m)
magazine rivista (f)
magnet magnete (m)
magnifying glass lente di ingrandimento (f)
mailbox cassetta delle lettere (f)
main entrance portale (m)
mainland continente (m)
male nurse infermiere (m)
management expert commercialista (m/f)
manager manager (m), direttore (m)
mango mango (m)
mangold bietola (f)
manufacturer fabbricante (m)
many molti
map cartina (f)
maple acero (m)
March marzo (m)
margarine margarina (f)
marjoram maggiorana (f)
market mercato (m)
marketing marketing (m)
married sposato
mascara rimmel (m)
mashed potatoes purea (f)

mason muratore (m)
master capo (m)
matches fiammiferi (m)
material materiale (m)
matte opaco
mattress materasso (m)
maximum values valori massimi (m)
May maggio (m)
mayonnaise maionese (f)
mayor's office ufficio del sindaco (m)
meadow prato (m)
measles morbillo (m)
measuring tape metro (m)
meat carne (f)
meat knife coltello da carne (m)
meat loaf polpettone (m)
mechanic meccanico (m), macchinista (m)
medication medicina (f)
medicine medicina (f)
medieval medievale
medium media
medlar nespole (f)
meet conoscere
meeting place punto di incontro (m)
melon melone (m)
menu menu (m)
merchant commerciante (m)
meter metro (m)
microfiber microfibra (f)
microwave forno a microonde (m)
Middle Ages medioevo (m)
middle finger medio (m)
midnight mezzanotte (f)
midwife ostetrica (f)
migraine emicrania (f)
milk latte (m)
milk jug bricco per il latte (m)
millimeter millimetro (m)
mineral water acqua minerale (f)
minibar minibar (m)
minimum (values) valori minimi (m)
minister sacerdote (m)
mint menta (f)
minute minuto (m)
mirabelle mirabella (f)
mirror specchio (m)
miscarriage aborto spontaneo (m)
mixed salad insalata mista (f)
mocha moka (f)
modem modem (m)

moderately warm temperato
Monday lunedì (m)
money denaro (m)
money exchange cambio di valuta (m)
money order vaglia (m)
month mese (m)
monument monumento (m)
mooring approdo (m)
more più
mosquito net rete per zanzare (f)
motel motel (m)
mother madre (f)
mother-in-law suocera (f)
motor motore (m)
motorboat motoscafo (m)
mottled mélange
mountain montagna (f)
mountain climbing alpinismo (m)
mountain hut baita di montagna (f)
mountain peak cima della montagna (f)
mountain spring fonte (f)
mountaineering alpinismo (m)
mouth bocca (f)
mouthwash collutorio (m)
movie cinema (m)
much molto
mudguard parafango (m)
mug brocca (f)
mugging aggressione (f)
mulberries bacche del gelso (f)
mullet muggine (m)
mumps orecchioni (m)
mural pittura murale (f)
muscle muscolo (m)
museum museo (m)
mushrooms funghi (m)
music musica (f)
musical musical (m)
musician musicista (m)
Muslim musulmano (m)
mussel cozze (f), conchiglia (f)
must dovere
mustache baffi (m)
mustard senape (m)
mutton montone (m)
mysterious misterioso
mystery novel giallo (m)

N

nail chiodi (m)
nail file limetta da unghie (f)

nail polish smalto (per unghie) (m)
nail polish remover acetone (per unghie) (m)
nail scissors forbicine (per unghie) (f)
name badge targhetta (f)
nape of the neck nuca (f)
napkin tovagliolo (m)
narcissus narciso (m)
narrow stretto
national highway strada statale (f)
national park parco nazionale (m)
nature park parco naturale (m)
nausea nausea (f)
nave navata (f)
neck collo (m)
necklace collana (f)
negotiation trattativa (f)
nephew nipote (m)
nerve nervo (m)
network cable cavo di rete (m)
network card scheda di rete (f)
new nuovo
New Year's day Anno nuovo (m)
New Year's eve San Silvestro
news notizie (f)
newsagent edicola (f)
newspaper giornale (m)
newsstand chiosco (m)
niece nipote (f)
night table comodino (m)
nightclub nightclub (m)
nightshirt camicia da notte (f)
nipples succhietto (m)
no no
nonfiction saggistica (f)
non-smoking section non fumatori (m)
non-swimmers non nuotatore (m)
noodle soup pasta in brodo (f)
noodles pasta (f)
nose naso (m)
nosebleed emorragia nasale (f)
notary notaio (m)
notebook quaderno di appunti (m)
notepad blocco note (m)
nothing niente
notions merceria (f)

novella novella (f)
November novembre (m)
now adesso
nurse infermiera (f)
nut vite (f)
nutmeg noce moscata (f)
nuts noci (f)

O
oak quercia (f)
oars pagaia (f)
oatmeal pappa di avena (f)
oats avena (f)
occupied occupato
ocean oceano (m)
ocean view vista sul mare (f)
October ottobre (m)
off season bassa stagione (f)
offer offerta (m)
office hours orario di visita (m)
office supplies cartoleria (f)
official impiegato pubblico (m)
oil olio (m)
oil filter filtro dell'olio (m)
oil paints colori ad olio (m)
oil pastels gessetti (m)
ointment for burns pomata per bruciature (f)
okra okra (f)
old vecchio
old quarter centro storico (m)
olive oil olio di oliva (m)
omelet omelette (f)
on su
one-week ticket biglietto settimanale (m)
onions cipolle (f)
only solo
open hours orari di apertura (m)
opera opera (f)
operation operazione (f)
operetta operetta (f)
opinion opinione (f)
optician ottico (m)
or o
orange arancia (f)
orange juice succo di arancia (m)
orchid orchidea (f)
order ordinare
oregano origano (m)
organic food prodotti biologici (m)

ornithology ornitologia (f)
other altr-i/-e
out (of) fuori
outfit tailleur (m)
outside esterno
outside cabin cabina esterna (f)
outstanding eccellente
oysters ostriche (f)
ozone ozono (m)

P
pacifier succhietto (m)
padlock lucchetto (m)
pain dolori (m)
painkillers antidolorifici (m)
paintbrush pennello (m)
painter imbianchino (m)
painting quadro (m), pittura (f)
painting course corso di pittura (m)
pair paio (m)
pajamas pigiama (m)
palette tavolozza (f)
pancake frittata (f)
panhandler mendico (m)
panties mutandine (f)
pants pantaloni (m)
papaya papaia (f)
paper carta (f)
paper clips fermagli (m), graffette (f)
paper napkins tovaglioli di carta (m)
parachute jumping paracadutismo
paragraph paragrafo (m)
paralysis paralisi (f)
parcel pacco (m)
park parco (m)
parking fee tassa di parcheggio (m)
parking garage autosilo (m)
parking place parcheggio (m)
parliament parlamento (m)
parsley prezzemolo (m)
part riga di lato (f)
partridge pernice (f)
pass passo (m)
passenger passeggero (m)
passion fruit frutta della passione (f)
passport passaporto (m), carta di identità (f)
pastels tinte pastello (f)
pastries pasticcerie (f)

pastry shop pasticceria (f)
pawnbroker monte di pietà (m)
pay phone telefono a gettoni (m)
payment terms condizioni di pagamento (f)
peach pesca (f)
peanut arachidi (f)
pearl perla (f)
pearl necklace collana di perle (f)
pears pere (f)
peas piselli (m)
pebble beach spiaggia di ghiaia (f)
pecan nut noci di pecan (f)
pedal pedale (m)
pedal boat pedalò (m)
pedestrian zone zona pedonale (f)
pediatrician pediatra (m)
pencil matita (f)
pencil sharpener temperino (m)
pendant ciondolo (m)
pepper pepe (m), peperone (m)
perch pesce persico (m)
perfume profumo (m)
perfume store profumeria (f)
perm permanente (f)
persimmon cachi (m)
pharmacy farmacia (f)
pheasant fagiano (m)
philosophy filosofia (f)
phone call chiamata telefonica (f)
phone card scheda telefonica (f)
photo store fotografo (m)
photographer fotografo (m)
physics fisica (f)
pickpocket borsaiolo (m)
picture book libro illustrato (m)
pie torta di frutta (f)
pig maiale (m)
pigeon piccione (m)
pike luccio (m)
pike perch spigola (f)
pilgrim pellegrino (m)
pillow cuscino (m)
pin spillo (m)
PIN numero segreto (m)
pincers tenaglie (f)
pine cone cono d'abete (m)
pine nuts pinoli (m)

pineapple ananas (m)
ping-pong ping-pong (m)
ping-pong ball pallina da ping-pong (f)
ping-pong racket racchetta da ping-pong (f)
pinkie mignolo (m)
pipe pipa (f)
pipe cleaner scovolino (m)
pipe filters filtro per pipa (m)
pipe implements scovolino (m)
pistachios pistacchi (m)
piston pistone (m)
plane ticket biglietto aereo (m)
planetarium planetario (m)
plastic bags borsa di plastica (f)
plastic wrap sacchetto per alimenti (m)
platform marciapiede (m)
platinum platino (m)
playing cards carte (da gioco) (f)
please per favore
pliers pinze (f)
plug tappo (m), spina (f)
plum susina (f)
plumber idraulico (m)
pneumonia polmonite (f)
poached egg uovo affogato (m)
pocket calculator calcolatrice tascabile (f)
pocket watch orologio da tasca (m)
poisoning avvelenamento (m)
police polizia (f)
police station distretto di polizia (m)
policeman poliziotto (m)
political refugee richiedente di asilo politico (m)
politics politica (f)
polka-dotted a pois
pollution sporcizia (f)
pomegranate melograno (m)
pomelo pomelo (m)
pond stagno (m)
poor circulation, tablets for medicine per la circolazione (f)
poplin popeline (f)
porridge pappa di avena (f)

port babordo
portable crib letto da viaggio (m)
porter facchino (m), portinaio (m)
post office posta (f)
post office box (P.O. Box) casella postale (f)
postage affrancatura (f)
postcard cartoline (illustrate) (f)
pot casseruola (f), pentola (f)
potatoes patate (f)
pottery ceramica (f)
poultry pollame (m)
pound mezzo chilo (m)
powder polvere (f)
powder (snow) neve farinosa (f)
powder room toiletta (f)
power corrente (f)
prawn gamberetti (m)
preferably preferibilmente
pregnancy gravidanza (f)
pregnancy test test di gravidanza (m)
pregnant incinta
pre-season bassa stagione (f)
president presidente (m)
press stampa (f)
press conference conferenza stampa (f)
pretty bello
previously prima
price prezzo (m)
priest prete (m)
printed a fantasia
printed matter stampa (f)
prison prigione (f)
private beach spiaggia privata (f)
private guest house camera privata (f)
procession processione (f)
processor processore (m)
production produzione (f)
professor professore (m)
profit guadagno (m)
programmer programmatore (m)
propane gas propano (m)
Protestant protestante (m)
psychiatrist psichiatra (m)
psychologist psicologo (m)
psychology psicologia (f)
public school collegio (m)
public service servizio pubblico (m)
puddle pozzanghera (f)

pulpit pulpito (m)
pumpkin zucca (f)
purchase contract contratto di acquisto (m)
purchase price prezzo di acquisto (m)
purple viola
purse portamonete (m)
putty knife spatola (f)

Q

quail quaglia (f)
quarter quarto (m)
quay banchina (f)
quiet tranquillo
quince mela cotogna (f)

R

rabbit coniglio (m)
racing bike bici da corsa (f)
radiator radiatore (m)
radio radio (f)
radish ravanelli (m), ravanello (m)
railroad ferrovia (f)
railway station stazione (f)
rain pioggia (f), piovere
raincoat impermeabile (m)
raisins uva passa (f)
RAM memoria di lavoro (f)
ramboutan rambutan (m)
rape violentare, stupro (m)
rash eruzione cutanea (f)
raspberries lamponi (m)
raw crudo
razor rasoio (m)
razor blades lame del rasoio (f)
read leggere
rear parte posteriore (f)
rear axle assale posteriore (m)
rear window lunotto (m)
rearview mirrors specchietto retrovisore (m)
rebate sconto (m)
receipt ricevuta (f)
reception reception (f)
reception desk registrazione (f)
recipient destinatario (m)
recommend consigliare
record store dischi musica (m)
red rosso
red beets rape rosse (f)
red cabbage cavolo rosso (m)
red perch persico rosso (m)
red wine vino rosso (m)

redneck villano (m)
reduction riduzione (f)
referee arbitro (m)
reflector riflettore (m)
refrigerator frigorifero (m)
regatta regata (f)
regional regionale
registered mail raccomandata (f)
regular benzina normale (f)
relief rilievo (m)
religion religione (f)
remains rovine (f)
remittance vaglia (m)
remote control telecomando (m)
rent noleggiare, affittare, affitto
rental fee tariffa di noleggio (f)
repair riparare
repair kit kit di riparazione gomme (m)
repeat ripetere
report verbale (m)
representative deputato (m), rappresentante (m)
reservation *(nature)* riserva naturale (f)
reservation *(tickets)* prenotazione (f)
reserve prenotare
restaurant ristorante (m)
restroom toilette (f)
retail vendita al dettaglio (f)
retired person pensionato (m)
retraining riqualificazione (f)
return flight volo di ritorno (m)
rheumatism reumatismo (m)
rhubarb rabarbaro (m)
rib costola (f)
rice riso (m)
ride montare
right destra, giusto
right to remain silent diritto di astensione dalla testimonianza (m)
rim cerchione (m)
ring anello (m)
ring finger anulare (m)
rinse risciacquare
river fiume (m)
riverboat trip gita sul fiume (f)
roast arrosto (m)

roast beef roastbeef (m)
rob rapinare
rocky shoreline scogliera (f)
roe uova di pesce (f)
roll panino (m)
rollerblades roller-blade (m)
rollerblading pattinaggio su roller-blade (m)
rolling pin matterello (m)
romanesque romanico (m)
romantic romantico
roofer muratore (m)
room camera (f)
room number numero di camera (m)
room service servizio camere (m)
rooster gallo (m)
root *(of the tooth)* radice del dente (f)
root canal work trattamento della radice (m)
rope corda (f)
rose rosa (f)
rosemary rosmarino (m)
rosette rosone (m)
rouge rouge (m)
round steak ossobuco (m)
round trip giro (m)
round trip ticket biglietto di andata e ritorno (m)
rowing canotaggio (m)
rowing boat barca a remi (f)
rubber boots stivali di gomma (m)
rubber dinghy canotto gonfiabile (m)
rubber raft aeroscivolante (m)
rubber soles suole in gomma (f)
rubberneck ficcanaso (m)
rudder remo (m)
rugby rugby (m)
ruins rovina (f)
ruler metro (m), righello (m)
rump steak costata di manzo (f)
rutabaga navone (m)
rye bread segala (f)

S

sacristy sagrestia (f)
saddle sella (f)
saddle *(of lamb)* schiena (f)
saddlebags borse portaattrezzi (f)

safe cassaforte (f)
safety pin spilla di sicurezza (f)
saffron zafferano (m)
sage salvia (f)
sail vela (f)
sailing vela (f)
sailing boat barca a vela (f)
sailing license patente nautica (f)
sailor marinaio (m)
salad insalata (f)
salesperson commesso (m)
salmon salmone (m)
salmonella salmonella (f)
salsify scorzonere (f)
salt sale (m)
salt cod stoccafisso (m)
salutation titolo (m)
same stesso
sand sabbia (f)
sand pail secchiello (m)
sandals sandali (m)
sandy beach spiaggia di sabbia (f)
sanitary napkins assorbenti (m)
sarcophagus sarcofago (m)
sardines sardine (f)
satin raso (m)
Saturday sabato (m)
sauerkraut crauti (m)
sauna sauna (f)
sausage salsiccia (f)
savoy cabbage verza (f)
saw sega (f)
say dire
scale bilancia
scales bilancia (f)
scallion cipollini (m)
scallop petonchio (m)
scanner scanner (m)
scarf sciarpa (f)
schedule orario (m)
schnapps grappa (f)
sciatica sciatica (f)
scientist scienziato (m)
scissors forbici (f)
scrambled egg uova strapazzate (f)
screen schermo (m)
screwdriver cacciavite (m)
screws viti (f)
scrubbing brush spazzola per bagno (f)
sculpture scultura (f)
sea mare (m)
sea bream pesce persico (m)

sea pike merluzzo (m)
sea snail lumaca di mare (f)
seahorse cavalluccio marino (m)
seasick mal di mare (m)
season ticket abbonamento (m)
seat sedile (m)
seat belt cintura di sicurezza (f)
seaweed alghe (f)
second secondo
second-hand store secondamano (f)
security cauzione (f)
security check controllo di sicurezza (f)
sedative sedativo (m)
see vedere
self-timer cavo dell'autoscatto (m)
sell vendere
semolina semolino (m)
sender mittente (m)
September settembre (m)
sewing kit attrezzatura per il cucito (f)
sewing needle ago (m)
shadows ombra (f)
shaken sbattuto
shampoo shampoo (m)
shares azioni (f)
shark squalo (m)
shaving brush pennello da barba (f)
shaving cream schiuma da barba (f)
sheep pecora (f)
sheet ice strade ghiacciate (f)
shellfish frutti di mare (m)
sheriff sceriffo (m)
shiny brillante
shirt camicia (f)
shit merda (f)
shoe brush spazzola per scarpe (f)
shoe polish lucido per scarpe (m)
shoelaces lacci delle scarpe (m)
shoemaker calzolaio (m)
shoes scarpe (f)
shopping bag borsa (f)
shopping basket cestino per gli acquisti (m)
shopping carts carrelli per la spesa (m)
shopping center centro commerciale (m)

shore excursion escursione a terra (f)
short corto
short circuit cortocircuito (m)
shorts pantaloncini (m)
short-sighted miope
shoulder spalla (f)
shoulder bag borsa a tracolla (f)
shovel paletta (f)
shower doccia (f)
showers scroscio di pioggia (m)
shutters serranda (f)
shuttlecock volano (m)
sick ammalato
side aisle navata laterale (f)
side dishes contorni (m)
sideburns basette (f)
sideview mirrors specchietto esterno (m)
sidewalk marciapiede (m)
signature firma (f)
silk seta (f)
silver argento (m)
silverware posata (f)
single *(person)* celibe
single bed letto singolo (m)
single cabin cabina singola (f)
sinker piombino (m)
sister sorella (f)
size taglia (f)
skate razza (f)
skateboard skateboard (m)
sketch pad blocco da disegno (m)
ski sci (m)
ski boots scarpone da sci (m)
ski instructor istruttore di sci (m)
ski lift skilift (m)
ski pass ski-pass (m)
ski pole bastoncino da sci (m)
ski run pista (f)
skiing sciare
skilled worker lavoratore specializzato (m)
skin pelle (f)
skirt gonna (f)
skyscraper grattacielo (m)
sledge slitta (f)
sleeper carrozza con cuccette (f)
sleeping bag sacco a pelo (m)
sleeping car vagone letto (m)

sleeping pills sonniferi (m)
sleet nevischio (m)
sleeve manicha (f)
slide frames telaietto per diapositive (m)
slip sottogonna (f)
slippers pantofole (f)
slow lento
small piccola
small parcel pacchetto (m)
smallpox vaiolo (m)
smell sentire
smelt sperlano (m)
smoke fumare
smoked affumicato
smoked salmon salmone affumicato (m)
smoking section fumatori (m)
snaphook carabina (f)
snorkel tubo respiratore (m)
snow nevicare, neve
snow chains catene da neve (f)
snowboard snowboard (m)
soap sapone (m)
soccer calcio (m)
soccer ball pallone (m)
socket presa di corrente (f)
socks calzini (m)
soft drink limonata (f)
soft-boiled egg uovo à la coque (m)
sole suole (f), sogliola (f)
some alcuni
son figlio (m)
son-in-law genero (m)
sore throat mal di gola (m)
sorry Scusi!/Scusa!
sound card scheda audio (f)
soup zuppe (f)
sour cream panna acida (f)
souvenir shop negozio di souvenirs (m)
soy sauce salsa di soia (f)
spaghetti spaghetti (m)
spare parts ricambi (parti di ricambio) (m)
spare ribs costoletta (f)
spare wheel ruota di scorta (f)
spark plug candele (f)
speak parlare
speaker altoparlante (m)
specialist lavoratore specializzato (m)

speedometer tachimetro (m)
spices spezie (f)
spider crab granseola (f)
spin dryer centrifuga (f)
spinach spinaci (m)
spin-dry centrifugare
spine spina dorsale (f)
spirits bevanda spiritosa (f)
splendid splendido
spoke raggio (m)
spoon cucchiaio (m)
sporting goods store articoli sportivi (m)
sports sport (m)
sprain slogatura (f)
spring primavera (f)
square piazza (f)
square kilometer chilometro quadrato (m)
square meter metro quadrato (m)
squash squash (m)
squid calamaro (m)
stadium stadio (m)
stag cervo (m)
stain remover smacchiatore (m)
stainless steel acciaio legato (m)
stairways scalini (m)
stamp francobollo (m)
starboard dritta
starfish stella marina (f)
starter motorino di avviamento (m)
statement dichiarazione (f)
stationery articoli di cancelleria (m), carta da lettere (f)
statue statua (f)
steak bistecca (f)
steal rubare
steamed cotto a vapore
steamer piroscafo (m)
steeple campanile (m)
steering sterzo (m)
steering wheel volante (m)
stereo system impianto Hifi (m)
stern poppa (f)
stew stufato (m)
still silenzioso
stirred sbattuto
stirring spoon mestolo (m)
stirring whisk frusta (f)
stitch in the side fitte ai fianchi (f)
stockings calze (f)
stomach pancia (f), stomaco (m)

stomachache mal di pancia (m), mal di stomaco (m)
stop fermata (f)
stopover scalo (m), sosta (f)
stopwatch cronometro (m)
storm tempesta (f)
straight ahead diritto
strain stiramento (m)
strands ciocche (f)
strange strano
straw paglia (f)
strawberries fragole (f)
street strada (f)
street number numero civico (m)
streetcar tram (m)
string corda (f)
string beans fagioli rampicanti (m)
strong forte
student scolaro (m), studente (m)
stuffed ripieno
subway metropolitana (f)
suckling pig maialino (m)
suction pump ventosa (f)
suede pelle di daino (f)
sugar zucchero (m)
suit abito (m)
suitcase valigia (f)
suite suite (f)
summer estate (f)
sun sole (m)
sun glasses occhiali da sole (m)
sun umbrella ombrellone (m)
sunblock crema da sole (f)
sunburn scottatura (f)
Sunday domenica (f)
sunflower girasole (m)
sunflower oil olio di girasole (m)
sunflower seeds semi di girasole (m)
sunrise alba (f)
sunroof tettuccio scorrevole (m)
sunset tramonto (m)
sunstroke insolazione (f)
super bellissimo, benzina Super (f)
supermarket supermercato (m)
supplier fornitore (m)
surcharge supplemento (m)
surf risacca (f)
surfboard tavola da surf (f)

surfing surf (m)
surgeon chirurgo (m)
suspenders bretelle (f)
swab striscio (m)
swamp pantano (m)
sweater pullover (m)
sweet dolce
sweet potatoes patate dolci (f)
sweetbread animella (f)
sweetener dolcificante (m)
swell moto ondoso (m)
swelling gonfiore (m), bernoccolo (m)
swimmers nuotatore (m)
swimming goggles occhiali da sub (m)
swimming pool piscina (f)
swimming ring salvagente (m)
swimming trunks calzoncini da bagno (m)
swindler imbroglione (m)
switchboard centralino (m)
swollen gonfio
swordfish pesce spada (m)
synagogue sinagoga (f)
synthetic fiber fibra sintetica (f)
syringes siringhe (f)
syrup sciroppo (m)

T

table tavola (f)
tablecloth tovaglia (f)
tachometer contagiri (m)
tail coda (f)
taillight luci retromarcia (f)
tailor sarto (m)
take prendere
takeoff decollo (m)
tamarind tamarindo (m)
tampons tamponi (m)
tangerine mandarino (m)
tangy piccante
tank serbatoio (m)
tarragon dragoncello (m)
taste assaggiare
tax advisor consulente fiscale (m)
taxes tasse (f)
taxi driver tassista (m)
tea tè (m)
teacher insegnante (m)
teaspoon cucchiaino (m)
technical book libro specialistico (m)
telegram telegramma (m)
telephone telefono (m)

telephone book elenco telefonico (m)
telephone booth cabina telefonica (f)
telephone line linea (f)
telephone number numero di telefono (m)
telephoto lens teleobiettivo (m)
television televisione (f)
telex telex (m)
tell raccontare
temple tempio (m)
tendon tendine (m)
tennis tennis (m)
tennis ball palla da tennis (f)
tennis racket racchetta da tennis (f)
tent tenda (f)
tent peg chiodo di fissaggio (m)
tent pole palo da tenda (m)
terrace terrazza (f)
terrific formidabile
terry cloth spugna (f)
tetanus tetano (m)
Thank you Grazie
that quell-o/-a
that one quello
thaw disgelo (m)
theater teatro (m)
theft furto (m)
then poi
there là
therefore quindi
thermometer termometro (m)
thermos termos (m)
thief ladro (m)
thighs coscia (f)
thimble ditale (m)
think pensare
thirst sete (f)
this one questo
thread filo (m)
through mediante
thumb pollice (m)
thumbtacks chiodini (m)
thunder tuono (m)
thunderstorm temporale (m)
Thursday giovedì (m)
thyme timo (m)
ticket biglietto (m)
ticket counter biglietteria (f)
ticket inspector controllore (m)
ticket vending machine distributore di biglietti (m)

tie cravatta (f)
tie pin fermacravatta (m)
tight stretto
tights collant (m)
time of delivery termine di consegna (m)
timetable orario (m)
tiny green peas piselli dolci (m)
tip mancia (f)
tired stanco
tires pneumatici (m)
tissues fazzoletti di carta (m)
toast toast (m)
toaster tostapane (m)
tobacco tabacco (m)
tobacco store tabaccheria (f)
today oggi
toe dito del piede (m)
toilet paper carta igienica (f)
tomato juice succo di pomodoro (m)
tomatoes pomodori (m)
tomorrow domani
ton tonnellata (f)
tongue lingua (f)
tonsillitis tonsillite (f)
tonsils tonsille (f)
too much troppo
tool attrezzo (m)
tooth dente (m)
toothache mal di denti (m)
toothbrush spazzolino da denti (m)
toothpaste dentifricio (m)
tornado tornado (m)
tossed salad insalata mista (f)
tow rimorchiare
tower torre (f)
towing cable fune di rimorchio (f)
town hall municipio (m)
tow service servizio rimorchio (m)
toy giocattolo (m)
toy store giocattoli (m)
track binario (m)
track and field atletica leggera (f)
tractor trattore (m)
trademark marchio di fabbrica (m)
traffic light semaforo (m)
tragedy tragedia (f)
trailer roulotte (f)
trainee apprendista (m/f)
tranquilizer sedativo (m)

transept navata trasversale (f)

transfer bonifico (m), cambiare ()

transit viaggio (m)

transparent adhesive tape nastro adesivo (schotch) (m)

trash bag sacchetto dell'immondizia (m)

travel agency agenzia di viaggi (f)

traveler's check travel cheque (m)

traveling bag borsa da viaggio (f)

tree albero (m)

trial processo (m)

trillion trilione (m)

tripe trippa (f)

tripod treppiede (m)

trout trota (f)

trunk bagagliaio (m)

try on provare

t-shirt t-shirt (f)

Tuesday martedì (m)

tuna tonno (m)

turbot rombo (m)

turkey tacchino (m)

turnips rape (f)

turnpike autostrada (f)

tuxedo smoking (m)

TV televisore (m)

tweezers pinzetta (f)

twine spago (m)

typhoon tifone (m)

U

ugly brutto

ulcer ulcera (f)

umbrella ombrello (m)

uncle zio (m)

unconscious senza sensi

underpants mutande (f)

undershirt canottiera (f)

understand comprendere

underwear biancheria intima (f)

unit unità (f)

United States Stati Uniti

university università (f)

unleaded senza piombo

urologist urologo (m)

uterus utero (m)

V

vacation apartment appartamento (per villeggiatura) (m)

vacation house casa di villeggiatura (f)

vacation spot residence (m)

vacuum cleaner aspirapolvere (m)

vagina vagina (f)

vaginitis vaginite (f)´

valley valle (f)

valuables oggetti di valore (m)

valve valvola (f)

vanilla vaniglia (f)

v-belt cinghia trapezoidale (f)

VCR videoregistratore (m)

vegetable soup minestra di verdura (f)

vegetables verdura (f)

vein vena (f)

velvet velluto (m)

vertically striped a strisce longitudinali

very molto

veterinarian veterinario (m)

videocassette cassetta per videoregistratore (f)

vinegar aceto (m)

vineyard vigna (f)

vintage vendemmia (f)

viral illness malattia virale (f)

vision grado visivo (m)

volcano vulcano (m)

volleyball pallavolo (f)

voltage tensione elettrica (f)

vote votazione (f)

W

waffles wafer (m)

waistcoat gilet (m)

waiter cameriere (m)

waiting room attesa (f)

wall clock orologio a parete (m)

wallet portafoglio (m)

walnut noce (f)

wardrobe guardaroba (m)

warm caldo

warning triangle triangolo (m)

washbasin lavandino (m)

washing machine lavatrice (f)

washroom lavatoio (m)

wastepaper basket cestino (m)

watch orologio da polso (m)

watchmaker orefice (m)

water acqua (f)

water bottle bottiglia dell'acqua (f)

water connection allacciamento dell'acqua (m)

water jug tanica di acqua (f)

water polo pallanuoto (f)

water pump pompa dell'acqua (f)

water wings braccioli (m)

watercolor crayons pastelli (m)

watercolor paper carta per acquerelli (f)

watercolors colori ad acquerello (m), acquerelli (m)

watercress crescione (m)

waterfall cascata (f)

watering can annaffiatoio (m)

watermelon anguria (f)

waterproof resistente all'acqua

waterskiing sci nautico (m)

wave onda (f)

wax cera (f)

wax beans fagiolini (m)

weak debole

Wednesday mercoledì (m)

weekend fine settimana (f)

weight peso (m)

weight belts cintura di piombo (f)

well fontana (f)

wetland regione paludosa (f)

wetsuit tuta subaquea (f)

what che cosa

wheat grano (m)

wheel ruota (f)

wheelchair sedia a rotelle (f)

when quando

where dove

whipped cream panna montata (f)

white bianco

white beans fagioli bianchi (m)

white bread pane bianco (m)

white wine vino bianco (m)

Whitsun Pentecoste (f)

who che

whole wheat bread pane integrale (m)

whooping cough pertosse (f)

why perché

wide largo

wife moglie (f)
wig parrucca (f)
wild duck anatra selvatica (f)
win vittoria (f)
wind vento (m)
windbreaker giacca a vento (f)
window pane vetro della finestra (m)
window seat posto accanto al finestrino (m)
windows finestra (f)
windshield parabrezza (m)
windshield wiper tergicristallo (m)
windsurfing windsurf (m)
windward sopravvento (m)
wine vino (m)
wine menu menu dei vini (m)
wine store vini & liquori
winter inverno (m)

wisdom tooth dente del giudizio (m)
with con
without senza
wolf perch spigola (m)
wool lana (f)
work lavorare
worker lavoratore (m)
worsted tessuto pettinato (m)
wound ferita (f)
wrench chiave (f)
wrestling lotta libera (f)
wrinkle-free da non stirare
wrist polso (m)
wristband cinturino (m)
write scrivere
wrong sbagliato

X........................
X-ray radiografo (m)

Y........................
yacht yacht (m)
year anno (m)
yellow giallo
yellow pages pagine gialle (f)
yes sì
yesterday ieri
yogurt yoghurt (m)
young giovane
young fattened hen pollastro da ingrasso (m)
youth hostel ostello della gioventù (m)

Z........................
zip code codice postale (m)
zipper chiusura lampo (f)
zoo zoo (m)
zoology zoologia (f)
zucchini zucchine (f)
zwieback fette biscottate (f)

Italian – English

A

a colori colorful, colored
a fantasia printed
a mezzogiorno at noon
a pois polka-dotted
a quadretti checkered
a strisce longitudinali vertically striped
a strisce trasversali diagonally striped
abbastanza enough
abbazia (f) abbey
abbigliamento (m) clothing store
abboccato full-bodied
abbonamento (m) season ticket
abito (m) suit
aborto (m) abortion
aborto spontaneo (m) miscarriage
accappatoio (m) bathrobe
acceleratore (m) gas pedal
accendino (m) lighter
accensione (f) ignition
accensione difettosa (f) backfire
acchiappamosche (m) fly swatter
acciaio legato (m) stainless steel
acciughe (f) anchovies
accordo (m) agreement
accusa (f) acknowledgment
acero (m) maple
aceto (m) vinegar
aceto balsamico (m) balsamic vinegar
acetone *(per unghie)* (m) nail polish remover
acqua (f) water
acqua alta (f) high tide
acqua calda (f) hot water
acqua di raffreddamento (f) coolant
acqua minerale (f) mineral water
acqua potabile (f) drinking water
acquerelli (m) watercolors
adattatore (m) adapter
adesso now
aerobica (f) aerobics
aeroporto (m) airport
aeroscivolante (m) rubber raft

a farfalla *(cravatta)* (f) bowtie
affittare rent
affitto (m) rent
affrancatura (f) postage
affumicato smoked
agenzia di viaggi (f) travel agency
aggressione (m) mugging
aglio (m) garlic
agnello (m) lamb
ago (m) sewing needle
agosto (m) August
agricoltore (m) farmer
aiutare help
aiuto (m) help
al completo full
alba (f) sunrise
albergatore (m) hotelier
albergo (m) hotel
albero (m) tree
albicocca (f) apricot
alcuni some
al forno baked
alghe (f) seaweed
aliscafo (m) hydrofoil
allacciamento dell'acqua (m) water connection
allacciamento elettrico (m) electrical connection
allegato (m) enclosure
allergia (f) allergy
alloro (m) laurel
alpinismo (m) mountaineering, mountain climbing
alta marea (f) high tide
alta stagione (f) high season
altare (m) altar
alto high
altoparlante (m) speaker
altr-i/-e other
amabile light
amaca (f) hammock
ambasciata (f) embassy
ambulanza (f) ambulance
amico (m) friend
ammalato sick
amministrazione (f) administration
amore (m) darling
ananas (m) pineapple
anatra (f) duck
anatra selvatica (f) wild duck
anca (f) hip

ancora again
àncora (f) anchor
andare go
anello (m) ring
anestesia (f) anesthetic, anesthesia
aneto (m) dill
angina (m) angina
anguilla (f) eel
anguria (f) watermelon
animella (f) sweetbread
annaffiatoio (m) watering can
anno (m) year
Anno nuovo (m) New Year's day
antidolorifici (m) painkillers
antiquariato (m) antique store
anulare (m) ring finger
apparecchio per i denti (m) braces
appartamento (m) apartment
appartamento *(per villeggiatura)* (m) vacation apartment
appendice (f) appendix
appendicite (f) appendicitis
apprendista (m/f) trainee
approdo (m) mooring
appuntamento (m) appointment
appuntamento di lavoro (m) business meeting
apribottiglie (m) bottle opener
aprile (m) April
apriscatole (m) can opener
aquilone (m) kite
arachidi (f) peanut
aragosta (f) crawfish
arancia (f) orange
arbitro (m) referee
archeologia (f) archaeology
architetto (m) architect
architettura (f) architecture
argento (m) silver
aria (f) air
aringa (f) herring
armadietto (m) locker
arrabbiato angry

arresto (m) arrest
arrivo (m) date of arrival
arrostito fried
arrosto (m) roast
arte (f) art
arteria (f) artery
articolazione (f) joint
articoli di cancelleria (m) stationery
articoli sportivi (m) sporting goods store
artigianato (m) handicrafts
artigianato artistico (m) arts and crafts
artigiano (m) craftsperson
artista (m/f) artist
asamblea (f) convention
ascensore (m) elevator
ascesso (m) abscess
asciugabiancheria (f) clothes dryer
asciugacapelli (m) hairdryer
asciugamano (m) bath towel, hand towel
asciugare al fon blow-dry
asciugatrice (f) dryer
ascoltare listen
asino (m) donkey
asma (f) asthma
asparagi (m) asparagus
aspirapolvere (m) vacuum cleaner
assaggiare taste
assale anteriore (m) front axle
assale posteriore (m) rear axle
asse da stiro (f) ironing board
assegno (m) check
assicurazione (f) insurance
assistente del medico (f) doctor's assistant
assistenza meccanica (f) breakdown assistance
assorbenti (m) sanitary napkins
atletica leggera (f) track and field
attaccapanni (m) hanger
atterraggio (m) landing
attesa (f) waiting room
attore (m) actor
attrezzatura per il cucito (f) sewing kit
attrezzo (m) tool
attrice (f) actress
autocaravan (m) camper
autore (m) author
autosilo (m) parking garage

autostrada (f) turnpike
autotraghetto (m) car ferry
autunno (m) autumn
avena (f) oats
avere have
avocado (m) avocado
avvelenamento (m) poisoning
avvocato (m) lawyer
azioni (f) shares

B ....
babordo port
baccalà (m) haddock
bacche del gelso (f) mulberries
baffi (m) mustache
bagagli (m) baggage, luggage
bagagliaio (m) trunk
bagaglio a mano (m) hand baggage
bagnino (m) life guard
bagno (m) bath
baita di montagna (f) mountain hut
balcone (m) balcony
balletto (m) ballet
ballo (m) dance
bambini (m) children
banana (f) banana
banca (f) bank
banchina (f) quay
bancomat (m) ATM
barba (f) beard
barca (f) boat
barca a remi (f) rowing boat
barca a vela (f) sailing boat
baseball (m) baseball
basette (f) sideburns
basilico (m) basil
bassa marea (f) low tide
bassa stagione (f) low season, pre-season, off season
basso low
bastoncino da sci (m) ski pole
batista (f) batiste
battello di salvataggio (m) lifeboat
batteria (f) battery
bellissimo super
bello pretty, beautiful
benchè although
bende (f) bandage
benzina (f) gas
benzina normale (f) regular

benzina Super (f) super
bere drink
bernoccolo (m) lump, swelling
berretto (m) cap, baseball cap
bevanda spiritosa (f) spirits
biancheria intima (f) underwear
bianco white
bibita (f) beverage
biblioteca (f) library
bicchiere (m) glass
bici da corsa (f) racing bike
bidone dell' immondizia (f) garbage can
bietola (f) mangold
biglietteria (f) ticket counter
biglietto (m) ticket
biglietto aereo (m) plane ticket
biglietto di andata e ritorno (m) round trip ticket
biglietto giornaliero (m) day ticket
biglietto per famiglia (m) family ticket
biglietto per gruppo (m) group card
biglietto settimanale (m) one-week ticket
bigodino (m) curler
bikini (m) bikini
bilancia (f) scales
bilanza scale
biliardo (m) billiards
binario (m) track
biologo (m) biologist
birilli (m) bowling
biro (f) ballpoint pen
birra (f) beer
biscotti (m) baked goods
bistecca (f) steak
bistecca di filetto (f) fillet steak
blazer (m) blazer
blocco da disegno (m) sketch pad
blocco note (m) notepad
blu blue
bocca (f) mouth
bocchino per sigarette (m) cigarette holder
bollito cooked
bollitore a immersione (m) immersion heater
bombola del gas (f) gas cylinder

bonifico (m) transfer
borsa (f) shopping bag
borsa a tracolla (f) shoulder bag
borsa da golf (f) golf bag
borsa da viaggio (f) traveling bag
borsa dell'acqua calda (f) hot water bottle
borsa delle fotografie (f) camera bag
borsa di plastica (f) plastic bags
borsa frigo (f) insulated box
borsa portadocumenti (f) briefcase
borsa termica (f) insulated bag
borsaiolo (m) pickpocket
borse porta-attrezzi (f) saddlebags
borsetta (f) handbag
botanica (f) botany
bottiglia (f) bottle
bottiglia dell'acqua (f) water bottle
bottiglie ad aria compressa (f) compressed-air bottles
bottone (m) button
bouclé knotted
boxe (f) boxing
braccialetto (m) bracelet
braccio (m) arm
braccioli (m) water wings
bretelle (f) suspenders
brevetto da sub (m) diving license
bricco per il latte (m) milk jug
brillante shiny
brividi di freddo (m) chills
brocca (f) mug
broccoli (m) broccoli
brodo di manzo (m) beef broth
brodo di pollo (m) chicken broth
bronchi (m) bronchial tubes
bronchite (f) bronchitis
bruciore di stomaco (m) heartburn
brutto ugly
bucato lavabile a 90 gradi (m) hot-water wash
bungalow (m) bungalow
buon good
Buon giorno! Hello!
burro (m) butter

bussola (f) compass
busta (f) envelope

C

cabaret (m) cabaret
cabina (f) cabana, cabin, berth
cabina doppia (f) double cabin
cabina esterna (f) outside cabin
cabina interna (f) inside cabin
cabina singola (f) single cabin
cabina telefonica (f) telephone booth
cacao (m) cocoa
cacciavite (m) screwdriver
cachi (m) persimmon
cadere fall
caffè (m) coffee
caffé gelato (m) coffee with ice cream
cagliata (f) curd
caiacco (m) kayak
calamaro (m) squid
calcio (m) soccer
calcolatrice tascabile (f) pocket calculator
caldo warm, hot
calendario (m) calendar
calore (m) heat
calze (f) stockings
calzini (m) socks
calzolaio (m) shoemaker
calzoncini da bagno (m) swimming trunks
cambiare transfer
cambiavalute (m) exchange bureau
cambio (m) exchange rate, gears
cambio di valuta (m) money exchange
camera (f) room
camera da letto (f) bedroom
camera doppia (f) double room
camera privata (f) private guest house
cameriera (f) chambermaid
cameriere (m) waiter, bellboy
camicetta (f) blouse
camicia (f) shirt
camicia da notte (f) nightshirt
camino (m) chimney

campana (f) bell
campananello (m) call button
campanile (m) steeple
campeggio (m) campsite
campo (m) field
canale (m) canal
cancro (m) cancer
candela (f) candle
candele (f) spark plug
candeliere (m) candlestick
cane (m) dog
canna da pesca (f) fishing rod
cannella (f) cinnamon
cannocchiale (m) binoculars
canoa (f) canoe
canocchie (f) jacob mussel
canotaggio (m) rowing, canoeing
canottiera (f) undershirt
canotto gonfiabile (m) rubber dinghy
canyon (m) canyon
caparra (f) deposit
capelli (m) hair
capi colorati (m) colored laundry
capitano (m) captain
capo (m) master
capo (di) reparto (m) department head
capolinea (m) last stop
cappella (f) chapel
cappello (m) hat
capperi (m) capers
cappone (m) capon
cappotto (m) coat
cappotto di pelle (m) leather coat
cappuccino (m) cappuccino
capra (f) goat
capretto (m) kid
capriolo (m) deer, buck
capsula (f) crown
carabina (f) snaphook
carambola (f) carambola
carboncini (m) charcoal pencils
carbone (m) charcoal
carburatore (m) carburetor
carciofi (m) artichokes
carne (f) meat
caro expensive
carote (f) carrots
carpa (f) carp
carpentiere (m) carpenter
carrelli per la spesa (m) shopping carts

carrello portabagagli (m) baggage carts
carrozza con cuccette (f) sleeper
carta (f) paper
carta da lettere (f) stationery
carta da regalo (f) gift wrap
carta da visita (f) business card
carta di credito (f) credit card
carta di identità (f) passport
carta igienica (f) toilet paper
carta per acquerelli (f) watercolor paper
carta stagnola (f) aluminum foil
carte *(da gioco)* (f) playing cards
cartellone (m) billboard
cartina (f) map
cartoleria (f) office supplies
cartoline (illustrate) (f) postcard
casa di villeggiatura (f) vacation house
casa natale (f) birthplace
casalinga (f) housewife
casalingo (m) homemaker
cascata (f) waterfall
casco (m) helmet
caseificio (m) dairy
casella postale (f) post office box (P.O. Box)
casinò (m) casino
cassa (f) cash register
cassaforte (f) safe
casseruola (f) pot
cassetta delle lettere (f) mailbox
cassetta per videoregistratore (f) videocassette
castagne (f) chestnuts
castagno (m) chestnut
castello (m) castle
catalogo (m) catalog
catena (f) chain
catene da neve (f) snow chains
cattedrale (f) cathedral
cattivo bad
cattolico (m) Catholic
cauzione (f) security
cavalletto (m) easel
cavallo (m) horse
cavalluccio marino (m) seahorse

cavatappi (m) corkscrew
caverna (f) cave
caviglia (f) ankle
cavo (m) cables
cavo dell'autoscatto (m) automatic shutter release, self-timer
cavo di alimentazione (m) electrical cord
cavo di rete (m) network cable
cavo per avviamento con cavi ponte (m) jumper cables
cavolfiore (m) cauliflower
cavolo (m) cabbage
cavolo bianco (m) cabbage
cavolo di Bruxelles (m) brussel sprouts
cavolo rosso (m) red cabbage
ceci (m) chickpeas
celibe single (person)
cellulare (m) cell phone
cena (f) dinner
centimetro (m) centimeter
centralino (m) switchboard
centrifuga (f) spin dryer
centrifugare spin-dry
centro commerciale (m) shopping center
centro storico (m) old quarter
centro urbano (m) downtown
cera (f) wax
ceramica (f) ceramics, pottery
cercare look for
cerchione (m) rim
cerfoglio (m) chervil
cerotti (m) band-aid
cervello (m) brain
cervo (m) stag
cestino (m) wastepaper basket
cestino per gli acquisti (m) shopping basket
cesto della biancheria (m) laundry basket
cetriolo (m) cucumber
che who
che cosa what
chiamata a carico del destinatario (f) collect call
chiamata di emergenza (f) emergency
chiamata telefonica (f) phone call
chiaro light
chiave (f) key, wrench

chiave per viti ad esagono cavo (f) Allen wrench
chiedere ask
chiesa (f) church
chilo (m) kilo
chilometro (m) kilometer
chilometro quadrato (m) square kilometer
chimica (f) chemistry
chimico (m) chemist
chiodi (m) nail
chiodi di garofano (m) clove
chiodini (m) thumbtacks
chiodo di fissaggio (m) tent peg
chiosco (m) newsstand
chiostro (m) cloister
chirurgo (m) surgeon
chiuso closed
chiusura lampo (f) zipper
ciabatte da spiaggia (f) bath slippers
cibo per neonati (m) baby food
ciclismo (m) cycling
ciclista (m) bicycle store
ciclo delicato (m) delicate wash
cicoria (f) chicory
ciliegie (f) cherry
cima della montagna (f) mountain peak
cimitero (m) cemetery, graveyard
cinema (m) cinema, movie
cinghia trapezoidale (f) v-belt
cinghiale (m) boar
cintura (f) belt
cintura di piombo (f) weight belts
cintura di sicurezza (f) seat belt
cintura per scalatori (f) climbing belt
cinturino (m) wristband
ciocche (f) strands
cioccolatini (m) chocolates
cioccolato (m) chocolate
ciondolo (m) pendant
cipolle (f) onions
cipollini (m) scallion
circo (m) circus
cistifellea (f) gallbladder
clacson (m) horn
clavicola (f) collarbone
climatizzatore (m) air conditioning
coalizione (f) coalition
cocco (m) coconut

cocktail di gamberi (m) crab cocktail

coda (f) tail

codice postale (m) zip code

cofano (m) hood

colazione (f) breakfast

colla (f) glue

collana (f) necklace

collana di perle (f) pearl necklace

collant (m) tights

collega (m) colleague

collegio (m) public school

collegio sindacale (m) board of trustees

colletto (m) collar

collina (f) hill

collo (m) neck

collutorio (m) mouthwash

colori ad acquerello (m) watercolors

colori ad olio (m) oil paints

colpo della strega (m) lumbago

coltellino da tasca (m) jacknife

coltello (m) knife

coltello da carne (m) meat knife

come like, as

comitato civico (m) citizens' initiative

commedia (f) comedy

commercialista (m/f) management expert

commerciante (m) businessman, merchant

commesso (m) salesperson

commissione (f) commission

comodino (m) night table

comprare buy

comprendere understand

con with

concerto (m) concert

conchiglia (f) mussel

condizioni di consegna (f) delivery terms

condizioni di pagamento (f) payment terms

condominio (m) condominium

conducente (m) driver

conferenza (f) conference

conferenza stampa (f) press conference

confessione (f) confession

confetto (m) candy

coniglio (m) rabbit

cono (m) ice cream cone

cono d'abete (m) pine cone

conoscente (m) acquaintance

conoscere meet

consegna dei bagagli (f) baggage claim

conserve (f) canned food

consigliare recommend

consolato (m) consulate

consulente fiscale (m) tax advisor

contabile (m) bookkeeper

contagiri (m) tachometer

contea (f) county

continente (m) mainland

conto (m) bill, invoice

contorni (m) side dishes

contrabbandiere di liquori (m) bootlegger

contrassegno (m) COD

contratto (m) contract

contratto di acquisto (m) purchase contract

controllo di sicurezza (m) security check

controllo doganale (m) customs check

controllore (m) conductor, ticket inspector

contusione (f) bruise

convegno (m) convention

convento (m) cloister

cooperazione (f) cooperation

coperta (f) blanket

copertone (m) cover

copricatena (m) chain guard

corda (f) rope, string

corda per il bucato (f) clothesline

cornetto (m) croissant

coro (m) choir

corrente (f) power, current

corridoio (m) aisle

corsa automobilistica (f) car racing

corsa dei cavalli (f) horse racing

corso (m) course

corso di cucina (m) cooking course

corso di lingua (m) language course

corso di pittura (m) painting course

cortile posteriore (m) backyard

corto short

cortocircuito (m) short circuit

coscia (f) thighs

costa (f) coast

costata di manzo (f) rump steak

costipazione (f) constipation

costituzione (f) constitution

costola (f) rib

costoletta (f) spare ribs

cotoletta (f) cutlet

cotone (m) cotton

cotto a vapore steamed

cotto al forno baked

cotto alla griglia grilled

cozze (f) mussel

crampo (m) cramp

crauti (m) sauerkraut

cravatta (f) tie

cravatta a farfalla (f) bowtie

credere believe

crema da sole (f) sunblock

crema per bambini (f) baby cream

crema per mani (f) hand cream

cren (m) horseradish

crescione (m) cress, watercress

crespo (m) crepe

crimine (m) crime

cripta (f) crypt

cristianesimo (m) Christianity

cristiano (m) Christian

crocchette (f) croquettes

croce (f) cross

crocicchio (m) crossroads

crociera (f) cruise

cronometro (m) stopwatch

crostata di mele (f) apple flan

crudo raw

cubetto di ghiaccio (m) ice cube

cucchiaino (m) teaspoon

cucchiaio (m) spoon

cucina (f) kitchen

cucina a gas (f) gas range

cucina elettrica (f) electric range

cucinetta (f) kitchenette

cuffia (f) bathing cap

cuffie (f) headphones

cugina (m) cousin

cugino (m) cousin

culla (f) child's bed

cultura (f) culture
cumino (m) caraway seed bread
cuoco (m) cook
cuoio (m) leather
cuore (m) heart
cuoretto (m) cockle
cupola (f) dome
cuscino (m) pillow
custodia *(per occhiali)* (f) glasses case

D
da non stirare wrinkle-free
dare give
data (f) date
datteri (m) dates
debole weak
decollo (m) takeoff
decoratore (m) decorator
deltaplano (m) hang-gliding
democrazia (f) democracy
denaro (m) money
dente (m) tooth
dente del giudizio (m) wisdom tooth
dentiera (f) denture
dentifricio (m) toothpaste
dentista (m) dentist
denuncia (f) complaint
deodorante (m) deodorant
depliant (m) brochure
deposito dei bagagli (m) checkroom
depresso depressed
deputato (m) representative
deserto (m) desert
dessert (m) dessert
destinatario (m) recipient
destra right
destro cute
detersivo (m) laundry detergent (powder), cleaning products
detersivo *(per piatti)* (m) dishwashing liquid
di mattina in the morning
di notte at night
di pomeriggio in the afternoon
di sera in the evening
diabete (m) diabetes
diamante (m) diamond
diarrea (f) diarrhea
dicembre (m) December
dichiarazione (f) statement
dichiarazione doganale (f) customs declaration
Diesel (m) diesel

differite (f) diphteria
diga (f) dam
dimenticare forget
dinamo (f) dynamo
dipendente (m) employee
diplomata (f) alumna
dire say
diretto (m) express train
direttore (m) manager
diritto straight ahead
diritto di astensione dalla testimonianza (m) right to remain silent
discesa (f) descent, downhill skiing
dischi musica (m) record store
discoteca (f) disco, discotheque
disgelo (m) thaw
disinfettante (m) disinfectant
Diskman (m) diskman
dislivello (m) gradient
distante far
distretto di polizia (m) police station
distributore (m) gas pump, distributor
distributore di benzina (m) gas station
distributore di biglietti (m) ticket vending machine
disturbi circolatori (m) circulatory disorder
ditale (m) thimble
dito (m) finger
dito del piede (m) toe
divertente amusing
dizionario (m) dictionary
doccia (f) shower
documenti della macchina (m) car documents
dogana (f) customs
dolce sweet
dolcificante (m) sweetener
dolciumi (m) candies
dolori (m) pain
domani tomorrow
domenica (f) Sunday
dopo afterward
dopodomani day after tomorrow
dorata (f) golden bream
dottore in legge (m) lawyer
dove where
dovere must
dozzina (f) dozen
dragoncello (m) tarragon
dramma (m) drama

dritta starboard
drive per CD-ROM (m) CD-ROM drive
droga (f) drug
droghiere (m) druggist
duna (f) dune
duomo (m) cathedral
durante la giornata during the day

E
e and
ebreo (m) Jew
eccellente outstanding, great, excellent
economia (f) economy
economico cheap
edicola (f) newsagent
edificio (m) building
elastico (m) elastic
elastico per capelli (m) elastic
elenco telefonico (m) telephone book
elettricista (m) electrician
elettricità (f) electricity
elezioni (f) elections
ematoma (m) hemorrhage
emicrania (f) migraine
emoraggia nasale (f) nosebleed
emorragia (f) bleeding
entrata (f) arrival
equipaggio (m) crew
equitazione (f) horseback riding
erba cipollina (f) chive
eruzione cutanea (f) rash
esca (f) bait
escursione a terra (f) shore excursion
esente da dazio doganale duty-free
esercito (m) army
esperto EDP (m) computer expert
esportazione (f) export
esposimetro (m) light meter
espositore (m/f) exhibitor
esposizione (f) exhibition
espresso (m) espresso, express mail
estate (f) summer
esterno outside, external
etichette (f) labels

F
fabbrica (f) factory
fabbricante (m) manufacturer

fabbro (m) locksmith
facchino (m) porter
faggio (m) beech
fagiano (m) pheasant
fagioli (m) beans
fagioli bianchi (m) white beans
fagioli nani (m) bush beans
fagioli rampicanti (m) string beans
fagioli rossi (m) kidney beans
fagioli verdi (m) green beans
fagiolini (m) wax beans
falegname (m) carpenter
fame (f) hunger
fantastico fantastic
faraona (f) guinea fowl
fare do
fare escursioni hiking
fare la tinta color
fari (m) headlight
farina (f) flour
farmacia (f) pharmacy, drugstore
faro (m) lighthouse
fattoria (f) farm
fax (m) fax
fazzoletti di carta (m) tissues
febbraio (m) February
febbre (f) fever
fegato (m) liver
feltro (m) felt
ferire injure
ferita (f) wound, injury
fermacravatta (f) tie pin
fermagli (m) paper clips
fermaglio (m) barrette
fermata (f) stop
ferro da stiro (m) iron
ferrovia (f) railroad
festival (m) festival
fette biscottate (f) zwieback
fiammiferi (m) matches
fibra sintetica (f) synthetic fiber
ficcanaso (m) rubberneck
fichi (m) figs
fichi d'india (m) cactus fruit
fidanzata (f) fiancée
fidanzato (m) fiancé
fieno (m) hay
fiera (f) fair
figlia (f) daughter
figlio (m) son
filo (m) thread
filo interdentale (m) dental floss

filosofia (f) philosophy
filtro dell'olio (m) oil filter
filtro di scarico (m) drain
filtro per pipa (m) pipe filters
fine settimana (f) weekend
finestra (f) windows
finocchi (m) fennel
fioraio (m) florist
firma (f) signature
fisica (f) physics
fissatore (m) fixative
fitte ai fianchi (f) stitch in the side
fiume (m) river
flanella (f) flannel
flash (m) flashbulb
flatulenza (f) flatulence
foglie d'alloro (f) bayleaves
folclore (m) folklore
fontana (f) well
fonte (f) mountain spring
fonte battesimale (m) font
footing (m) jogging
forbici (f) scissors
forbicine *(per unghie)* (f) nail scissors
forcella ruota anteriore (f) front wheel fork
forchetta (f) fork
forcine (f) hairpins
forfora (m) dandruff
formaggio (m) cheese
formaggio caprino (m) goat's milk cheese
formaggio di crema (m) fresh cheese
formaggio pecorino (m) ewe's-milk cheese
formato (m) format
formidabile terrific
formula di saluto (f) greeting
fornello a gas (m) gas stove
fornitore (m) supplier
forno a microonde (m) microwave
forte strong
fortezza (f) fortress
foruncolo (m) boil
fotografo (m) photographer, photo store
fragole (f) strawberries
francobollo (m) stamp
fratello (m) brother
frattura *(ossea)* (f) fracture
frecce (f) blinker
freccette (f) darts
freddo cold

fregio (m) frieze
frenare brake
freno (m) brake
freno a mano (m) hand brake
freno a tamburo (m) drum brake
freno di emergenza (m) emergency brake
frigorifero (m) refrigerator, cooler
frittata (f) pancake
fritto deep-fried
frizione (f) clutch
frusta (f) stirring whisk
frustrato frustrated
frutta (f) fruit
frutta della passione (f) passion fruit
frutta e verdura (f) fruit stand, fresh produce stand
fruttato fruity
frutti di mare (m) shellfish
fumare smoke
fumatori (m) smoking section
fune di rimorchio (f) towing cable
fune freno (f) brake cable
funghi (m) mushrooms
funivia (f) cable railway
fuoco (m) fire
fuori out (of)
furto (m) theft
fusibile (m) locking system

G

galleggiante (m) float
galleria (f) choir loft, gallery
galleria d'arte (f) art gallery
galletto (m) chicken
gallo (m) cock, rooster
gamba (f) leg
gamba *(sotto il ginocchio)* (f) lower leg
gamberetti (m) prawn
gambero (m) crab
gambero di mare (m) lobster
gara ciclistica (f) bicycle racing
garage (m) garage
garanzia (f) guarantee
garofano (m) carnation
garretto (m) leg
gas butano (m) butane gas
gas propano (m) propane
gastronomia (f) delicatessen

gatto (m) cat
gelato (m) ice cream
gelo (m) frost
gemelli (m) cufflinks
genero (m) son-in-law
gengiva (f) gum
gennaio (m) January
geologia (f) geology
gessetti (m) oil pastels
gesso (m) chalk
ghiaccio (m) ice
giacca (f) jacket
giacca a vento (f) windbreaker
giacca di pelle (f) leather jacket
giallo yellow, mystery novel
giardiniere (m) gardener
giardino (m) garden
giardino botanico (m) botanical gardens
giglio (m) lily
gilet (m) waistcoat
ginecologo (m) gynecologist
ginnastica (f) gymnastics
ginocchio (m) knees
giocattoli (m) toy store
giocattolo (m) toy
gioielliere (m) jeweler
giornale (m) newspaper
giornalista (m) journalist
giorno (m) day
giorno della partenza (m) date of departure
giovane young
giovedì (m) Thursday
giradischi (m) CD player
girasole (m) sunflower
giro (m) round trip
giro del porto (m) harbor tour
gita sul fiume (f) riverboat trip
giubbetto di salvataggio (m) life jacket
giudice (m) judge
giugno (m) June
giurisprudenza (f) law
giusto right
glassato glazed
glossario (m) glossy
gocce per le orecchie (f) ear drops
golf (m) golf
gomito (m) elbows
gomma (f) eraser
gonfio swollen
gonfiore (m) swelling
gonna (f) skirt

gotico (m) Gothic
governo (m) government
grado di difficoltà (m) degree of difficulty
grado visivo (m) vision
graffette (f) paper clips
grammo (m) gram
granchio (m) crab
grande large
grande magazzino (m) department store
grandine (f) hail
grano (m) grain, wheat
granseola (f) spider crab
grappa (f) schnapps
grattacielo (m) skyscraper
gravidanza (f) pregnancy
Grazie Thank you
grembiule (m) apron
grigio gray
griglia (f) grill
gruppo sanguigno (m) blood type
guadagno (m) profit
guanti (m) gloves
guardaroba (m) wardrobe, baggage deposit, cloakroom
guaritore (m) healer
guarnizione (f) gaskets
guarnizione del freno (f) brake lining
guida (f) guidebook
gusto (m) flavor

H
harddisk (m) hard disk
hockey sul ghiaccio (m) ice hockey

I
ibisco (m) hibiscus
idraulico (m) plumber
ieri yesterday
il fermo posta general delivery
imbarco (m) boarding pass
imbianchino (m) painter
imbroglione (m) swindler
imbuto (m) funnel
immersione (f) diving
immigrazione (m) immigration
immondizia (f) garbage
impanato breaded
impermeabile (m) raincoat
impianto Hifi (m) stereo system
impianto lampeggio emergenza (m) emergency flashers

impiegato (m) employee, civil servant
impiegato pubblico (m) official
importare import
importazione (f) import
imprenditore (m) businessman
impressionante impressive
in in
in bianco e nero black-and-white
inchiostro (m) ink
incidente (m) accident
incinta pregnant
incrocio (m) crossroad
indice (m) forefinger
indirizzo (m) address
industria (f) industry
infarto (m) heart attack
infermiera (f) nurse
infermiere (m) male nurse
infezione (f) infection
infiammazione (f) inflammation
infiammazione alla vescica (f) inflammation of the bladder
influenza (f) flu
informazioni (f) information
ingannare deceive, cheat
ingegnere (m) engineer
Inghilterra (f) England
ingresso (m) entrance
iniettore (m) fuel injector pump
iniezione (f) injection
innamorarsi fall in love
innesto marce (m) gearshift
inondazione (f) flood
insalata (f) salad
insalata mista (f) tossed salad, mixed salad
insalata verde (f) green salad
insegnante (m) teacher
inserzione publicitaria (f) ad
insetticida (m) insect repellent
insolazione (f) sunstroke
internista (m) internist
interno (m) direct dialling, internal, inside
interprete (m) interpreter
interruttore della luce (m) light switch
interurbana (f) long-distance call
intestazione (f) letterhead

intestino (m) intestine
inverno (m) winter
invito (m) invitation
ippoglosso (m) halibut
istituto di bellezza (m)
  cosmetics store
istruttore di sci (m) ski instructor
Italia (f) Italy
Italo-americano (m) Italian-American
itterizia (f) jaundice

J
jazz (m) jazz
judo (m) judo

K
karatè (m) karate
kit di riparazione gomme
  (m) repair kit
kiwi (m) kiwi

L
là there
labbro (m) lip
laca (f) hair spray
lacca (f) hairspray
lacci delle scarpe (m)
  shoelaces
ladro (m) thief
lago (m) lake
l'altro ieri day before yesterday
lame del rasoio (f) razor
  blades
lampada (f) lamp
lampada a petrolio (f)
  kerosene lamp
lampadina (f) light bulb
lampeggiatore (m) headlight flasher
lampo (m) lightning
lamponi (m) raspberries
lana (f) wool
lancetta (f) hands
lardellato larded
largo wide
lasciare let
lassativo (m) laxative
latte (m) milk
latte per il corpo (m) body
  lotion
latticini (m) dairy products
lattina (f) can
lattuga (f) garden lettuce
  salad
lavanderia (f) dry cleaning
lavanderia a gettone (f)
  laundromat
lavandino (m) washbasin

lavastoviglie (f) dishwasher
lavatoio (m) washroom
lavatrice (f) washing machine
lavorare work
lavoratore (m) worker
lavoratore edile (m) construction worker
lavoratore specializzato
  (m) skilled worker, specialist
legge (f) law
leggere read
lente di ingrandimento (f)
  magnifying glass
lenti a contatto (f) contact
  lenses
lenticchie (f) lentils
lento slow
lenza (f) fishing line
lenzuolo (m) bed sheets
lepre (f) hare
lettera (f) letter
letteratura (f) literature
letto (m) bed
letto da viaggio (m)
  portable crib
letto doppio (m) double
  bed
letto singolo (m) single
  bed
lettore CD (m) CD player
lettore DVD (m) DVD player
leva del cambio (f)
  gearshift lever
libraio (m) bookseller
libreria (f) bookstore
libro di cucina (m) cookbook
libro illustrato (m) picture
  book
libro per bambini (m) children's book
libro specialistico (m)
  technical book
licenza di pesca (f) fishing
  license
limetta (f) lime
limetta da unghie (f) nail
  file
limonata (f) soft drink
limone (m) lemon
linea (f) telephone line
lingua (f) tongue
lino (m) linen
liquido dei freni (m) brake
  fluid
liquore (m) liqueur
litro (m) liter
locatore (m) landlord

locomotiva (f) locomotive
lombata (f) loin steak
lombo (m) loin
lotta libera (f) wrestling
lucchetto (m) padlock
luccio (m) pike
luce anteriore (f) headlight
luci retromarcia (f) taillight
lucido per scarpe (m) shoe
  polish
luglio (m) July
lumaca di mare (f) sea
  snail
lunedì (m) Monday
lungo long
lunotto (m) rear window

M
maccheroni (m) macaroni
macchina (f) car
macchina del caffè (f) coffee machine
macchina fotografica (f)
  camera
macchinista (m) mechanic
macellaio (m) butcher
macinino del caffè (m)
  coffee grinder
madre (f) mother
maggio (m) May
maggiorana (f) marjoram
magnete (m) magnet
magnifico gorgeous
maiale (m) pig
maialino (m) suckling pig
maionese (f) mayonnaise
mais (m) corn
mal di denti (m) toothache
mal di gola (m) sore throat
mal di mare (m) seasick
mal di pancia (m) stomachache
mal di schiena (m) backache
mal di stomaco (m) stomachache
mal di testa (m) headache
malattia virale (f) viral illness
male al cuore (m) heart
  problems
manager (m) manager
mancia (f) tip
mandarino (m) tangerine
mandorle (f) almond
mangiare eat
mango (m) mango
manicha (f) sleeve
maniglia *(della porta)* (f)
  door handle

mano (f) hand
manubrio (m) dumbbell, handlebars
manzo (m) beef
marca (f) brand
marchio di fabbrica (m) trademark
marciapiede (m) sidewalk, footpath, platform
mare (m) sea
margarina (f) margarine
margherita (f) daisy
marinaio (m) sailor
marito (m) husband
marketing (m) marketing
marmellata (f) jam
martedì (m) Tuesday
martello (m) hammer
martinetto (m) jack
marzo (m) March
mascella (f) jaws
masterizzatore (m) CD burner
materassino (m) air mattress
materasso (m) mattress
materiale (m) material
matita (f) pencil, concealer
matita colorata (f) color pen
matita per le sopracciglia (f) eyebrow pencil
matite colorate (f) crayon
matterello (m) rolling pin
mazza da golf (f) golf clubs
meccanico (m) mechanic
meccanico per automobili (m) car mechanic
media medium
mediante through
medicina (f) medication, medicine
medicine per la circolazione (f) poor circulation, tablets for
medico (m) doctor
medievale medieval
medio (m) middle finger
medioevo (m) Middle Ages
medusa (f) jellyfish
mela (f) apple
mela cotogna (f) quince
mélange mottled
melanzana (f) eggplant
melograno (m) pomegranate
melone (m) melon
memoria di lavoro (f) RAM
mendico (m) panhandler
menta (f) mint

menu (m) menu
menu dei vini (m) wine menu
meraviglioso awesome
mercantile (m) freighter
mercato (m) market
mercato delle pulci (m) flea market
merceria (f) notions
mercerie (f) dry goods
mercoledì (m) Wednesday
merda (f) shit
merluzzo (m) sea pike, codfish
mese (m) month
messa (f) church service
mestolo (m) stirring spoon
metà (f) half
metro (m) ruler, meter, measuring tape
metro quadrato (m) square meter
metropolitana (f) subway
mezza pensione (f) half board
mezzanotte (f) midnight
mezzo half
mezzo chilo (m) pound
microfibra (f) microfiber
miele (m) honey
mietitrebbiatrice (f) harvester
mignolo (m) pinkie
miliardo (m) billion
millimetro (m) millimeter
minestra di verdura (f) vegetable soup
minibar (m) minibar
minuto (m) minute
miope short-sighted
mirabella (f) mirabelle
mirtilli (m) blueberries
mirtilli rossi (m) cranberries
misterioso mysterious
misuratore di profondità (m) depth meter
mittente (m) sender
mobili (m) furniture
moda (f) fashion
modem (m) modem
modificare alter, change
moglie (f) wife
moka (f) mocha
mollette *(per la biancheria)* (f) clothespins
molti many
molto much, very
molto contrastato high-contrast
monarchia (f) kingdom
monete (f) coins

mongolfiera (f) hot-air balloon
montagna (f) mountain
montanaro rustico (m) hillbilly
montare ride
monte di pietà (m) pawn-broker
montone (m) mutton
monumento (m) monu-ment
morbillo (m) measles
more (f) blackberries
morso (m) bite
motel (m) motel
moto ondoso (m) swell
motore (m) motor
motorino di avviamento (m) starter
motoscafo (m) motorboat
mozzo (m) hub
muggine (m) mullet
mulattiera (f) climbing path
municipio (m) town hall
muratore (m) mason, roofer
muscolo (m) muscle
museo (m) museum
musica (f) music
musical (m) musical
musicista (m) musician
musulmano (m) Muslim
mutande (f) underpants
mutandine (f) panties

N ....
narciso (m) narcissus
naso (m) nose
nastro adesivo *(scotch)* (m) transparent adhesive tape
Natale (m) Christmas
nausea (f) nausea
navata (f) nave
navata centrale (f) center nave
navata laterale (f) side aisle
navata trasversale (f) transept
navone (m) rutabaga
nebbia (f) fog
nebbioso hazy
negozio di alimentari (m) grocery store
negozio di casalinghi (m) household merchandise
negozio di computer (m) computer store
negozio di elettrodomesti-ci (m) electrical appli-ances store

negozio di ferramenta (m) hardware store
negozio di souvenirs (m) souvenir shop
nero black
nervo (m) nerve
nespole (f) medlar
neve (f) snow
neve farinosa (f) powder (snow)
nevicare snow
nevischio (m) sleet
niente nothing
nightclub (m) nightclub
nipote (f) niece, grandson, nephew
no no
nocciole (f) hazelnut
noce (f) walnut
noce moscata (f) nutmeg
noci (f) nuts
noci del Parà (f) Brazil nuts
noci di pecan (f) pecan nut
nodo (m) knots
noleggiare rent
noleggio imbarcazioni (m) boat rental
non fumatori (m) non-smoking section
non nuotatore (m) non-swimmers
nonna (f) grandmother
nonno (m) grandfather
norme doganali (f) customs regulations
notaio (m) notary
notizie (f) news
novella (f) novella
novembre (m) November
nubi (f) clouds
nuca (f) nape of the neck
numero civico (m) street number
numero del vagone (m) car number
numero del volo (m) flight number
numero di camera (m) room number
numero di telefono (m) telephone number
numero segreto (m) PIN
nuora (f) daughter-in-law
nuotatore (m) swimmers
nuovo new
nuvoloso cloudy

O..........................
o or
obiettivo (m) lens
oca (f) goose

occhiali da sole (m) sun glasses
occhiali da sub (m) swimming goggles
occhio (m) eye
occupato occupied
oceano (m) ocean
odontotecnico (m) dental technician
offerta (m) offer
oggetti di valore (m) valuables
oggi today
ogni each
ogni ora hourly
okra (f) okra
olio (m) oil
olio di girasole (m) sunflower oil
olio di oliva (m) olive oil
ombra (f) shadows
ombrello (m) umbrella
ombrellone (m) sun umbrella
ombretto (m) eye shadow
omelette (f) omelet
onda (f) wave
opaco dull, matte
opera (f) opera
operazione (f) operation
operetta (f) operetta
opinione (f) opinion
ora (f) hour
orari di apertura (m) open hours
orario (m) schedule, timetable
orario *(dei voli)* (f) flight schedule
orario di arrivo (m) arrival time
orario di decollo (m) departure time
orario di visita (m) office hours
orchidea (f) orchid
ordinare order
orecchini (m) earrings
orecchio (m) ear
orecchioni (m) mumps
orefice (m) watchmaker
origano (m) oregano
ornitologia (f) ornithology
oro (m) gold
orologio a parete (m) wall clock
orologio da polso (m) watch
orologio da tasca (m) pocket watch
orologio subacqueo (m) diving clock

ortodontista (m) dental surgeon
orzo (m) barley
ospedale (m) hospital
ossa (f) bones
ossobuco (m) round steak
ostello della gioventù (m) youth hostel
ostetrica (f) midwife
ostriche (f) oysters
otorinolaringoiatra (m) ear, nose, and throat specialist
ottico (m) optician
ottobre (m) October
otturazione (f) filling
ovaia (f) fallopian tubes
ozono (m) ozone

P..........................
pacchetto (m) small parcel
pacco (m) parcel
sovraccarico (m) excess baggage
padella (f) bedpan
padiglione (m) hall
padre (m) father
pagaia (f) oars
pagamento in contanti (m) cash payment
pagine gialle (f) yellow pages
paglia (f) straw
paio (m) pair
paletta (f) shovel
palla (f) ball
palla da tennis (f) tennis ball
pallacanestro (f) basketball
pallamano (f) handball
pallanuoto (f) water polo
pallavolo (f) volleyball
pallina da golf (f) golf ball
pallina da ping-pong (f) ping-pong ball
palloncino (m) balloon
pallone (m) soccer ball
palo da tenda (m) tent pole
palpebra (f) eyelid
pancia (f) stomach
pane (m) bread
pane bianco (m) white bread
pane croccante di segala (m) cracker
pane integrale (m) whole wheat bread
pane nero (m) black bread
panetteria (f) bakery

panettiere (m) baker
panino (m) roll
panna (f) cream
panna acida (f) sour cream
panna montata (f) whipped cream
pannolini (m) diapers
panorama (m) landscape
pantaloncini (m) shorts
pantaloni (m) pants
pantano (m) swamp
pantofole (f) slippers
papaia (f) papaya
pappa di avena (f) porridge, oatmeal
parabrezza (m) windshield
paracadutismo parachute jumping
parafango (m) mudguard, fender
paragrafo (m) paragraph
paralisi (f) paralysis
paraurti (m) bumper
parcella (f) fees
parcheggio (m) parking place
parco (m) park
parco naturale (m) nature park
parco nazionale (m) national park
parcogiochi (m) children's playground
parlamento (m) parliament
parlare speak
parrucca (f) wig
parrucchiere (m) hairdresser
parte posteriore (f) rear
partecipazione (f) investment
partenza (f) departure
partner *(commerciale)* (m) business partners
Pasqua (f) Easter
passaporto (m) passport
passeggero (m) passenger
passera di mare (f) flounder
passerella (f) jetty
passo (m) pass
pasta (f) noodles
pasta in brodo (f) noodle soup
pastelli (m) watercolor crayons
pastello (m) crayon
pasticceria (f) pastry shop
pasticcerie (f) pastries
pasticcino (m) cookies

pastiglie per mal di gola (f) cough drops
pastiglie per mal di testa (f) headache tablets
patate (f) potatoes
patate arrostite (f) fried potatoes, hash browns
patate dolci (f) sweet potatoes
patatine fritte (f) french fries
patente nautica (f) sailing license
pattinaggio su roller-blade (m) rollerblading
pattinaggio sul ghiaccio (m) ice skating
pattinatore su roller-blade (m) inline skates
pattini sul ghiaccio (m) ice skates
pattumiera (f) dustpan
pausa (f) intermission
pecora (f) sheep
pedale (m) pedal
pedalò (m) pedal boat
pediatra (m) pediatrician
pelle (f) skin
pelle di daino (f) suede
pellegrino (m) pilgrim
pelletteria (f) leather goods
pellicceria (f) furrier
pellicola (f) film
penna (f) fountain pen
pennarello (m) felt tip pen
pennello (m) paintbrush
pennello da barba (m) shaving brush
pensare think
pensionato (m) retired person
pensione completa (f) full board
Pentecoste (f) Whitsun
pentola (f) pot
pepe (m) pepper
peperoncino (m) chili
peperone (m) pepper
peperoni (m) green pepper
per for
per favore please
perché why
perchè because
perdita (f) loss
pere (f) pears
perla (f) pearl
permanente (f) perm
pernice (f) partridge
persico dorato (m) golden perch

persico rosso (m) red perch
pertosse (f) whooping cough
pesca (f) peach
pesca con l'amo (f) fishing
pesce (m) fish
pesce gatto (m) catfish
pesce persico (m) sea bream, perch
pesce spada (m) swordfish
pescivendolo (m) fish store
peso (m) weight
petonchio (m) scallop
pettine (m) comb
petto (m) breast
pezzi d'antiquariato (m) antiques
piacere like
piano (m) floor
pianta della città (f) city map
piatti a base di uova (m) egg dishes
piatto (m) dish
piazza (f) square
piccante tangy
piccione (m) pigeon
piccola small
piccolo little
piede (m) foot
pigiama (m) pajamas
ping-pong (m) ping-pong
pinne (f) fins
pinoli (m) pine nuts
pinze (f) pliers
pinzetta (f) tweezers
pioggia (f) rain
piombino (m) sinker
piovere rain
pioviggine (f) drizzle
pipa (f) pipe
piroscafo (m) steamer
piscina (f) swimming pool
piselli (m) peas
piselli dolci (m) tiny green peas
pista (f) ski run
pistacchi (m) pistachios
pistone (m) piston
pittura (f) painting
pittura murale (f) mural
pittura su vetro (f) glass painting
più more
più tardi later
planetario (m) planetarium
platino (m) platinum
pneumatici (m) tires

poco contrastato low-contrast
poco grasso low-fat
poi then
politica (f) politics
polizia (f) police
poliziotto (m) policeman
pollame (m) poultry
pollastro da ingrasso (m) young fattened hen
pollice (m) thumb
pollo (f) chicken
pollo arrosto (m) grilled chicken
polmone (m) lung
polmonite (f) pneumonia
polpaccio (m) calf
polpettone (m) meat loaf
polsini (m) cuffs
polso (m) wrist
poltrona (f) armchair
polvere (f) powder
pomata per bruciature (f) ointment for burns
pomelo (m) pomelo
pomodori (m) tomatoes
pompa (f) air pump
pompa *(della bicicletta)* (f) bicycle pump
pompa dell'acqua (f) water pump
pompelmo (m) grapefruit
ponte (m) dental bridge, bridge, deck
popeline (f) poplin
poppa (f) stern
porro (m) leek
porta (f) door
portafoglio (m) billfold, wallet
portale (m) main entrance
portamonete (m) purse
portinaio (m) porter
porto (m) harbor
posacenere (m) ashtray
posata (f) silverware, cutlery
posta (f) post office
posta aerea (f) airmail
posto accanto al finestrino (m) window seat
posto sul corridoio (m) aisle seat
potere can
povero di calorie low-calorie
povero di colesterolo low cholesterol
pozzanghera (f) puddle
pranzo (m) lunch
prato (m) meadow

preferibilmente preferably
prefisso (m) area code
prendere take
prenotare reserve
prenotazione (f) reservation (tickets)
presa di corrente (f) socket
presbite far-sighted
presentare introduce
preservativo (m) condom
presidente (m) president
pressione alta (f) high blood pressure
prete (m) priest
prezzemolo (m) parsley
prezzo (m) price
prezzo di acquisto (m) purchase price
prigione (f) prison
prima before, earlier, previously
primavera (f) spring
primo early, first
principiante (m) beginner
processione (f) procession
processo (m) trial
processore (m) processor
procuratore (m) authorized officer
prodotti biologici (m) organic food
prodotti dietetici (m) health food store
produzione (f) production
professore (m) professor
profondo deep
profumeria (f) perfume store
profumo (m) perfume
programmatore (m) programmer
prolunga (f) extension cord
prosciutto (m) ham
prostituta (f) hooker
protestante (m) Protestant
provare try on
prua (f) bow
psichiatra (m) psychiatrist
psicologia (f) psychology
psicologo (m) psychologist
pubblico ministero (m) district attorney
pulcino (m) chick
pulizia a secco (f) dry-cleaning
pullover (m) sweater
pulpito (m) pulpit
punto di incontro (m) meeting place
puntura d'insetto (f) insect bite

purea (f) mashed potatoes

Q
quaderno di appunti (m) notebook
quadro (m) painting
quaglia (f) quail
quando when
quanto how much
quanto tempo how long
quarto (m) quarter
quello that one
quell-o/-a that
quercia (f) oak
questo this one
qui here
quindi therefore
quotidiano daily

R
rabarbaro (m) rhubarb
racchetta da ping-pong (f) ping-pong racket
racchetta da tennis (f) tennis racket
racchetta da volano (f) badminton racket
raccoglitore *(ad anelli)* (m) loose-leaf notebook
raccomandata (f) registered mail
raccontare tell
radiatore (m) radiator
radice del dente (f) root (of the tooth)
radio (f) radio
radiografo (m) X-ray
raffreddore (m) cold, head cold
raffreddore da fieno (m) hay fever
raggio (m) spoke
rambutan (m) rambutan
rame (m) copper
rampone (m) crampons
rana pescatrice (f) anglerfish
rape (f) turnips
rape rosse (f) red beets
rapido fast
rapinare rob
rappresentante (m) representative
raso (m) satin
rasoio (m) razor
ravanelli (m) radish
ravanello (m) radish
razza (f) skate
reception (f) reception
regalo (m) gift
regata (f) regatta

reggiseno (m) bra
regionale regional
regione paludosa (f) wet-land
registratore (m) cassette recorder
registrazione (f) reception desk
religione (f) religion
remo (m) rudder
reni (m) kidneys
reparto (m) department
residence (m) vacation spot
resistente all'acqua water-proof
responsabilità (f) liability
rete per zanzare (f) mosquito net
reumatismo (m) rheuma-tism
ribes (m) currants
ricambi *(parti di ricambio)* (m) spare parts
ricci (m) curls
ricevere get
ricevuta (f) receipt
richiedente di asilo politi-co (m) political refugee
riduzione (f) reduction, discount
riflesso (m) color rinse
riflettore (m) reflector
riga di lato (f) part
riga in mezzo (f) center part
righello (m) ruler
rilievo (m) relief
rimmel (m) mascara
rimorchiare tow
riparare repair
ripetere repeat
ripieno stuffed
riqualificazione (f) retrain-ing
risacca (f) surf
riscaldamento (m) heater
riscaldamento a carbone (m) coal heating
riscaldamento centralizza-to (m) central heating
riscaldamento elettrico (m) electric heating
risciacquare rinse
riserva naturale (f) reser-vation (nature)
riso (m) rice
ristorante (m) restaurant
ritardo (m) delay
rivista (f) magazine
roastbeef (m) roast beef
roller-blade (m)

rollerblades
romanico (m) romanesque
romantico romantic
rombo (m) turbot
rompere break
rosa (f) rose
rosmarino (m) rosemary
rosolato browned
rosolia (f) German measles
rosone (m) rosette
rossetto (m) lipstick
rosso red
rouge (m) rouge
roulotte (f) trailer
rovina (f) ruins
rovine (f) remains
rubare steal
rubinetto (m) faucet
rugby (m) rugby
ruota (f) wheel
ruota dentata (f) gear
ruota di scorta (f) spare wheel
rupe (f) cliff
ruscello (m) brook

S ....
sabato (m) Saturday
sabbia (f) sand
sacchetto dell'immondizia (m) trash bag
sacchetto per alimenti (m) plastic wrap
sacco a pelo (m) sleeping bag
sacerdote (m) minister
saggistica (f) nonfiction
sagrestia (f) sacristy
sala concerti (m) concert hall
sala ricreazione (f) child care
sale (m) salt
salita (f) ascent
salmone (m) salmon
salmone affumicato (m) smoked salmon
salmonella (f) salmonella
salsa di soia (f) soy sauce
salsiccia (f) sausage
salvagente (m) life pre-server, swimming ring
salvia (f) sage
sambuco (m) elderberries
San Silvestro New Year's eve
sandali (m) sandals
sangue (m) blood
sapere know
sapone (m) soap

sarcofago (m) sarcophagus
sardine (f) sardines
sarto (m) tailor
sauna (f) sauna
sbagliato wrong
sbattuto shaken, stirred
scacchi (m) chess
scala (f) ladder
scala mobile (f) escalator
scaldabagno (m) hot water heater
scalini (m) stairways
scalo (m) stopover
scaloppina (f) deep-fried cutlet
scanner (m) scanner
scarico (m) exhaust
scarpe (f) shoes
scarpe da ginnastica (f) gym shoes
scarpe da montagna (f) climbing boots
scarpe per bambini (f) children's shoes
scarpe per scalatori (f) climbing boots
scarponcini (m) hiking boots
scarpone da sci (m) ski boots
scavi (m) excavations
sceriffo (m) sheriff
scheda audio (f) sound card
scheda di rete (f) network card
scheda grafica (f) graphics card
scheda telefonica (f) phone card
schermo (m) screen
schermo parasole (m) lens shade
schiarita (f) clearing
schiena (f) saddle (of lamb)
schiuma da barba (f) shaving cream
sci (m) ski
sci di fondo (m) cross-country skiing
sci nautico (m) waterski-ing
sciare skiing
sciarpa (f) scarf
sciatica (f) sciatica
scienziato (m) scientist
sciroppo (m) syrup
sciroppo per la tosse (m) cough syrup
scodella (f) bowl

scogliera (f) rocky shoreline
scolapiatti (m) dishrack
scolaro (m) student
scompartimento (m) compartment
sconfitta (f) defeat
sconto (m) rebate, discount
scopa (f) broom
scorzonere (m) salsify
scottatura (f) sunburn
scovolino (m) pipe cleaner, pipe implements
scrittore (m) author
scrivania (f) desk
scrivere write
scroscio di pioggia (m) showers
scultura (f) sculpture
scuro dark
Scusi!/Scusa! sorry
se if
secchiello (m) sand pail
secchio (m) bucket
secco dry
secondamano (m) second-hand store
secondo second
sedano (m) celery, leafy celery
sedativo (m) sedative, tranquilizer
sedia (f) chair
sedia a rotelle (f) wheelchair
sedia a sdraio (f) deck chair
sedia ripiegabile (f) folding chair
sedia sul ponte (f) deck chair
sedile (m) seat
sega (f) saw
segala (f) rye bread
seggiolone (m) highchair
seggiovia (f) chairlift
segreteria telefonica (f) answering machine
sella (f) saddle
semaforo (m) traffic light
semi di girasole (m) sunflower seeds
semolino (m) semolina
senape (f) mustard
sensale (m) agent
sentiero (m) footpath
sentire hear, smell, feel
senza without
senza piombo unleaded
senza sensi unconscious
serbatoio (m) tank

serranda (f) shutters
serratura (f) lock
servizio camere (m) room service
servizio clienti (m) customer service
servizio pubblico (m) public service
servizio rimorchio (m) tow service
seta (f) silk
sete (f) thirst
settembre (m) September
sgombro (m) mackerel
shampoo (m) shampoo
sì yes
sigarette (f) cigarettes
sigari (m) cigars, cigarillos
signale libero (m) dial tone
silenzioso still
similpelle (f) artificial leather
sinagoga (f) synagogue
sinistra left
siringa usa-e-getta (f) disposable needles
siringhe (f) syringes
skateboard (m) skateboard
skilift (m) ski lift
ski-pass (m) ski pass
slitta (f) sledge
slogatura (f) sprain
smacchiatore (m) stain remover
smalto *(per unghie)* (m) nail polish
smoking (m) tuxedo
snowboard (m) snowboard
soggetto a dazio doganale dutiable
soggiorno (m) living room
sogliola (f) sole
sole (m) sun
solo only
sonniferi (m) sleeping pills
sopravento (m) windward
sopracciglia (f) eyebrow
sorella (f) sister
sorprendente amazing
sosta (f) stopover
sottogonna (f) slip
sottovento (m) leeward
sovraccarico (m) excess baggage
spaghetti (m) spaghetti
spago (m) twine
spalla (f) shoulder
spatola (f) putty knife
spaventoso dreadful
spazzacamino (m) chimney sweep

spazzola (f) hairbrush
spazzola *(per vestiti)* (f) clothes brush
spazzola per bagno (f) scrubbing brush
spazzola per scarpe (f) shoe brush
spazzolino da denti (m) toothbrush
specchietto esterno (m) sideview mirrors
specchietto retrovisore (m) rearview mirrors
specchio (m) mirror
speck (m) bacon
sperlano (m) smelt
spese (f) costs
spese aggiuntive (f) extra costs
spese di trasporto (f) freight charges
spettacolo (m) event
spezie (f) spices
spezzatino (m) goulash
spia serbatoio (f) fuel gauge
spiaggia (f) beach
spiaggia di ghiaia (f) pebble beach
spiaggia di sabbia (f) sandy beach
spiaggia privata (f) private beach
spiccioli (m) change
spiga (f) ear of grain
spigola (m) wolf perch, pike perch, bluefish
spilla (f) brooch
spilla di sicurezza (f) safety pin
spillo (m) pin
spina (f) plug
spina dorsale (f) spine
spinaci (m) spinach
spirale (f) intrauterine device
splendido splendid
sporcizia (f) pollution
sport (m) sports
sportello (m) counter
sposato married
spremiagrumi (m) lemon squeezer
spugna (f) bath sponge, kitchen sponge, terry cloth
squalo (m) shark
squash (m) squash
stadio (m) stadium
stagno (m) pond
stampa (f) press, printed matter

stampante a getto d'inchiostro (f) inkjet printer
stampante laser (f) laser printer
stanco tired
Stati Uniti United States
statua (f) statue
stazione (f) railway station
stella marina (f) starfish
stendibiancheria (m) clothes racks
sterzo (m) steering
stesso same
stiramento (m) strain
stivali (m) boots
stivali di gomma (m) rubber boots
stoccafisso (m) salt cod
stomaco (m) stomach
stop *(luci freno)* (m) brake light
storia (f) history
stoviglie (f) dishes
straccio (m) cleaning rag
strada (f) street
strada provinciale (f) country road
strada statale (f) national highway
strade ghiacciate (f) sheet ice
straniero (m) foreigner
strano strange
stressato annoyed
stretto tight, narrow
striscio (m) swab
strofinaccio per lavare (m) face cloths
studente (m) student
stufato (m) stew, braised
stupro (m) rape
su on
succhietto (m) nipples, pacifier
succo di arancia (m) orange juice
succo di frutta (f) fruit juice
succo di mela (m) apple juice
succo di pomodoro (m) tomato juice
succo di uva (m) grape juice
suite (f) suite
suocera (f) mother-in-law
suocero (m) father-in-law
suole (f) sole
suole in gomma (f) rubber soles
suole in pelle (f) leather soles

superiore (m) chairman
supermercato (m) supermarket
supplemento (m) surcharge, appendix
surf (m) surfing
susina (f) plum
sveglia (f) alarm clock

T

tabaccheria (f) tobacco store
tabacco (m) tobacco
tacchino (m) turkey
tacco (m) heel
tachimetro (m) speedometer
taglia (f) size
tagliatelle (f) flat noodles
taglio (m) gash
tailleur (m) outfit
tallone (m) heel
tamarindo (m) tamarind
tamponi (m) tampons
tanica di acqua (f) water jug
tanica di benzina (f) gas can
tappo (m) corks, plug
tardi late
targhetta (f) name badge
tariffa (f) charge
tariffa di noleggio (f) rental fee
tassa di licenza (f) licensing fees
tassa di parcheggio (f) parking fee
tasse (f) taxes
tassista (f) taxi driver
tastiera (f) keyboard
tavola (f) table
tavola da surf (f) surfboard
tavolo ripiegabile (m) folding table
tavolozza (f) palette
tazza (f) cup
tè (m) tea
tè alla frutta (f) fruit tea
tè nero (m) black tea
teatro (m) theater
tegame (m) frying pan
teglia (f) frying pan
tela (f) canvas
telaietto per diapositive (m) slide frames
telecomando (m) remote control
telefono (m) telephone
telefono a gettoni (m) pay phone

telefono a scheda (m) card telephone
telegramma (m) telegram
telemetro (m) distance meter
teleobiettivo (m) telephoto lens
televisione (f) television
televisore (m) TV
telex (m) telex
telo da spiaggia (m) beach towel
temolo (m) grayling
temperato moderately warm
temperino (m) pencil sharpener
tempesta (f) storm
tempio (m) temple
temporale (m) thunderstorm
tenaglie (f) pincers
tenda (f) curtain, tent
tendine (m) tendon
tennis (m) tennis
tensione elettrica (f) voltage
tergicristallo (m) windshield wiper
termine (m) appointment, deadline
termine di consegna (m) time of delivery
termocoperta (f) electric blanket
termometro (m) thermometer
termos (m) thermos
termosifone (m) heating
terrazza (f) terrace
tessuti (m) fabric store
tessuto pettinato (m) worsted
test di gravidanza (m) pregnancy test
testa (f) head
testata cilindri (f) cylinder head
tetano (m) tetanus
tettuccio scorrevole (m) sunroof
tifone (m) typhoon
tiglio (m) lime tree
timo (m) thyme
tinta per riflessi (f) hair dye
tinte pastello (f) pastels
tisana (f) herbal tea
titolo (m) salutation
toast (m) toast
toiletta (f) powder room
toilette (f) restroom
tomba (f) grave

tonnellata (f) ton
tonno (m) tuna
tono (di) occupato (m) busy signal
tonsille (f) tonsils
tonsillite (f) tonsillitis
torcia (f) flashlight
tornado (m) tornado
torre (f) tower
torta (f) cake
torta di frutta (f) pie
torta di mela (f) apple pie
tosse (f) cough
tostapane (m) toaster
tovaglia (f) tablecloth
tovaglioli di carta (m) paper napkins
tovagliolo (m) napkin
tragedia (f) tragedy
traghetto (m) ferry
tram (m) streetcar
tramonto (m) sunset
tranquillo quiet
trapano (m) drill
trasfusione di sangue (f) blood transfusion
trattamento della radice (m) root canal work
trattativa (f) negotiation
trattore (m) tractor
trauma cranico (m) concussion
travel cheque (m) traveler's check
treno diretto (m) express train
treno navetta (m) car-train
treno suburbano (m) commuter train
treppiede (m) tripod
triangolo (m) warning triangle
trilione (m) trillion
trippa (f) tripe
tritato ground, chopped
troppo too much
trota (f) trout
trovare find
t-shirt (f) t-shirt
tubo dell'acqua (m) hose
tubo flessibile (m) inner tube
tubo respiratore (m) snorkel
tuono (m) thunder
tuta subaquea (f) wetsuit
tutt-i/-e all

U
udienza (f) legal proceedings

ufficio del sindaco (m) mayor's office
ufficio oggetti smarriti (m) lost-and-found office
ufficio stranieri (m) immigration authority
ulcera (f) ulcer
umidità (f) humidity
un po' a little
un, una a, an
unità (f) unit
università (f) university, college
uova di pesce (f) roe
uova strapazzate (m) scrambled egg
uovo à la coque (m) soft-boiled egg
uovo affogato (m) poached egg
uovo al tegamino (m) fried egg
uovo sodo (f) hard-boiled egg
uragano (m) hurricane
urbana (f) local call
urologo (m) urologist
uscita (f) departure, exit
uscita *(il cancello)* (f) gate
uscita di emergenza (f) emergency exit
ustione (f) burn
utero (m) uterus
uva (f) grape
uva passa (f) raisins
uva spina (f) gooseberry

V
vacca (f) cow
vagina (f) vagina
vaginite (f) vaginitis
vaglia (m) remittance, money order
vagone letto (m) sleeping car
vagone ristorante (m) dining car
vaiolo (m) smallpox
valigia (f) suitcase
valle (f) valley
valori massimi (m) maximum values
valori minimi (m) minimum (values)
valuta (f) currency
valvola (f) valve
vaniglia (f) vanilla
vano posaoggetti (m) glove compartment
varicella (f) chickenpox
vasca da bagno (f) bathtub

vecchio old
vedere see
vela (f) sail, sailing
vellutino (m) corduroy
velluto (m) velvet
vena (f) vein
vendemmia (f) vintage
vendere sell
vendita al dettaglio (f) retail
venerdì (m) Friday
Venerdì santo (m) Good Friday
venire come
ventilatore (m) fan
vento (m) wind
ventosa (f) suction pump
verbale (m) report
verde green
verdura (f) vegetables
verza (f) savoy cabbage
vescica (f) bladder
vestaglia (f) housecoat
vestito (m) dress
veterinario (m) veterinarian
vetraio (m) glazier
vetro della finestra (m) window pane
viaggio (m) transit
vicolo (m) alley
videoregistratore (m) VCR
vigili del fuoco (m) fire department
vigna (f) vineyard
villano (m) redneck
vini & liquori wine store, liquor store
vino (m) wine
vino bianco (m) white wine
vino rosso (m) red wine
viola purple
violentare rape
viso (m) face
vista sul mare (f) ocean view
vite (f) nut
vitello (m) calf
viti (f) screws
vittoria (f) win
volano (m) badminton, shuttlecock
volante (m) steering wheel
volo (m) flight
volo di coincidenza (m) connecting flight
volo di ritorno (m) return flight
volume illustrato (m) illustrated book
vongola (f) clam

votazione (f) vote
vulcano (m) volcano
vuoto empty

W
wafer (m) waffles
walkman (m) cassette player
windsurf (m) windsurfing

Y
yacht (m) yacht
yoghurt (m) yogurt

Z
zafferano (m) saffron
zaino (m) backpack
zenzero (m) ginger
zia (f) aunt

zio (m) uncle
zona pedonale (f) pedestrian zone, crosswalk
zoo (m) zoo
zoologia (f) zoology
zucca (f) pumpkin
zucchero (m) sugar
zucchine (f) zucchini
zuppe (f) soup

© Copyright 2001 by Koval Verlag GmbH, Weilerbachstrasse 44, D-74423 Unterfischach, Germany
First edition for the United States and Canada published in 2003 by Barron's Educational Series, Inc.

All inquiries should be addressed to:
Barron's Educational Series, Inc.
250 Wireless Boulevard
Hauppauge, New York 11788
http://www.barronseduc.com

International Standard Book Number 0-7641-2282-7
Library of Congress Catalog Card Number 2002101237

Printed in Hong Kong
9 8 7 6 5 4 3 2 1